H

Help Yourself to Health

HELP YOURSELF TO HEALTH

Linda A. Clark, M.A.

PYRAMID HOUSE
NEW YORK

HELP YOURSELF TO HEALTH

ISBN: 0–515–09301–7

Library of Congress Catalog Card Number: 74-189529

Printed in the United States of America

Pyramid House Books are published by Pyramid Communications, Inc.
Its trademarks, consisting of the word "pyramid" and the portrayal
of a pyramid, are registered in the United States Patent Office.

PYRAMID HOUSE
Pyramid Communications, Inc.
919 Third Avenue
New York, New York 10022, U.S.A.

*I dedicate this book to the angels
and the many people who made it possible.*

Acknowledgements

My sincere and loving appreciation goes to:

The Browns, Harper and Eve, who started the ball rolling by stimulating my reading and thinking in this field through thousands of telephone words.

Dorothy Wynn Smith, backed up by her husband, Melvin O. Smith, who urged me to write this book and kept after me until I did.

Dorie D'Angelo, who introduced me to the angels as "friends," and their delightful participation in everyday life.

Eleanore Thedick, known as "Ladye" to her grateful followers, who enlarged on the subject of the angels, particularly upon their protection.

Ann Ree Colton and Jonathan Murro, who provided me with invaluable help and information and patiently answered unlimited questions, provided references when they were needed, and supplied wise counsel based on years of experience in writing, teaching, and ministering to their loving congregation.

Many other assorted helpers, including Joanna Briggs, who acted as a sounding board for ideas, tested theories, and shared every shred of information she could find; Paul Jones, who relayed teaching principles he acquired in many years of attendance at Esalen Institute; Nancy Rushmer and my daughter Karen Kelly who typed, suggested, and bore with me in preparing the manuscript; and Martha Volf who contributed priceless findings from her late husband's brilliant research on sound therapy.

And last, but by no means least, the angels who helped me at every step of the way to find and make this information available, sometimes in the most miraculous ways.

LINDA CLARK

Explanation

This book, coming from me, a nutrition reporter, will surprise many of my readers. True, it contains some new findings about nutrition and health, but it is not devoted exclusively to the subject as are my other books. Whereas I have previously shown how correct nutrition has restored the health of thousands upon thousands of people and is still continuing to do so, I have learned that it is not the *whole* story for everyone. Something more is needed for a growing majority. I have discovered from people themselves as well as from voluminous research that other, unusual methods are needed in order to turn the tide of such failures in the right direction. Coupled with nutrition, these surprising methods have brought health and success as well as a new way of life.

This book is designed for a new age in which civilization, problems, and people are different from those of the traditional past. What formerly was sufficient to assure peace, happiness, contentment, and good health, is becoming badly out of date. New thinking and new guidelines are needed for a new age. If you feel that the information I have reported is too far out, let me ask you these questions: If the old way of life is adequate, why are more and more people becoming ill, frightened, depressed, and disillusioned? Why is there more insanity, more rioting and crime, more fear? We have international problems never before known, including pollution of air, water, food, even thought; continuing wars; atom bombs poised precariously over our heads. What worked for our forefathers no longer applies to us. Frank McCarthy says, "A new world is in the making but many of us cannot really see this because we are part of the changes. It is difficult for all of us to live through these

9

times since we are *unprepared* for such massive changes."*

This book presents some guidelines which *will* prepare us for living more successfully in this new world. The information will no doubt startle many of you. But because you have never heard of it, nor thought of it, nor tried it, is no reason to reject it. If you really want to keep abreast with the changing scene you will have to maintain an open mind and get with it or be left behind.

So give this book a fair trial if you are in trouble of any kind: worried, depressed, ill, desperate, or just plain weary from trying to cope with the many problems we all face these days. There are solutions here. We all differ—if one section does not appeal to you, read another, then another until you *do* find one that rings a bell. If none of them rings a bell, then lay the book aside. You are not ready for it.

I am a reporter and researcher and have looked far and wide for the information you will find here. This information is not my opinion alone, but a compilation of the work of talented, dedicated and sincere experts in various fields. I am proud to introduce these authors to you. I have given them due credit and have quoted only highlights of their findings, many verbatim. Because of their vast experience they have clarified a concept far better than I could. A few of these books are now out of print, but I urge you to read those available in full to learn their message in greater detail. I believe you will agree that they have made a wonderful contribution to all of mankind.

I have shared this information with you because it has helped so many. It is also changing my life for the better. I hope it will do the same for you.

I regret that I cannot correspond with readers in connection with this book under *any* circumstances. My work load is too great.

LINDA CLARK

---

*1971 *Moon Sign Book*. Llewellyn Publications, St. Paul, Minn. 55101.

Table of Contents

PART ONE:

The Incredible Power of Your Mind

1 *There IS Help for You*

Nearly everyone is suffering from *something* these days. It may be a minor or a major illness, or it may be a recurring feeling of dread, uncertainty, an obsession of fear, or overwhelming tension. One type of disturbance can cause another. Since the body is not compartmentalized but intricately interwoven, emotional tension can cause physical problems and vice versa, as you will soon see.

Most people do not know how to sort out their problems and get rid of them. Instead, they hide their heads, ostrichlike, in the sand and hope they will go away. Even worse, they may use drugs or tranquilizers to numb their reactions in order to not suffer so greatly. This method does not really solve the problem; it merely postpones it. Furthermore, there is now abundant research to prove that drugs can eventually cause deterioration of mind, emotions, and body.

As an example, here is a letter written to a famous advice-giving columnist:

Dear Ann Landers:
I used to think, "Oh, hell, why not take drugs — get as much pleasure out of life as possible. The world is in lousy shape. Trouble everywhere you look." Then one day I met a woman with a mentally retarded child.

15

He was a sweet little boy about eight, but he couldn't do much for himself. He was like a two-year-old. The mother had taken the boy all over, trying to get help — hoping and praying that maybe somewhere a doc had something new, something that would help her boy's mind develop.

I began to think about what I was doing to myself. Here was a mother who would give anything in the world if her boy could have a normal brain, and I was screwing mine up with pot and LSD — freaking out four nights a week. It was like wild.

I'm off the junk now and it was easier than I thought. All I needed was to keep reminding myself of that mother and her little boy. The preaching and scare stuff didn't make a dent, but somehow that mother got to me, Ann. Please print my letter. It might mean something to somebody.

—Off It

There are safer therapies which can help to remove difficulties once and for all. Some of these therapies are comparatively new. Others are as old as the hills but have either been forgotten or are lying unused, waiting to be rediscovered as keys to recovery. Many people are using them with surprising success.

As I describe these therapies, many specialists will scoff at them or challenge me and insist that they are either useless or superficial. I accept these challenges. *The proof of the pudding is in the eating;* the methods have worked for too many people to disqualify them. You have to watch these specialists. They are usually so concentrated upon their own area of endeavor that they may believe their method is the *only* road to recovery. For example, an exercise specialist may believe that exercise is all that is needed to regain physical health. A psychiatrist may believe that psychiatric therapy is the only way to achieve emotional health. A physician may believe that his treatment, including drugs, is the only way to bring about a complete remission of all the ills of the body. There is one value to the general practitioner; he takes an overall view of his patient, does what he can, and can refer the person, if necessary, to a specialist. This is the ideal solution. Specialists are invaluable, but in my opinion they should work *with* each other, not independently, for the good of the whole person.

Some specialists, such as psychiatric or psychological counselors, are not always available to the average person. Many people cannot afford them even if they could find them. For this reason, the books written by the authors mentioned in this book may help you to help yourself. If you can find a specialist, fine. If you can't, learning what self-help you can is certainly better than doing nothing.

Now I would like to tell you a true story of a man (let's call him John) who became seriously ill and recovered his health by using a combination of the therapies in this book. His experience startled me into changing my own thinking.

One of the reasons that John's health failure surprised me is that he works in my field as a nutrition specialist. Up to this time I admit to guilt in believing that correct nutrition could reverse *any* health condition. John has studied, lectured, and written about nutrition so long that there is little about the subject he does not know. Yet several years ago, he began to show signs of illness. I, and others who knew him, thought, "Well, what's the matter with *him?* He should follow the precept, 'Physician, heal thyself.'" He certainly had all the knowledge to work with, or so we thought. And John tried. The worse he felt, the more nutritional remedies he used to correct his problem. But he continued to deteriorate until he was in complete confusion as to the cause or cure of his illness. Finally, much to his embarrassment, as well as the rest of us in the nutrition field who had preached that nutrition, single-handed, could cure or prevent all ills, it became obvious that it was not doing so in his own case.

He finally turned himself over to other experts. They found that his body had become a jangling orchestra, completely out of tune. Every gland, every organ, his entire nervous system was completely out of balance and operating inefficiently. His resistance was so depleted that he had also picked up a deep-seated infection.

It was during some of these tests that a chance remark from a therapist who was examining him suddenly threw everything into focus. The therapist said, "You must have been under severe emotional stress in order to bring about this severe condition."

It was indeed true, John suddenly realized. Several years prior to his illness, a family member had become mentally imbalanced. The burden was placed upon John's shoulders since he was closer to this relative than anyone else. The problem brought crisis after crisis, a day-and-night worry, until it was finally necessary, after trying everything else, to remove the ailing individual from the family environment.

Meanwhile the years of unnerving experience had taken their toll on John without his realizing it. Not until the therapist made his bombshell remark, was John jolted into realizing the impact on his own health. He was then reminded of the findings of Dr. Hans Selye, the world authority on stress. Dr. Selye's experiments with rats revealed that when the animals were exposed to undue stress, their glands — including the adrenal and thymus glands which help control the body — as well as their stomach linings, became almost unrecognizable. Photographs showed these organs were gorged with blood, enlarged, and diseased, although those of a control group of the same species *not* exposed to stress were smooth and healthy. And remember, the changes had occurred not because of germs, a virus, poison, or even disease, but as a *result only of emotional stress.*[*]

[*]Hans Selye, M.D., *The Stress of Life.* McGraw-Hill Book Co. Inc., New York, 1956. *See also* Gross, Nancy E. (Foreword by Hans Selye), *Living With Stress.* McGraw-Hill Book Co. Inc., New York, 1958.

What happens to animals can usually happen to people. John now belatedly recognized what had happened to him. But why, nutrition converts will ask, with his good diet *could* such a thing happen? The reason has become clear: one may eat the best diet in the world, containing the proper nutrients which usually help a body to repair itself, but if there is stress, an organ can become so tense that it resists these repair materials. The organ, gland, or cell does not accept or assimilate the nutrients needed for its survival and health, and thus disease results.

Dr. Selye found stress the most common cause of disease. He found that not only can it upset the glandular system (the body regulators) but it can lead to high blood pressure, diabetes, coronaries, ulcers, allergies, kidney trouble, and a host of other conditions. Yet the person may not suspect what is happening to his own body.

Each person has his weak spot. When stress occurs, a person may tense up somewhere. It may be his heart, or his gall bladder, or some other area. I have already told the story in another book, of a man who, as long as he worked at his tense executive job in the city, suffered from gall bladder trouble. (No doubt he unconsciously tensed his gall bladder so that it could not work properly.) Yet when he moved to the country, away from his exacting job, his gall bladder trouble disappeared. When he returned to the job, his gall bladder trouble also returned.

Poor digestion can also interfere with proper assimilation of a good diet. And there is one other reason why the best possible diet may not do the job: poor circulation. The older you get, the slower the circulation. A sluggish blood stream cannot properly deliver repair nutrients to all parts of your body. This problem, however, is comparatively easy to solve. Daily exercise can improve circulation. This usually does not include housework because so many housewives hate it they tense up as they work. Walking, golf, swimming, gardening, bowling, yoga, or something you *do* enjoy can

encourage relaxation, relieve tension, and increase circulation. Even negative thoughts such as fear, worry, resentment, and even hurry can interfere with circulation and
create tension. So watch your thinking!

In order to get well, John found he needed to make
some changes in his thinking and way of life. When, in addition to his nutrition knowledge, he learned to understand
the effect of emotions on his body and the need for some
physical and other types of therapies, he began to get well.
It took time, but he did it.

There is no need to fear tension. Everyone faces stress.
It happens to everyone, everyday. The body can adjust to
small and fleeting tensions. In fact, they may even prove
stimulating in many cases. It is the prolonged unsolved
stress, or the *individual's reaction to stress,* that can cause
trouble.

So we must consider the body as a whole mechanism.
This book tells how to recognize tensions, how to eliminate
them, or how to adjust to them without damaging results.
It also tells you how to prevent or reverse illness due to such
causes so that you can acquire and maintain radiant health.

The next chapter tells you how to begin.

2 *The Hidden Iceberg*

Most people struggle through life feeling weak and ineffectual. Because they are not successful or happy or healthy, they conclude they are not supposed to be—that fate has given them a raw deal and that it is the other fellow who gets all the breaks. Nothing could be farther from the truth! They, too, could be successful, happy, and healthier if they only knew how.

Each person has a dynamo within him, a sleeping giant. He has the ability, though perhaps not the know-how, to call on that power which can completely transform his life for the better, once he has learned its operational laws. Those who are already successful have not become so through wishful thinking. They have, consciously or unconsciously, discovered and harnessed these laws to work for them in their lives and thus help them receive all good things.

If you are accomplished in any area and of course you are — it may be swimming, playing the piano, driving a car, carpentry, or cooking — it came by learning the rules and by *practicing them* until you became proficient. From then on, you scarcely gave it a second thought; its performance became automatic. You had, whether you realized it or not, turned the responsibility over to your subconscious mind, which is a genie if there ever was one. If you can be successful in one accomplishment, however unimportant, you can be successful in other endeavors as well.

The first requirement for success is that you must *want* something very much. Although this great power of accomplishment is open to and at the disposal of everyone, we may not all want the same things. Each of us has come into this existence with some potential, some talent, large or small, so that we like to do some things better than others. We will have greater — and easier — success if we harness the great powers to that interest. Not everyone wants to be a figure skater or a ballet dancer. But those who *do,* can use their natural interests as a clue to getting, with the help of the dynamo within them, successful results in half the time it would take someone else who does not like the same thing. Your particular talent may not be yet clear to you, but you have it! Self-seeking can eventually unearth it.

In addition to being born with a talent (the psychologists call it an aptitude because you like it and do that thing more easily) you were also born with a *mind.* These gifts were not bestowed upon you at birth for nothing; you are expected to use them to the fullest if you wish to be successful, happy, and healthy. Feeling disgruntled, futile, and unfulfilled can actually make you ill. Yet, this mind of yours can do *anything* you really want it to, and it can do some things you don't want it to, unless you know how to handle it correctly.

This power, a performer of magic when you know how to use it, is not the conscious mind or intellect, but the subconscious mind which is like a submerged iceberg. Psychologists tell us that the subconscious comprises nine-tenths of our mind and lies below the level of consciousness. It successfully controls our bodies and affairs if we let it.

Dr. Joseph Murphy[1] writes, "While you are awake or sound asleep the ceaseless, tireless action of your subconscious mind controls all the vital functions of your body without the help of your conscious mind. For example,

---

[1]Dr. Joseph Murphy, *The Power of Your Subconscious Mind.* Prentice-Hall, Englewood Cliffs, New Jersey, 1963.

while you are asleep your heart continues to beat rhythmic-ally, your lungs do not rest, and the process of inhalation and exhalation whereby your blood absorbs fresh air goes on just the same as when you are awake. Your subconscious controls your digestive processes and glandular secretions as well as all the other mysterious operations of your body. Your hair continues to grow whether you are asleep or awake. Scientists tell us that the skin secretes much more perspiration during sleep than during waking hours. Your eyes, ears and other senses are active during sleep. For in-stance, many of our great scientists have received answers to perplexing problems while they were asleep. They saw the answers in a dream.

"Your subconscious mind works 24 hours a day and makes provisions for your benefit, pouring all the fruit of your habitual thinking into your lap . . . . The main point to remember is once the subconscious mind accepts an idea it begins to execute it . . . . It works for good and bad ideas alike.

"Remember your subconscious mind does not engage in proving whether your thoughts are good or bad, true or false, but it responds according to the nature of your thoughts of suggestions. It does not reason; this is the job for the con-scious mind."

The conscious mind, by comparison, is less important. Many people deny this. They think, "I am smart" or "I know it all," but, as just one example, you do not know how to operate each integral part of your body so that it works successfully for you. It is a highly intricate engine, believe me, and none of us is a successful enough mechanic to run it ourself. The conscious mind, or intellect, is only one-tenth of consciousness. Often it gets us into more trouble than success because it tries to push itself to the front, be-comes egotistical and thus a pain in the neck to ourselves as well as to others. It can of course cope with everyday problems of living, but it is not a match for the subconscious if the larger mind decides to become recalcitrant. The thing the conscious mind is best for is to give commands and control the subconscious, which it must learn to do exactly as if it were training a dog.

Dr. Murphy adds, "Oftentimes your conscious mind interferes with the normal rhythm of the heart, lungs and functioning of the stomach and intestines by worry, anxiety, fear and depression. Thus these patterns of thought interfere with the harmonious functioning of your subconscious mind."

Agnes Sanford[2] explains, "The subconscious mind does not respond to reason but only to suggestion. Every time we think . . . 'I'm afraid I'm catching cold,' the subconscious mind picks up the suggestion and begins to work on it . . . so by our own contrary thought suggestions we constantly destroy the protective and life building energies of the body."

The English authors, Grace and Ivan Cooke,[3] add, "The subconscious mind makes its appearance with the birth of the baby, and immediately takes charge of its welfare. Most people say all this happens automatically or by instinct. They are wrong. This is part of the plan of life obeyed by all creatures endowed with life. What it wants it will get, the subconscious being a one-track mind. We must picture this mind so wholly engrossed with bodily things, with the appetites and pleasures of the body, its aches and pains, that it is always organizing its functions. Why not, when it is both engineer in charge and unwearying worker for the body having undertaken a lifetime job from the womb to the grave? This mind is our companion for every hour of the 24 hours of the day, since we sleep with it, and it wakes us, trudges along with us during our working hours and flops down to sleep with us at night. Not that

[2]Agnes Sanford, *The Healing Light*. Macalester Park Publishing Co., St. Paul, Minnesota, 19th Edition, 1955.
[3]Ivan and Grace Cooke, *Healing*. The White Eagle Publishing Trust, New Lands, Liss, Hampshire, England, 1955.

the subconscious ever sleeps! We should perish if it did, and at once."

Agnes Sanford says, "Moreover, the subconscious mind, psychologists tell us, keeps everything we've ever stored within it. By the time we are middle-aged, most of us have accumulated in the subconscious all manner of thought suggestions of fear, illness, limitations and lack . . . . From this storeroom of memories there floats into the subconscious mind a continual stream of doubts, fears and negations."

Ivan and Grace Cooke agree: "Not only are childhood memories infallibly registered, but everything else which happens during an entire human lifespan. Every thought and feeling passing through the conscious mind sinks down into the body, into the subconscious and is recorded there. Furthermore, such memories become an actual part of the subconscious which in itself is largely built up and composed of bodily memories, which in turn color the conscious mind's outlook on life. So if we store away a healthy outlook in our subconscious, we keep ourselves healthy and happy. We can also reverse this simple process."

A teacher who is engaged in showing others how to make the most of the potential of their subconscious, makes some claims that are extravagant sounding but true about the results that can be brought about once you learn the operational laws of the subconscious. This teacher (who is one of many who have seen these laws work) states, "Learning to harness the subconscious mind often leads to improvement in business and professional success, more money, and new happiness. Many people often report improvement in health. Others tell of increased physical strength, magnetic personality, courage, poise. This subconscious mind has the equivalent of the conscious mind power of a thousand men and can be trained to help anyone to be more successful in his daily affairs and life work."

Now let us learn more about this exciting power so that it will work for you.

3 *As a Man Thinketh*

The statement, "As a man thinketh, so is he," means exactly what it says. I know hundreds of people who have changed or are changing their lives for the better by merely changing their thinking. It is like learning a new game; you must learn the rules and then follow them to the letter. The way you think can make you a slave or a king. If you are dissatisfied with your lot in life, there is no need for self-pity, but *action*.

Here are methods to use and proof that thought really can be used as a controlling force in your life. Whatever your problem is, you can change it through your thinking. Skip Eldridge[1] explains: "The mind of man is divided into at least two parts — the conscious mind, and the subconscious mind. The conscious part is the thinking and sorting station. It receives information from the five senses and decides which is important, which to act upon, and which to ignore. The conscious mind is the door through which all information is channeled into the subconscious. (In hypnosis the door is blocked open so that information and suggestion can be fed directly into the subconscious mind.) The subconscious does not reason, it does not choose. Like a computer it accepts, records, and stores information, and delivers the results. Its power to deliver results is seemingly unlimited. No one has ever approached the limits of the

[1]Skip Eldridge, "Prayer," *Pep Talk*. P. O. Box 677, Auburn, Wash. 98002, October 1970.

awe-inspiring power or the magnificent capacity of the subconscious mind. It is the perfect slave — unquestioning, completely willing, and possessing tremendous powers to perform whatever it believes its owner wishes to be done. It is the genie of Aladdin's Wonderful Lamp. Gaining conscious control of the subconscious is probably the greatest and most important of all human achievements.

"To be successful we must know two things — we must know what we want (or what we do NOT want), and we must know (believe) without question or a shred of doubt that what we want is available to us without depriving anyone else.

"Many of us do not know what we really want. We vacillate. We hem and haw. We change our minds. We expect things that we do not want. Our subconscious slave is confused. It has no idea of what to deliver or when to deliver it.

"Negative thinking is one of the most common roadblocks to success. It is extremely powerful and must be avoided at all costs if we are to have what we want and avoid that which we do not want. Listen for these phrases and hundreds of others like them: 'I can't seem to . . . .' 'I can't afford it.' 'I'm always broke before payday.' 'I have a hard time . . . .' 'This is my unlucky day.' 'Everything I eat turns to fat!' 'I can remember faces, but I can't remember names.' 'Everything I touch turns out wrong.' 'I can't stand. . . .' 'I'm afraid that. . . .' The list is endless, and all of us have our pet negative phrases. With this type of data being fed into the computer, what results could one expect? We must weed these phrases out of our conversation and out of our thoughts.

"Your subconscious mind does not know good from bad, except as you have taught it. It will deliver without question whatever it thinks you want, or what you believe to be true. If you say, 'This is my unlucky day,' it will see to it that it IS your unlucky day. If you say, 'I can't remember names,' it will see to it that you can't remember names.

If you say, 'Everything I eat turns to fat,' it will see to it that everything you eat turns to fat. If you say, 'I'd like to quit smoking, but I just can't seem to do it,' it will see to it that you are not able to quit.

"Habits of a lifetime are difficult to change. [A negative statement if I ever heard one.] And habits of thought are certainly no exception."

So every time a negative thought appears, substitute a positive one. This reminds me of the story of Ellen, a waitress in a retirement home. Everyone who came to the dining room avoided this waitress because she looked unpleasant; she *was* unpleasant. Her tone of voice was sharp; she was apparently full of resentment and bitterness and she made everyone feel uncomfortable when she waited on them. There were several other waitresses in this dining room and people would deliberately try to find the table which was not under Ellen's domain, in order to avoid her. One day one of the women in the retirement project decided that she would see what she could do to help Ellen.

She said, "Ellen, why are you so unpleasant all of the time?"

Ellen looked a little surprised and said, "Well, why shouldn't I be unpleasant? Look how ugly I am!"

The woman said, "But you needn't be ugly; if you smile and look pleasant you would look entirely different."

Ellen answered, "I don't know that I could do that. Every morning when I look into the mirror I say to myself, 'Ellen, you ugly thing!' and it just puts me out of sorts for the whole day."

The woman said, "And it puts everyone else out of sorts who sees you, too. Why don't you try talking to yourself in the mirror and say, 'Ellen, you are loving; you are kind; you are radiating warmth and affection to all the people on whom you wait.' "

The advice was apparently followed because Ellen made a complete change in her personality. She became pleasant and sweet. Her face became relaxed, more attractive looking, and people no longer avoided her. She reconditioned herself and her looks by a change of thought.

Many people are careless in their thinking, not realizing the tremendous power which exists behind thought as well as words. They think critically of themselves or others, forgetting that every person needs the help of constructive positive thought. When people hurl critical and destructive words or thoughts at each other they are pulling their fellows down and hurting them.

Thought can make or break your health too, and there is scientific proof. David M. Horvik[2] reported, "Skeptical behaviorists ... began to sit up and take notice when science declared that many dedicated Zen and Yoga meditators were indeed capable of asserting mind over matter. Researchers wired them to electroencephalogram (EEG) machines and found that meditators could by sheer force of will, beefed up by years of training, produce on command profound trance states, raise and lower blood pressure, reduce body temperature, slow heart rates and, in general, tap into physiological functions thought to be forever beyond the reach of conscious control."

Another study was conducted at Yale University several years ago in which a professor discovered that the power of thought applied to various parts of the body indeed stimulated the blood flow freely to whatever part of the body the thought was directed and as a result of a change of thought the parts of the body could be influenced for good or bad. In other words, wherever your attention is directed, energy flows to that part. The early Egyptians and Brahmins knew this secret of healing and used it.

Catherine Ponder[3] says, "In the laws of physics you know that force started at one point acts simultaneously at

[2]David M. Horvik, "Brainwaves," *Look*, October 6, 1970.
[3]Catherine Ponder, *The Healing Secret of the Ages*. Prentice-Hall, Englewood Cliffs, New Jersey, 1964.

every other point in the substance. So it is with disease and with healing: it is never confined to just a single organ but affects the whole body . . . . You can rest assured that the subconscious phases of the mind which control the automatic functions of your body will respond in their own time and way . . . . Peace of mind precedes bodily healing. When you get a sense of peace, that is an indication that healing is taking place."

Reward tests with animals have shown that heartbeat, intestinal contractions, dilation of blood vessels, and blood pressure can be voluntarily changed. As a result of these animal tests some physicians are now teaching people to control their blood pressure by thought. Patients are learning to keep blood pressure down by watching for a signal light when it is at a proper level. This technique has been developed as a result of 12 years of specialized research by doctors at six major medical centers: Cornell University, the Massachusetts Mental Health Center in Boston, as well as Boston's City Hospital of Behavioral Medicine Laboratory, Rockefeller University in New York, a gerontology institute in Baltimore, and the University of California School of Medicine in San Francisco.

James C. G. Conniff[4] tells about it: "Humans are enabled to utilize a little-appreciated 'mind-body' faculty they possess after going through a process called 'operant conditioning' or 'visceral learning.'

"Convinced that if the mind can make the body ill (as it can in psychosomatic disorders), it should also be able to help it get better and stay well, a handful of pioneers began groping their way along unexplored avenues to find out *how*.

"Now they have developed a simple, Yoga-like technique — which they are the first to admit they themselves do not yet fully understand — and are teaching it to selected patients at these half a dozen major medical centers.

---

[4]James C. G. Coniff, "Can You Control Your Heart?" *Family Weekly*, October 11, 1970.

"These patients do not just imagine they're sick: they really *are* sick. But by applying the new technique to their afflictions, many of them have begun to experience successfully a kind of 'psychosomatic illness in reverse.' That is to say, they literally think themselves well again. Once they have mastered the method, they can go on using it to help themselves stay that way. Within hours the patient can slow or advance his own heart rate at will, lower his blood pressure, regulate an erratic pulse, or soothe a spastic colon . . . .

"Research psychologist Neal E. Miller, formerly at Cornell and now at the Rockefeller University, has applied successfully to people with too rapid heartbeat the knowhow he and his associates derived from some milestone studies with rats.

"A Harvard team of Drs. David Shapiro, Bernard Tursky, and Gary Schwartz has also done and reported scientifically exquisite work in using operant conditioning to lower systolic blood pressure among persons with essential hypertension (high blood pressure of unknown origin).

"To accomplish this, the Miller team, then working with Cornell Medical Center physicians, simply told patients that a mutual effort would be made to reduce their speeded-up heartbeat and that a beep would sound whenever even a small slowing occurred.

"Other labs accompany the beep with a pleasing picture flashed briefly on a screen, but the only reward the Cornell patients needed was the prospect of getting well. They did their level best to keep that beep sounding and, in case after case, they succeeded until their racing hearts were normal.

"How did they do it? Nobody really knows. But as Dr. Gary E. Schwartz of Harvard's Psychophysiology Lab at the Massachusetts Mental Health Center sees it, 'We don't have an answer to the truly basic question of how we move our arm, either. We *do* it, but we cannot say exactly *how* we do it. That goes for things a lot more mysterious than raising or lowering blood pressure, such as how people self-direct their entire behavior.'

"Miller's team developed the feat of inducing rats to dilate blood vessels in the right ear without affecting those in the left ear, and then reversed the process! Now a team is working with Dr. Herbert Benson at Boston City Hospital's Thorndike Memorial Research Lab to train individuals to raise the temperature in feet. By actually training people to raise the temperature in their icy soles and toes, the medical profession stands to earn a special vote of gratitude from many a married couple.

"Doctor Schwartz feels operant conditioning may even be applicable to the prevention of baldness because one of the causes of baldness is loss of blood flow to the scalp. If rats can learn to dilate the blood vessels in *one* ear and thus upgrade the flow of blood to that ear, Doctor Schwartz sees no reason why people cannot be trained to dilate blood vessels in the scalp and ward off hair loss.

"Even so, to the layman it borders on the occult to know that medical science has now proved beyond doubt that we can actually learn to make heart, brain, circulation, and so on do our bidding."

Until I read of this scientific research, I took with a grain of salt the remarks of two of my closest friends who told me they could bring their blood pressure down by thought. After reading the research I called them and asked them how they did it. The first, a woman doctor, told me that she gave a command, either silently or audibly, that her blood pressure and heart action become entirely normal. Then she took her mind off the problem and left it completely alone. Within an hour when she took tests, her blood pressure, accustomed to soar, and her heart action, also erratic at times, both gave normal readings.

The second friend, a man who has had both medical and psychiatric training, had an experience which surprised himself. He was under the care of a doctor for general physical debility after a long period of work on a very difficult project. Among other findings in his medical check-up, his blood pressure had registered a consistent 180/100 week after week. The doctor considered this too high. After two or three weeks, my friend decided on the way to the doctor's that he would bring his blood pressure down. As he drove along in his car, he told me, he gave a strong direction or command that every part of his body apparatus which controls blood pressure should operate to bring his pressure down to 120/80, a good level for him. He strongly visualized the reading at these exact numbers.

When he reached the doctor's office, the nurse who was to take his pressure said, "I suppose this will be up again though let's hope it won't be as high." The man said nothing. The nurse gasped at the reading and said jubilantly, "It has come down! It is only 120/80!" She rushed into the doctor's office with the report.

The following week the man decided this was cheating both himself and the doctor and decided he had better not do it again. Without thought control, the reading had gone up again. Only after continued treatment by the doctor who used nutritional therapy did it become permanently lower. But my friend had demonstrated to his satisfaction that he could accomplish the same result by thought, if necessary.

Dr. Edna Lister[5] writes, "Man's imagination cannot build a goal too great for him to achieve. Man's controlled thinking can accomplish anything his mind gives him provided he accepts and believes it. Man's controlled desire can call to him any amount of power needed for his whole structure of living.

"Twenty-four hours a day must be filled with picture patterns and thinking which is so strong that it can ignore any idea which seeks to creep back into the mind — the portals must be kept closed to the old ways. A desire to con-

---

[5]Dr. Edna Lister, *Eternal Youth at Eighty and Beyond*. NCS Publishing Co., 16324 Hawthorne Boulevard, Lawndale, Calif. 90260, 1969.

quer must be cultivated until it takes over in such strength that nothing unwanted can come between it and the goal. Man is a creator in his own right but once he makes up his mind to accomplish a certain thing, he must remain steadfast to that idea with no wavering; all outside enticements must be ignored. Man is usually his own delay. He allows himself to grow lukewarm just when he needs to turn on the heat of desire to reach his goal. There must be no interference allowed from the subconscious causing one to detour from his new plan of life.

"Everyone is free to choose either the sun or the shadow. We can limp through life half awake, half alive, unhappy and pitying ourselves or we can choose to change our thinking and revolutionize our whole life. We can draw upon the power to be or to do anything we desire with enough flame under it to hold us to the plan."

While you are trying to break the habit of thinking negative thoughts so that the subconscious won't pick them up when your back is turned, what do you do if suddenly you make a mistake and realize that you have said something negative that your subconscious may be greedily picking up? It is very simple. All you have to do is to say, "Cancel that thought." In other words, you can talk to your subconscious.

I remember seeing an article on a bulletin board as I waited in the reception room of a veterinarian's office. The article stated that a man gave his dog an oral command. The dog obeyed. Then the man went behind a screen so that the dog could not see his lips move as he gave a different command. The dog again obeyed. Finally, the man merely made a mental picture of a different command as clearly as possible. He did not make a sound. The dog obeyed the visualized command!

A friend of mine had a small dog that loved ice cream. After hearing me tell the above story, she tried it on her dog. He was lying at the foot of her bed one evening while she was reading. She made a clear-cut mental picture of some ice cream in a dish and the dog bounded out to the kitchen and met his owner at the refrigerator which contained the ice cream.

If you are going to dog-train your subconscious, you can use these same methods. You can talk to your subconscious as if it were a person. You can show love and affection in your voice. As a reward, you thank it for having done something you like. Should you want it to start doing something new, you state, as you would for a dog, not in complex, rambling terms, but in a single word or phrase, something like, "Find me the right job." Repeat this command often. Do not vary the words. You can think it, if it is not possible to say it aloud, or you can make a mental picture (the method for which I will describe later).

Do not get into the act yourself and try to figure out how this command is to be obeyed. This is the job of the subconscious. Turn it over to the subconscious completely. The less you think about it the better the results. I can promise you that the fulfillment usually does not come about as you would have expected. A friend may call you out of the blue with an idea, you may see an item in the newspaper; almost anything may happen to help fulfill your command, except what you expected.

Sometimes you may discover that, like a dog, your subconscious is not convinced you mean business. Perhaps you have changed the order, in thought or words, until it is confused. If you find, for instance, that you can't seem to get off the ground on that reducing program, you can blame it on the subconscious. In fact, if you embark on any plan of improvement and find yourself resisting the steps that are necessary, chalk it up to your subconscious. The subconscious does not like change! It feels more comfortable maintaining the status quo. But you are and must be the boss! You have to be in the driver's seat and issue the commands for the direction that you want to go. You must mean it, be persistent, and not put up with any dilly-dallying if you are going to change your life by thought.

There are two other rules that you can couple with thought if you wish more perfect as well as quick results. These rules are the use of *imagery* or visualization, and *feeling*. Let's see how they work.

4 *Feeling Your Way*

There are no "if's" about working with the subconscious. There are only "how's." So many people have discovered the good results of harnessing the subconscious to their needs and desires that the concept is in common usage by many different types of teachers and therapists: doctors, psychologists, psychiatrists, yogis, and religious healers. Jesus was an expert in giving commands to the subconscious of others and used them in his healing techniques. "Arise and walk" and "Be ye perfect as your Father in heaven is perfect" are only two examples.

Dr. Edna Lister[1] says, "Stripped of all nonessential and controversial matters, the Bible is just a textbook on how to live perfectly. The New Testament is the greatest book ever written on psychiatry: every how-not-to-do-it of today can be found there."

Yogi Ramacharaka[2] writes, "There is no mystery about self-suggestion. It is merely a matter of telling your subconscious mind to get to work and attend to its affairs properly. You can make up your own suggestions and affirmations. Just speak to the subconscious mind as if it were another person who had charge of your body and tell it what you expect it to do. Do not hesitate about being in earnest

[1]Edna Lister, *Eternal Youth at Eighty and Beyond.* NCS Publishing Co. 16324 Hawthorne, Lawndale, Calif. 90260.
[2]Yogi Ramacharaka, *Science of Psychic Healing.* Yoga Publication Society, Box 148, Des Plaines, Illinois 60016, 1934.

about it. Put some life into your commands. Talk to it in earnest. Say to it, 'Here, you subconscious mind, I want you to get down to work and manage things better for me. I'm tired of this old trouble and I intend to get rid of it. I am eating nourishing food and my stomach is strong enough to digest it properly and I insist upon your attending to it right away now. I am breathing properly and burning up the waste matter, and properly oxygenizing the blood and you must do the rest. Get to work. Get to work.'

"Add to this any instructions you think well and then the subconscious mind will get down to business. Then maintain the proper mental attitude, bracing yourself with strong affirmation until you get things going right. Say to yourself, 'I am getting strong and well; I am manifesting health.'"

Dr. Edna Lister[3] reminds us that these commands can work for any problem. Instead of using the words "command" or "suggest" she, like many other new thought ministers, uses the terms "declare" and "decree." She says, "Declare and decree for strength and for wealth. Declare that the body will answer any demand you desire to make upon it."

I will tell you later how Dr. Lister brought about her own amazing self-healing.

In addition to commands, still faster results can be accomplished by adding two other techniques: the use of feeling and imagination or visualization. These methods intensify the effect of commands and set up a strong rapport with your subconscious. Let's look at feeling first to see how to use it and what it can do for you. Neville,[4] the English author of a tiny book on this subject, gives some invaluable suggestions:

"Knowledge of the law of the subconscious and the method of operating this law will enable you to accomplish

---

[3] Edna Lister, *ibid*.
[4] Neville, *Feeling Is the Secret*. (Out of print at this writing).

all you desire in life. Armed with a working knowledge of this law, you can build and maintain an ideal world.

"The conscious impresses the subconscious while the subconscious expresses all that is impressed upon it.

"The subconscious does not originate ideas but accepts as true those which the conscious mind *feels* to be true and in a way known only to itself objectifies the accepted ideas. Therefore, through his power to imagine and feel and his freedom to choose the idea he will entertain, man has control over creation. Control of the subconscious is accomplished through control of your ideas and feelings.

"The conscious is male; the subconscious is female. The conscious generates ideas and impresses those ideas on the subconscious; the subconscious receives ideas and gives form and expression to them.

"The subconscious is the womb of creation. It receives the idea through the feelings of man. It never changes the idea received, but always gives it form. Hence the subconscious out-pictures the idea in the image and likeness of the feeling received.

"By this law—first conceiving an idea and then impressing the idea conceived on the subconscious — all things evolve.

"Ideas are impressed on the subconscious through the medium of feeling. No idea can be impressed on the subconscious until it is felt, but once felt — be it good, bad or indifferent — it is expressed. Feeling is the most important medium through which ideas are conveyed to the subconscious. Therefore, the man who does not control his feelings may easily impress the subconscious with undesirable states. By control of feeling is not meant restraint or suppression of your feeling, but rather the disciplining of self to imagine and entertain only such feeling that contributes to your happiness. Control of your feeling is all important to a full and happy life. Never entertain an undesirable feeling nor think sympathetically about negative conditions in any shape or form. Do not dwell on the imperfection of yourself or others. To do so is to impress the subconscious with these limitations. To feel a state as hopeless or impossible is to impress the subconscious with the idea of failure.

"Think feelingly only of the state you desire to realize. Feeling the reality of the state sought and living and acting on that conviction is the way of all seeming miracles. All changes of expression are brought about through a change of feeling. A change of feeling is a change of destiny. All creation occurs in the domain of the subconscious. What you must acquire is a reflective control of the operation of the subconscious, that is, control of your ideas and feelings.

"The subconscious never fails to express that which has been impressed upon it. The moment it receives an impression it begins to work out ways of its expression. It accepts the feeling impressed upon it, *your feeling,* as a fact existing within itself and immediately sets about to produce in the outer or objective world the exact likeness of that feeling. The subconscious never alters the accepted beliefs of man. It out-pictures them to the last detail whether or not they are beneficial.

"Chance or accident is not responsible for the things that happen to you, nor is predestined fate necessarily the author of your fortune or misfortune. Your subconscious impressions mainly determine the conditions of your world. The subconscious is not selective; it is impersonal and no respecter of persons. The subconscious is not concerned with the truth or falsity of your feeling. It always accepts as true that which you feel to be true. Feeling is the assent of the subconscious to the truth of that which is declared to be true. Because of this quality of the subconscious there is nothing impossible to man. Whatever the mind of man can conceive and feel as true, the subconscious can and must objectify. Your feelings create the pattern from which your world is fashioned, and a change of feeling is a change of pattern."

Neville tells how to do it: "Once asleep man has no freedom of choice. His entire slumber is dominated by his *last waking* concept of himself. It follows, therefore, that he should always assume the feeling of accomplishment and satisfaction before he retires in sleep. Your mood prior to sleep defines your state of subconsciousness. If, as you prepare for sleep, you assume and maintain the consciousness of success by feeling 'I am successful,' you must be successful. Feel as you would were you in possession of your wish and quietly relax into unconsciousness.

"Preparing to sleep, *feel* yourself into the state of the answered wish, and then relax into unconsciousness. This is the way to discover and conduct your wishes into the subconscious. Feel yourself in the state of the realized wish and quietly drop off to sleep.

"Night after night you should assume the feeling of being, having and witnessing that which you seek to be, possess and see manifested. Never go to sleep feeling discouraged or dissatisfied. Never sleep in the consciousness of failure. Your subconscious, whose natural state is sleep, sees you as you believe yourself to be, and whether it be good, bad, or indifferent, the subconscious will faithfully embody your belief.

"To be realized, then, the wish must be resolved into the feeling of being or having or witnessing the state sought. This is accomplished by assuming the feeling of the wish fulfilled. The feeling which comes in response to the question, 'How would I feel were my wish realized?' is the feeling which should monopolize and immobilize your attention as you relax into sleep. You must be in the consciousness of being or having that which you want to be or to have before you drop off to sleep.

"To impress the subconscious with the desirable state you must assume the *feeling that would be yours had you already realized your wish.* In defining your objective you must be concerned only with the objective itself. The manner of expression of the difficulties involved is not to be considered by you. To think feelingly on any state impresses it on the subconscious. Therefore, if you dwell on difficulties, barriers or delay, the subconscious, by its very nonselective nature, accepts the feeling of difficulties and obstacles as your request and proceeds to produce them in your outer world."

Harry Douglas Smith, minister of the Church of Life, Hollywood, California, one of the largest metaphysical churches in the United States, has successfully practiced the healing art for himself and others for many years. He has been a personal witness, he says, to hundreds of so-called "miraculous healings" which have been achieved under his direction and through his use of the principles he teaches and has encompassed in his book.[5]

Reverend Smith believes not only that negative feelings can induce disease, but that certain specific negative feelings can cause specific diseases. For instance, Reverend Smith points out that a feeling of irritation can lead to the following disturbances:

ALLERGIES
ASTHMA
COLD SORES
COLITIS
ECZEMA
GASTRITIS
HAY FEVER
INDIGESTION
LARYNGITIS
NEURITIS
SHINGLES
SINUSITIS
SKIN RASH
SKIN DISEASE

Reverend Smith states that it is impossible to be irritated by anything or anyone without your consent. When

[5]Harry Douglas Smith, *The Secret of Instantaneous Healing*. Parker Publishing Co., West Nyack, New York, 1965.

you allow something or someone to irritate you, it is only
then that they have power over your body, causing blood
to rise to your head, your voice to rise, your fingers to shake,
etc. By becoming irritated you have allowed the other person
to put you on the defensive and you are playing *his*
game. Reverend Smith's remedy for this is the following
statement: "I refuse to be irritated by anything or anyone."

Another set of disturbances, according to Reverend
Smith, is the result of a work overload or deadlines; a feeling
that no matter how hard you try to catch up, you are still
always behind. These illnesses, he says, include:

ALCOHOLISM
DIZZINESS
HEART PALPITATION
MUSCULAR TROUBLES
NERVOUS BREAKDOWN
NEUROSIS
PARALYSIS
RUPTURE
STROKES
SWOLLEN ANKLES
TUBERCULOSIS
VARICOSE VEINS
VOICE DEFECTS

He even tells of the case of the loss of hair that resulted
in a well-known baseball player. Reverend Smith told the
man that the falling out of his hair was a result of nerves,
and when his strain, which had been increasing for some
time, was over, his hair would grow back. This proved to be
true. Reverend Smith says to remind yourself that you are
in command of both yourself and your work load. He says
to tell yourself that you have the time and the strength to
do what you want to do and need to do. And that your best
is sufficient. You do not need to push yourself beyond your
endurance. As a matter of fact, success is more noticeable
from relaxation than from tension.

A third category of illness caused by a wrong feeling
is the underlying attitude of obstruction or delay which
seems to keep you from getting what you want. Reverend

Smith says, "The belief that you can be obstructed or delayed in any area of your life can lead not only to illness but to the obstruction and delay of your healing as well." He suggests that this type of negative thinking can produce:

CORONARY OCCLUSION
HARDENING OF THE
 ARTERIES
INDIGESTION
POOR CIRCULATION

His remedying affirmation is, "Nothing has the power to keep my good from me; nothing can obstruct or delay my reaching that state or condition of life that I choose."

A fourth category is a feeling of dislocation as if the person is never in the right place at the right time. Reverend Smith says that the conditions that can be traced to this negative point of view are:

ACCIDENTS
ARTHRITIS
FALLEN AND MISPLACED
 ORGANS
LOSING THINGS
SACROILIAC TROUBLE
SLIPPED DISC

His remedy: "I am always in my right place at the right time . . . every cell in my body is also in its right place."

A fifth group of illnesses, according to Reverend Smith, can result from hostility, which includes suspicion, doubt, hatred, antagonism and resentment. These conditions include:

ANEMIA
BACTERIAL DISEASE
CANCER
HIGH BLOOD PRESSURE
INDIGESTION
INFECTION
SORE THROAT

Reverend Smith adds, "Bacteria will not flourish destructively in an atmosphere in which they have not been 'invited'." Even arthritis has been found to be caused by smoldering or sudden resentment. Reverend Smith's remedying affirmation is: "I am surrounded by harmony and good will." And supplanting the feelings of hostility or resentment with feelings of love and blessing, no matter how you feel toward the other person, will eventually dissolve the state of mind and with it the disturbance. Remember that no one can control you unless you allow him to. *You are always in the driver's seat.* Reverend Smith's book contains a more complete list of the disturbances, illnesses, and diseases that result from various mental attitudes or negative feelings and the book abounds with constructive affirmations and many examples of healing successes through this method.

Fear is also considered one of the greatest causes of disease. Fear creates tension and tension can lead to ill health as we discovered in John's story, in Chapter 1. Remove fear, experts tell us, and the symptoms created by it will gradually disappear. Doubt also interferes with healing. However, getting rid of fear and doubt is easier said than done. Agnes Sanford[6] tells us what to do: "We ignore the old thought habits. We must also gently and patiently teach ourselves a new thought habit. We must re-educate the subconscious mind, replacing every thought of fear with the thought of faith; every thought of illness with the thought of health.

"This method to be practiced daily will gradually replace the old thought habits with new, and the subconscious will eventually accept these new thoughts as it did the old. And daily practice is just as important as learning to type, drive a car, or play the piano."

Constructive feeling can be applied to anything, including money. Wealthy people state that they seem to have a money consciousness. They *feel* affluent. They refuse to accept thought of poverty. So do not say that you cannot afford something. The minute that you do the subconscious picks it up and you will not be able to afford it. Dr. Joseph Mur-

---

[6]Agnes Sanford, *The Healing Light.* Macalester Park Publishing Co., St. Paul, Minnesota, 19th Edition, 1955.

phy[7] tells a story about a young girl who needed a traveling bag for a trip. She saw just what she wanted in a store window. She was about to say to herself, "I can't afford it." Then she remembered a statement of Dr. Murphy's which was: "Never finish a negative statement; reverse it immediately and wonders will happen in your life." So she said, "That bag is mine. It is for sale. I accept it mentally, and my subconscious sees to it that I receive it." Sure enough, in time for her trip, the bag arrived, a gift from her fiancé.

Feeling helps achieve faith that success is possible. This applies especially to health. Many a person has become well because a doctor supplied a medicine with the statement, "This medicine will make you well." Doctors have even given placebos with equal success. (A placebo is a dummy pill made of bread or some nonmedicated substance.) When doctors have impressed many patients that they would get well with placebos (which the patients thought were drugs) they *did* get well! Even Jesus, when he cured the blind man, applied spittle to the man's eyes, realizing that the man needed faith in something more than words.

One example of this form of therapy is that African witch doctors appear to effect some of their cures by convincing patients of their ability to make them well, and this may indicate that the mind plays an even greater part in disease than Western doctors now believe. Dr. Stephen Black, after investigating witch doctors in Nigeria, said he examined one woman who reported that ten years earlier she had suffered from what a hospital diagnosed as cancer of the skin. She had been unsuccessfully treated by x rays, so a year later she went to a witch doctor who gave her an ointment that cleared it up in a week. Dr. Black said that he had the ointment analyzed and it was found to contain nothing therapeutic, although it was mildly radioactive. This would

[7]Dr. Joseph Murphy, *The Power of Your Subconscious Mind*. Prentice-Hall, Englewood Cliffs, New Jersey, 1963.

indicate that either her mind or the mind of the witch doctor was involved in the cure.

Judge Troward[8] was convinced that feeling is a secret ingredient for accomplishment by the subconscious. He wrote, "The subconscious is infinitely susceptible to *feeling* and consequently it will reproduce with absolute accuracy whatever conception of itself we impress upon it."

Dr. Edna Lister[9] gives an account of how she achieved an amazing healing. She says, "My eyes were going blind and I needed to stand or fall by everything I had ever believed. I decided to act (and feel) as if my eyes were already restored. One must ignore the things that are contrary to our desires and keep on with declarations. My eyes did not come back to perfect vision all at once. It took two years of continued declaration each day, sight growing stronger, until one day I forgot all about my eyes. They were perfect. They still are at eighty while I use them all I desire without glasses of any kind."

Dr. Lister combined her declarations and the feeling as if her eyes were normal, with prayer, another method of conveying feeling to the subconscious, which we will take up in a later chapter.

So first, by using carefully chosen thoughts, you give your subconscious orders and commands *how* to operate. Next you supply strong, forceful feeling to provide a form of power like jet propulsion to get it off the ground into orbit. Next, we will see how to tell your subconscious *where* to go by means of visualization.

---

[8]Judge Troward, *The Edinburgh Lectures on Mental Science*. Robert M. McBride & Co., 1924.
[9]Edna Lister, *ibid*.

CHAPTER **5** *Seeing Is Believing*

Visualization can be fun. It gives the subconscious an exact blueprint to follow and thus brings you more quickly to your goal. Results can be fantastic. In fact you are, without realizing it, already sending your subconscious words, feelings, and pictures which are being created as the problems or the successes you are now enjoying. If you want good things, you have to, as with a radio, dial good things. If you picture yourself as a failure, or ill, or poor, the wheels of the subconscious are set in motion to produce just that. So you must use selective tuning, *controlled* imagination. Every architect, contractor, or inventor does this. They construct blueprints and the final results conform exactly.

In order to make your blueprint, Skip Eldridge,[1] mentioned in Chapter Three, says, "Decide what you want to have, to do, or to become. Visualize it. Feel it. Try to feel the way you would if you already had it. This will provide the emotional punch necessary to hasten the manifestations of your desires. Decide the kind of work you would like to do. Decide the kind of home you would like most to have — and where you would like to have it. Decide the kind of wife (husband) you would like to have. Decide the kind of person you would like to be. Decide how much money you would like to have. Decide, decide, decide!!! If you can't de-

---

[1]Skip Eldridge, "Prayer," *Pep Talk;* October 1970. P. O. Box 677, Auburn, Washington 98002.

cide, then decide not to decide, and table the question until another day."

After you decide what you want, stick to it! Deciding what you want one day and changing it the next, throws the poor subconscious into confusion. You can't blame it if it finally just lies down in bewilderment and does nothing. It's the same old story of dog training again. Make it clear. Make it simple. And to clinch it, repeat it whenever possible — certainly once a day, and more often if possible. If you have more than one wish, do not try to dramatize all of them at once. Work on the most important first and later add another, one at a time.

To visualize, make a moving picture in detail with yourself as the star, seeing and feeling and enjoying whatever it is you are visualizing. This intensifies the process. Whether it is health or something else you desire, many experts agree on the method of achieving it. William Wolff[2] writes: "Picture an image as though this feeling of well-being permeated every inch of your being. Especially be alert not to block blessings that might come from the most unlikely of areas. . . . After the proper incubation time your image will become a reality if you haven't replaced the feeling picture with a stronger image of impatience. . . . Feeling that perhaps it won't really work after all, you [can] create a 'counter image,' one that will negate one that you consciously desire."

Judge Troward[3] stated, "We are thus planting a seed which if left undisturbed will infallibly germinate into external fruition. The science of embryology shows that this rule holds good without exception. Similarly, the action of mind plants the nucleus, which, when allowed to grow undisturbed, will eventually attract to itself all the conditions necessary for its manifestation in outward form."

[2]William Wolff, *Psychic Development With Concept Therapy.* Grosset and Dunlap, New York, 1968, (paperback).
[3]Judge Troward, *The Edinburgh Lectures on Mental Science.* Robert M. McBride & Co., 1924.

Since positive thoughts bring positive results and negative thoughts bring negative results, Yogi Ramacharaka[4] cautions, "In giving suggestions it is important to picture yourself with the desired condition, the condition that you wish to bring about. Never make any reference to the disease condition but always speak of the condition as you wish it to be. Lead the mind away from the present unwanted condition and place it upon the expected condition."

Dr. Norman Vincent Peale adds, "Think success, visualize success, and you will set in motion the power force of the realizable wish. When the mental picture (thought)or attitude is strongly enough held it actually seems to control conditions and circumstances."

One need not huff and puff in order to get results. Easy does it. Yogi Ramacharaka says, "Transmitting the thought requires no strenuous effort on the part of the healer. The main difficulty lies in the ability to form the mental image. Once formed the thought is easily transmitted by *merely thinking of it as occurring.*"

The Tibetan Lama, T. Lobsang Rampa, also believes that imagination (visualization) is a powerful tool and far more effective than will power. It is also easier. I have been amazed at how a formula for getting something done without making myself do it by the use of will power has worked for me. Dr. William S. Casselberry[5] says you do not have to *make* yourself do things in order to accomplish them. You merely follow three steps: first, say the words; second, see yourself doing [or looking at] what you desire; and third, feel yourself as visualized.

Let me tell you how I put this formula to work. When I had a chore to accomplish and was lukewarm about it or even without time for getting it done, I formerly tried to

[4]Yogi Ramacharaka, *Science of Psychic Healing*, Yoga Publication Society, Box 148, Des Plaines, Illinois 60016, 1934.

[5]Dr. William S. Casselberry, *How to Work Miracles in Your Life, The Golden Secret of Successful Living*. Parker Publishing Co., Englewood Cliffs, New Jersey, Sixth Printing, 1966.

take myself in hand and say, "You must do this." Now I follow Dr. Casselberry's suggestion and I visualize the job as already done. It works almost like magic. For example, if I have a desk piled high with correspondence, I now, whenever I think about it, just visualize the desk absolutely clear and the correspondence going out in the mail; I give it no more thought. Before I realize it, I suddenly realize I *want* to do those letters, or get that piece of writing done, or whatever my assignment. And so I jump into it eagerly and before I know it, my desk is clean as a whistle and the correspondence has gone out in the mail. I have done this too many times to believe that this is just a chance occurrence. No doubt by making a picture of the deed accomplished, since the subconscious works in pictures, I have sent a picture of the desired result to the subconscious which then finds the time and willingness for me to get it done. When you are using the will power method, you can undoubtedly get a job done, but you fight yourself and the job all the way. When you do it by the previsualization method, it seems to go quickly and more enjoyably. So often as I have approached one of these formerly dreaded chores, I find myself saying, "I feel exactly like doing this right now" and I sit down and do it with true enjoyment as well as speed.

For longer projects, it is necessary to use your visualization technique according to certain conditions and at a particular time. Hypnosis provides a clue. Judge Troward[6] wrote, "Under the control of a practiced hypnotist the very personality of the subject becomes changed for the time being; he believes himself to be whatever the operator tells him he is: a swimmer breasting the waves, a bird flying in the air, a soldier in the tumult of battle, an Indian stealthily tracking his victim; in short for the time being he identifies himself with any personality that is impressed upon him by the will of the operator and acts the part with inimitable accuracy."

---

[6]Judge Troward, *ibid.*

Hypnosis is a method of putting the conscious mind out of the way so that a command for a desired condition can be impressed upon the subconscious without conscious interference. Hypnosis is common today. Doctors, dentists, therapists, and psychiatrists are using it when all else fails. And although we can learn from hypnotism how to better handle our own subconscious, we must also learn about its pitfalls. Many wonderful results have occurred at the hands of hypnotists but many tragedies have also occurred. Inadequately trained or amateur hypnotists, including some professional doctors, can be exceedingly dangerous. Lester David, writing in *Good Housekeeping*, gave these warnings in his article entitled, "Hypnotism Is Still Dangerous!": "When used in highly selective instances by qualified professional men, this mysterious and potent force can be of great help in medicine and dentistry, but according to the American Medical Association, used unwisely by the wrong people and on the wrong people, it can throw patients into a state of panic, cause coma, trigger mental illness, make neurotic habits considerably worse and even bring about suicides.

"One example was the case of the mother of three children whose doctor hypnotized away her severe and long-standing back pains. Two days later, though the back pains had disappeared on hypnotic treatment, the woman jumped to her death from a tall building. The pains had been serving as an emotional safety valve which had been covering up and 'protecting' her from an underlying suicidal depression. In other words, the doctor had treated her symptoms, not the underlying *cause*."

Dr. Harold Rosen, a Johns Hopkins University psychiatrist and chairman of the AMA committee on hypnotism, has stated that though hypnosis can be a valuable psychiatric tool, it can "threaten the sanity of the patient and sometimes of the hypnotist himself, if unskillfully employed."[7]

<hr>

[7]*Medical World News,* June 3 and Sept. 9, 1960.

An AMA two-year study showed that a group of doctors and dentists who had given 600 patients hypnotic treatment had personality defects themselves and some were even mentally ill. There are also many quacks promising quickie courses or help for everything from weight reducing, chain-smoking, or sleep-teaching, to assuring teenagers that they can cure their acne. Young children are even being hypnotized by unqualified therapists to "cure" bed-wetting, poor eating habits, and fighting with their brothers and sisters.

To show you how trouble can result from incorrectly used hypnotism, one woman went to a hypnotist to stop smoking. She did stop, but she soon began to eat compulsively and gained 50 pounds. The hypnotist then cured her of overeating. Next she became an alcoholic. This hypnotist, too, was treating the symptoms only, whereas a psychiatrist, trained to look for deeper causes of a problem, would have searched for the underlying emotional cause and eliminated that at the outset.

Another nonmedical hypnotist removed a woman's continuous headache successfully. It was later found to be caused by a brain tumor. I attended the autograph party of a nonmedical therapist who uses hypnotism for many problems including obesity and chain-smoking. This man, who was autographing his books, was himself chain-smoking! He looked at me and said with a wry grin, "It didn't work on me, did it?" The method did not work on others I know who went to him to lose weight and stop smoking, but it was not always the fault of the therapist; the patients were blocking their own recovery subconsciously, a problem which we will discuss later and show the way out of.

Dr. Rosen cautions:

Never allow anyone to treat you for complaints outside of his particular specialty.

Never ask a doctor or a dentist for hypnotic treatment.

It is up to the doctor to decide if the technique is necessary or advisable.

Never allow yourself to be hypnotized by an amateur or a stage entertainer. This may be a quick route to mental breakdown for people who are emotionally imbalanced.

On the other hand, hypnosis has accomplished some wonderful results. According to Robert Coughlan, in an article "What Hypnosis *Can* Do,"[8] it can help anxiety, stress, tension, compulsions, phobias, correction of bad habits, reducing, smoking, and alcoholism [if the underlying emotional cause is first spotted and treated]. It can also be a successful pain reducer. One of my friends, after her recovery from hipbone surgery, experienced great pain during the healing process. Her doctor hypnotized her and showed her how to use posthypnotic suggestion on herself when necessary. It proved to be a godsend during her recovery. Through self-suggestion she could discontinue her pain for as long as eight hours without the use of painkilling drugs.

However, as Robert Coughlan says, "Hypnosis is far from a cure-all. It is of no use whatever in certain medical conditions and it will not bring *recovery* (merely relief) from other illness except in conjunction with other medical measures." Good results, he says, do result with any ailment produced by stress: ulcers, dyspepsia, chronic gastritis, colitis, high blood pressure, rapid pulse and heart palpitation, sexual impotence and frigidity, poor bladder control, menstrual difficulties, speech disorders, asthma, and many skin disorders including eczema and hives.

Hypnosis can work! Mr. Coughlan tells of an interesting experiment by Dr. Lewis R. Wolberg, a New York psychiatrist and a dear friend of mine. "Dr. Wolberg hypnotized a subject and told him that exactly two years and two days from a certain date the man would read a certain poem by

8*Life,* March 7, 1960.

Tennyson. A week before that time, the subject developed a yearning to read poetry. Perusal of the bookshelves of a library caused him to finger through one of Tennyson's volumes. It interested him and he borrowed it. He placed it on his desk until suddenly, on the prescribed day, he found an opportunity to read the poem. He was positive that his interest in Tennyson was caused by a personal whim."

The advertisers have caught on to the effect of suggestion. Either by subliminal advertising (a mere flash of a suggestion on television) or an out-and-out commercial coupled with pictures which arouse feeling, they try to entrap the subconscious of the listeners and to make them want to run to the nearest store to buy the product. Children are excellent victims for such remote control.

I am sure you are wondering at this point if it is even safe to talk to your own subconscious by the methods we have discussed. Yes, it is safe because you are fully conscious and aware of what you are doing. Under hypnotism by someone else, you do not have the will power to reject any ideas being given you. There are some people, and I am one, who can't even be hypnotized. Yet I can get an idea through to my own subconscious.

Now, after warning you of the possible perils of being hypnotized by an unscrupulous or even inadequately trained operator, let's see how we can learn from the hypnotism principle to safely reach our own subconscious. As previously stated, hypnotism works because the conscious mind is sidetracked to allow a thought, feeling, picture—or all three wrapped up together—to get through to the subconscious without interference from the conscious mind.

Thus, in order to contact your own subconscious, you can get best results *without* hypnotism by getting your conscious out of the way yourself. Just as you go to sleep is an effective time because your conscious mind is already becoming drowsy and sleepy and is getting itself out of the way. At other times you will have to induce a drowsy, relaxed state in order to duplicate the same conditions. This is how reliable professionals tell us to do it:

Sit in a quiet room where you will not be interrupted by a telephone or people. It may help you to relax if the room is not too brightly lighted. Relax in a comfortable chair, but keep your spine straight, your feet flat on the floor, and your hands relaxed, palms facing upward in your lap. Talk to yourself, using your name if you wish, or say "I." Say, "Jane, you are (or I am) now relaxing your (my) foot and your (my) right leg." Pause and feel this relaxation. Repeat with the left foot and left leg. If you cannot produce a feeling of relaxation, tense each area first and then relax it. Don't hurry. Follow this area-by-area relaxing plan upward throughout your entire body — your lower torso, then the upper part including your chest. Next, relax your spine beginning at the lowest vertebra and working upward. Relax your shoulders, then your arms and hands and fingers. Relax your neck (this is a tense spot; you may have to do some stretching or wide circling to help out). Then relax your face and eyes. By this time you should begin to feel like a rag doll. Your conscious mind has calmed down to the point of nonresistance. You are now ready for your autosuggestion.

Charles Baudoin, a brilliant psychotherapist and professor at the Rousseau Institute in France, was extremely successful in teaching autosuggestion. He advised his students, once they had reached the sleepy state, to make a short condensed statement of what they desired and say it over and over as a lullaby in order to impregnate the subconscious with it. So do this next. Say, for example, over and over, "I am becoming strong and healthy."

Now is the time to start imaging. If you are working on a health problem, you can say, aloud if possible, "Jane, I see your . . ." or "My circulation" is now coursing through my veins all over my body until it comes to my stomach (or wherever you wish help). My stomach is becoming warm, warm, warm. This warmth is bringing fresh blood to my stomach to carry away all toxic accumulation, bring fresh nourishment to heal the condition. It feels good (and really *feel* deeply at this point). "Now, Jane, you are . . ." or "I am looking well because I am beginning to feel well."

Frederick Pierce, M.D.,[9] reports amazing success of the effect of visualizing or "imaging," as he calls it, on the vital organs and glands. He states that he has found that the liver, and the pancreas in supplying secretions to the digestive tract, can be stimulated by appropriate brain images. He has used this method with his patients and taught it to many students. He wrote: "In imaging, to imitate something there must be a model to imitate. In every form of imagination there is a wish feeling present as the moving force and the more highly emotionalized this wish feeling is, the more vividly will the emotion work and the images live in the mind."

For a model you might choose someone you admire for the particular thing you want to duplicate: good health, vitality, some particular trait such as hair, skin, or whatever you are visualizing. Seeing an actual person with that characteristic in your mind's eye helps you to pass that picture along to the subconscious. Later you can transfer the pictured condition to yourself.

Dr. Pierce continues, "What we need is an emotion which will always attach itself to a forward-looking and constructive image of any sort, and this I have found which I call ego maximation.

"Ego maximation is in my opinion assuredly one of instinct and one of great power . . . in the emotion attached to this instinct I have found an always serviceable quickener of autosuggestion images. The primary image must always be that of oneself physically and mentally what one wishes to be within the bounds of possible development. In every instance of the regular practice of autosuggestion there

[9]Frederick Pierce, *Mobilizing the Mid-Brain (The Technique for Utilizing Its Latent Power)*. E. P. Dutton & Co., New York, 1933.

must be a full release of the emotion of ego maximation. *We must not only construct an image of ourselves as we wish to be, but we must also train ourselves to visualize this image as perceived, esteemed, loved and as being admired by others.* Instead of imagination constantly being used only to bring up an image of ourselves experiencing all the benefits and values of freedom, with the ego maximating emotion of other people esteeming and admiring us for the result of our work, more success will occur."

You must make up your own words for autosuggestion; no one can do it for you. Dr. Pierce says that the exact words are not really important, anyway, so long as they express the image you are seeking and you incorporate into it the "ego maximating" factor. After seeing yourself as you want to be, you could add, "Your (or my) family and friends are beginning to compliment you (me) on your (my) health or your (my) appearance." And visualize them as doing so, including the actual words you would like to hear them say, such as "Richard, you look wonderful! What's the secret?"

Dr. Pierce adds, "The unsatisfactory condition must absolutely not appear in the image, or the autosuggestion will yield little or nothing. It should also be noted that the words should not state the corrected condition as a *present* fact. Experience has shown that autosuggestion is usually only defeated by stating a thing is true while the mind is unescapably aware it is not true. If we have a cold there is no point in frequently denying it, since only psychological confusion can result. The thing to do is to visualize the end result of correction, add the ego maximating factor, and then both regard and state the process as being underway, as moving toward the goal. This avoids the folly of lying to oneself or denying facts." One can say, "This condition is clearing up," or "It is going to be better soon, hour by hour, day by day."

Dr. Pierce admonishes, "One warning should be noted

here in connection with specific images; if they are too many and too varied in any given treatment, the results will be unsatisfactory. It is imperative that a selection be confined to two or three at a time and that one cultivate the patience to be satisfied with seeing a gradual development in himself of his corrective scheme.

"In addition to specific images we must not lose sight of the importance of a general overall image of physical and mental well-being. A simple statement such as, 'Day by day in every respect I am getting better and better and approaching nearer and nearer to this perfected picture of myself,' should become, as it were, a text of life. The chief point is that one must not only develop autosuggestive thought, but also must make *persistent* use of it. It does little good to use strongly affirmative autosuggestion before going to sleep at night and then at the first instance of discouragement in the morning, let one's mind slump into a helpless and negative attitude. The assurances given oneself in the treatment at night of moving toward the goal must be repeated the next morning and throughout the day many times.

"As an all-over treatment I have found most serviceable a mental image of oneself possessing a healthy body and a beautiful skin with its color and texture clearly visualized and a strong ego maximation factor developed in thinking intensively of others as sensing, admiring and even envying this acquired attribute of beauty. The word picture could be: 'Steadily, day by day all my glands are coming into more and more perfect balance, giving to blood and nerves their perfected chemistry. Hour by hour as nerves and bloodstream approach their normal, healthy state, my skin is becoming clearer, softer, more attractive to the touch and more beautiful to the eye. My entire body is becoming healthier, more youthful, more attractive.'"

Dr. Pierce also has a formula for controlling pain. He says, "I have never found anything more effective than

Coué's formula. If convenient one should lie down, but the method can be effectively used after a little practice when walking, riding, or even in a noisy group. It depends largely on acquiring the habit of quick concentration whenever it is used and consists simply of repetition with the utmost possible speed of some such words as: 'It's passing away,' or 'It's going, it's going, it's going,' continued often for seven or eight minutes. When, because of the presence of others the words cannot be whispered or spoken, relief often follows from very rapid mental repetition. Concentration on the words and the speed of repetition, which must be so great that the words run into each other in a flow as to be mere babble, takes the energy of attention from the pain or disturbance and there is also a slight automatic appeal to the imagination. Remarkable relief often results even under the most difficult conditions."

In concluding his teaching on how to reach the subconscious successfully, Dr. Pierce says, "This method taught to many pupils has worked over and over again and I have yet to encounter a failure when it is fully understood and properly used."

Dr. Joseph Murphy[10] gets results with similar methods. He tells of a psychologist who had an infection of the lungs. X ray and analysis confirmed the presence of tuberculosis. Just before going to sleep at night, the psychologist would say, quietly, "Every cell, nerve, tissue and muscle of my lungs are now being made whole, pure, and perfect. My whole body is being restored to health and harmony." A complete healing followed in about a month's time as proved by x rays.

Dr. Murphy gives another example: "A young man who came to my lectures on the healing power of the subconcious mind had severe eye trouble which his doctor said necessitated an operation. He said to himself, 'My subcon-

---

[10]Dr. Joseph Murphy, *The Power of Your Subconscious Mind.* Prentice-Hall, Englewood Cliffs, New Jersey, 1963.

scious made my eyes and it can heal me.' Each night as he went to sleep he entered into a drowsy meditative state, a condition akin to sleep. His attention was immobilized and focused on his eye doctor. He imagined the doctor in front of him and he plainly heard, or imagined he heard, the doctor saying to him, 'A miracle has happened!' He heard this over and over again every night for perhaps five minutes before going to sleep. At the end of three weeks he again went to the ophthalmologist who had previously examined his eyes, and the physician said to this man, 'This is a miracle! . . .' Through repetition, faith, and expectancy he had impregnated his subconscious mind and immediately it began to heal the eye.

"Similarly your subconscious mind is the master mechanic, the all-wise one who knows ways and means of healing any organ of your body as well as your affairs. Decree health and your subconscious will establish it, but relaxation is the key. 'Easy does it.' Do not be concerned with details and means, but know the end result. Get the *feel* of the happy solution to your problem, whether it is health, finances or employment. Remember how you felt after you had recovered from a severe state of illness. Bear in mind that your *feeling* is the touchstone of all subconscious demonstration. Your new idea must be felt subjectively in the finished state, not as the future, but as coming about now.

"You will find your intellect trying to get in the way, but persist in maintaining a simple childlike miracle-making faith. Picture yourself *without* the ailment or problem. Imagine the emotional accompaniment of the freedom state you crave.

"You avoid all conflict between your desires and imagination by entering into a drowsy sleepy state which brings all effort to a minimum. The conscious mind is submerged to a great extent within a sleepy state. The best time to impregnate your subconscious is prior to sleep. In this state the negative thoughts and imagery which tend to neutralize your desire and so prevent acceptance by your subconscious mind no longer present themselves. When you imagine the reality of the fulfilled desire and feel the thrill of accomplishment, your subconscious mind brings about the realization of your desire."

Dr. Murphy also tells how to use the subconscious to meet other needs, say, for instance, one involving a check. He suggests that the person get into a sleepy, drowsy state "which reduces all mental effort to a minimum." Then Dr. Murphy suggests that the person picture the check in his hands and go to sleep rejoicing that the check has come.

David Seabury,[11] the late practical psychologist, gave an example of acquiring the home he wanted. Every night he seated himself in a comfortable chair in a quiet room, relaxed his body and conscious mind, then began making a picture of the home he wanted. First, he visualized the area where he wanted it to be. Next, he imagined the house to include the desired number of rooms, the type of architecture, even the furnishings. He saw himself moving happily and contentedly through the house, enjoying it, feeling the pleasure of living in it. He created this moving picture as a scenario writer would produce a dynamic picture. He repeated the performance night after night. Within a few short months the house, exact in every detail, came on the market at a price he could afford and he bought it!

During his autosuggestion program he did not worry about how the subconscious was going to bring him his desire. He set the machinery in motion, then deliberately turned his attention elsewhere. He observed the old warning that "a watched pot never boils." This let-alone method prevents the conscious mind from getting into the act and gumming up the works.

Some people, who at first find it difficult to visualize, have been aided by cutting pictures from a magazine to

---

[11]David Seabury, *The Art of Living Without Tension.* Harper & Bros., New York, 1958.

gaze at during their daily imagery session. Another excellent method is a want list. I use this all the time. Take a card, date it, and make a list, numbered 1, 2, 3, etc., and put your wants in order of importance. Every day during your visualization session look at each item (keep it short), read the item aloud, and then visualize yourself having acquired it and feeling happy at its accomplishment. Your card could read something like this:

1. I wish radiant health and vitality.
2. I wish to have all my bills paid each month easily, without strain or sacrifice.
3. I would like to have people like me better.
4. I wish a perfect figure and/or perfect weight.

A friend of mine told me that she started her want list with a new refrigerator and ended it with the desire of becoming a better person. Later on she got to feeling uneasy about the order of the items. She changed her want list by putting at the top the item, "Being a better person (thoughtful, unselfish, kind)" and the refrigerator at the bottom. She soon got the refrigerator. She still keeps the personal improvement as her No. 1 goal. She feels she *is* improving but that there is always room for more improvement.

Occasionally, as I am going through old papers and belongings, I come across an old want list card I had tucked away. I am amazed at how the items have materialized and I had forgotten all about them. I usually stop and give a little word of thanks to my subconscious. Agnes Sanford believes we should be loving towards our subconscious and always thank it for service rendered. After all, if you follow the rules, the subconscious *will* cooperate and give you an excellent return on your investment of time, thought, feeling, and visualization. It deserves some thanks!

6 How to Prevent Your Subconscious from Talking Back

Occasionally, a tug of war develops between a person and his subconscious. Surprisingly, the subconscious often wins. This is what can happen: A person may *think* he wants to do something whereas actually he dreads it. He tells himself and others that he will be glad to do it, whereas "subconsciously" he really fears it. The subconscious picks up the fear message (a feeling, not words) and goes to work to save the situation, though the person himself is unaware of what has happened.

I have told the story in another book about a mature man who was ready to qualify for his Ph.D. degree after the required years of university training. His next step was to take a written examination. When the examination questions were given to him, he picked up his pen to write the answers and suddenly his arm froze; he could not move it! He was temporarily excused from the examination and sent to the university infirmary, where his arm was found to be paralyzed — a real, not an imagined condition. In due time his arm recovered and he was given another chance at the examination. The same thing happened *three times*. His arm became paralyzed the minute that he was faced with the ordeal of that examination! Finally he was afraid to try again and gave up. He never did receive his Ph.D. degree.

What had happened? He was afraid he would fail the examination so his subconscious dreamed up a "legitimate" excuse, a way out to save face for the man. I do not know whether he ever realized the cause of his failure. Psychologists who knew him told me the story.

A friend was in need of some added employment. She was offered a job teaching a subject in which she had formerly been extremely proficient, though she now felt she had become somewhat rusty and inadequate for the job. She, too, was supposed to pass an examination before she could qualify. She told me, "I don't know whether I really want this job or not. Except for the money, I am content living my life as it is. I really don't like change." (Since the subconscious resists change, this sounded suspiciously like the subconscious at the controls.)

Just before examination time, an old leg injury which had not bothered her for years, suddenly flared up and she could not even drive to the school to take the examination, let alone stand on her feet to do any later teaching. The leg injury was *real*. She suffered excruciating pain and was forced to be taken to her doctor numerous times by friends. Never once connecting her leg injury with her resistance to her prospective job, she decided she would take a refresher course in the subject and postpone the decision. Once relieved of the immediate problem, her subconscious had no need to "protect" her with the reactivated leg injury. So, once the decision was made, her leg immediately began to get well and finally returned to normal.

Though there are countless similar examples of the subconscious coming to the rescue, the solution may often be more drastic than the original problem. It is not unusual for a widowed parent to have a heart attack when an only child threatens to leave home. An insecure man unconsciously developed an ulcer as a ruse to cover up and "solve" the problem of failure to provide sufficient financial income for his family. The ulcer successfully kept his wife and family diverted from the real problem. They felt sorry for him and cushioned him with every possible attention because of his "condition." He thus could not be blamed for his failure to support them adequately so his subconscious ruse worked!

In other families it is not unusual to hear relatives cautioning, "Don't cross father, remember his blood pressure!" Such self-protective devices are noticeable among business executives, too. The inner conflict may be due to the fight against loneliness, lack of affection, a sense of guilt or inadequacy, or a fear of failure. The outward forms vary.

Dr. George A. Wilson[1] writes, "We readily recognize the red face of anger, the white face of fear, the set face of determination, the contorted face of pain, the flushed face of blushing or self-consciousness, but we do not always connect the outward expressions with an inner, unresolved form of tension. This tension can become visceral (interior body tension) and cause both emotional flare-ups as well as physical ailments.

"We know such tension can cause cold sweats, chills, or fever. Visceral tension can upset and alter the functions of many parts of the body. It can cause contraction of the liver (i.e. liver trouble), of the gall bladder (gall bladder trouble), of the stomach (indigestion), of the heart and/or blood vessels (heart attack or high blood pressure), as well as just plain, unrelieved tiredness. Anxieties, fears, frustrated desires and wishes can also lead to visceral tension and in turn overactivate or inhibit the sympathetic and parasympathetic systems. Nerves, headache, a speeded-up heartbeat, spastic colitis, bronchial asthma, constipation or diarrhea, chronic skin diseases, arthritis, and a host of other disturbances have been proved to be 'psychosomatic' or emotionally caused. Yet a patient in all good faith may deny he is under tension, will stoutly maintain that he has no reason to be upset, and rarely dreams that his ailment comes from anything but physical causes."

This interior disharmony or emotional conflict can and does register as a physical disturbance or actual disease.

[1]George A. Wilson, *Emotions In Sickness.* 1963 (Out of Print).

Sometimes the cause is recent, sometimes it may come from something buried since childhood in the subconscious, and still exists, unrelieved, like a thorn festering in its depths. Finding and uncovering the hidden cause of trouble, bringing it to the light of day so that the individual can recognize it, has often relieved and eliminated a physical ailment, as well as a personality problem. The question is, how is this done?

"The Psychological Approach to Healing"[2] states: "The situation in all cases is that the disease acts as a safety valve for some otherwise unbearable tensions at the thought-feeling level. Such disease is often an effective way of relieving the patient from the necessity of facing or dealing with an unpleasant situation.

"Often a patient may require treatment from a psychotherapist who will seek the interior cause of evident nervous tension. In favorable cases a cure may be established only after a single consultation, but in most cases the deeply seated nature of the disturbance will need a number of interviews. The list of illnesses recognized as 'psychosomatic' grows larger from year to year.

"We know that if therapeutic measures can be applied in the early stages of mental conflict, tensions may be resolved and true health may be restored. The general principle underlying all analytical techniques is that of bringing matters which are hidden or ignored into the field of consciousness, thus making the patient aware of the nature of his symptoms and of their relationship with underlying conflicts due to fear, guilt, frustration, ambition, and the like. At the present time there are many schools, each using its

---

[2]A chapter from *The Mystery of Healing*, by The Theosophical Research Center, Theosophical Publishing House, London, Ltd. 1958. (A Quest Book, revised edition, 1968, Theosophical Publishing House, a department of the Theosophical Society of America, Wheaton, Ill.) This book is the work of N. Beddow Bayly, M.R.C.S., L.R.C.P., Laurence J. Bendit, M.A., M.D., Mrs. Phoebe D. Bendit, H. Tudor Edmunds, M.B., B.S., and Mrs. Adelaide Gardner, B.A.

own characteristic technique and each having a different view of the symptoms revealed. For general principles we will divide these schools roughly into two groups: first, those that look backward into the history of the individual for the cause of his trouble; second, those that look forward.

"The first group works on reductive lines. It looks into the past, exploring the patient's childhood and seeking the cause of his disturbance in terms of repression. This group is frequently successful in relieving symptoms but offers no direct assistance in positive character development. It is true that the individual who has been thus analyzed often alters his behavior, but this is due more to the release of pressure and anxiety than to anything learned about conscious integration. As a result it can happen, and indeed has happened, that what is set free under reductive analysis is destructive and disruptive so that from the social point of view the last state of the patient is worse than the first.

"*The key to all psychological and psychosomatic therapy lies within the patient himself.* True, psychotherapy can and frequently does occur in an individual working by himself. The cure then takes place as a sequel to a *moment of insight,* a clear perception when the person suddenly sees himself as reacting automatically and needlessly to some particular situation. Such a realization of his own compulsive behavior puts him in a position to choose whether in the future he will go on behaving in that way. Obviously if the reaction is painful or shameful he will be ready enough to give it up if he can, but it sometimes happens that the symptom is in some way useful or gives the patient a sense of importance so that a weak character may cling to it even while partially realizing that he himself is creating it to his own detriment. Recovery from deep-seated or long established neurotic conditions *takes time.* Miracles do sometimes happen. Sudden release from compulsive behavior does occur but needs close watching lest the deeper layers of the disorder not yet touched reassert themselves.

"Emotional release, deliberate or accidental, can lead to a change of ideas. A rational perception of the possibility of a new outlook, of a wider view upon life, can react into emotion readjustment, freedom from guilt, or an outburst of forgiveness of an injury. For sound readjustment to take place, all that is needed is an experience of integration *within one's own field of consciousness*. One of the most important things that can happen in psychological treatment is the *discovery of volition, of the power of the inner man to take charge and to choose deliberately to think and act in ways that are more constructive than the old behavior pattern* [emphasis mine]."

Some people can reach this stage of self-understanding alone; others, as previously stated, may need the help of a psychoanalyst to weed out complexes, repressions, and conflicts from the subconscious. However, not everyone believes that psychoanalysis is the *only* way to solve such problems.

Carl Jung,[3] the world famed psychoanalyst, favored by many over Sigmund Freud, stated, "I simply contest the notion that all neuroses . . . arise without exception from some crucial experience of childhood. . . . This is frequently very harmful to the patient, for he is forced to search in his memory, perhaps over a course of years, for a hypothetical event in his childhood while things of immediate importance are grossly neglected.

"The unconscious is not a demonic monster, but a thing of nature that is perfectly neutral, as far as moral sense, esthetic tastes and intellectual judgment go. . . . The unconscious itself does not harbor explosive materials, but it may become explosive owing to the repressions exercised by a self-sufficient or cowardly conscious outlook.

"In my opinion every doctor should be aware of the fact that psychotherapy in general and analysis in particular is a procedure that breaks into a purposeful and continuous

---

[3]C. G. Jung, *Modern Man In Seach of a Soul.* Harcourt, Brace & World, Inc., New York, N. Y., 1933.

development, now here and now there, and thus singles out particular phases which may seem to follow opposing courses. Since every analysis by itself shows only one part or aspect of the deeper course of development, nothing but hopeless confusion [may] result from casuistic comparison."

Self-help *is* possible. Dr. Frederick Pierce,[4] the psychiatrist, suggests that in the case of a conflict, if professional analysis is not available, many people can achieve success by themselves by going back, year by year, analytically. Sometimes helped by word association (a word will raise a feeling of emotional disturbance which needs to be analyzed in order to find out why), an ailment or disturbance can be discovered tied up with a particular experience in one's earlier life. Sometimes if the experience does not come clearly into focus, just writing down the word, which promotes or provokes emotional discomfort, and elaborating and noting any thoughts that seem to come in connection with this word which produced emotional disturbance may reveal the cause.

When the experience is suddenly remembered by the individual, a word picture can then be given to the subconscious to suggest or command that this be dissolved and have no further effects upon the person; that the ailment will be diminished to the point of no return. Dr. Pierce states that he has seen many individuals recover by this method.

This is a do-it-yourself method well worth trying. Another self-help is to watch your dreams. The subconscious often tries to communicate through dreams (while the conscious mind is out of the way). Usually, however, this communication comes via symbols and few people are able to interpret the dreams without professional help. There are some books which list and define dream symbols. I particularly like Hugh Lynn Cayce's *Venture Inward*, Harper and

---

[4]Frederick Pierce, *Mobilizing the Mid-Brain (The Technique for Utilizing Its Latent Power).* E. P. Dutton & Co., New York, 1933.

Row, Publishers, New York, 1964. (Hugh Lynn Cayce is the son of the late Edgar Cayce.) Another book of dream symbology is in preparation by Ann Ree Colton. Mrs. Colton is an ordained minister, and with Jonathan Murro, has founded Niscience, Inc., a many faceted nondenominational group which provides the highest type of education of various kinds. (You will read more about her in Part 3). I have been greatly helped by Mrs. Colton's personal and accurate dream interpretations. You can write to Niscience, Inc., 336 West Colorado Street, Glendale, California, 91204, for further information on her book of dream symbology.

Other self-help in dealing with problems of the subconscious appears in this book in Part 3.

The late Dr. Eric Berne[5] provides a good summary of why the subconscious causes problems for many of us. He wrote, "The unconscious is a region where feelings are stored. This is not 'dead storage' but very much 'live storage' . . . feelings are stored by being attached to images just as electricity is stored by being condensed in something. One cannot store electricity by itself. It has to be stored *in* something. In the same way a feeling has to be stored *about* something. . . . The unconscious then is the source of energy, a thought factory and a storage place. It cannot think any more than an automobile factory can go on a trip. It can only feel and wish and it pays no attention to time, place, and the laws of the physical universe.

"The connections of the emotions with physical disease together with the effects of physical disease on the emotions are often spoken of as 'psychosomatic medicine.' The idea is that a sick mind may affect a healthy body, and a sick body may affect a healthy mind. If we think of the whole human being as a single energy system, we can understand that anything which affects the body will always affect the emotions as well and anything that affects the emotions will

---

[5]Eric Berne, M.D., *A Layman's Guide to Psychiatry and Psychoanalysis*, 3rd Edition, Simon & Schuster, New York, 1968.

also affect the body. In other words, all diseases are psychosomatic. There is no such thing as a disease of the body which does *not* affect the mind sooner or later."

So far, we have, for the most part, discussed emotions which reach or are stored in the subconscious and create tension-caused illnesses.

There are other factors, also stored in the subconscious, which create personality problems. A person may be unpopular, difficult to live with. He may experience failure in marriage, personal relationships, be unsuccessful in a job, feel shy, harassed, persecuted, unloved, and unhappy without knowing what to do about it.

Dr. Berne, also the author of the best-selling book, *Games People Play*, developed a form of therapy to solve such problems. His method is helping a growing number of people. It is called Transactional Analysis. It is relatively new, and is just beginning to be available throughout the U.S. It is a form of self-understanding provided by a trained professional leader and it is available either on a personal basis, or in group therapy.

Dr. Thomas A. Harris,[6] explains it as follows: "Transactional Analysis is a teaching and learning device rather than a confessional or an archeological exploration of the psychic cellars. It gives patients a tool that they can use. It is profoundly rewarding as an experience to see people begin to change from the first treatment hour, get well, grow and move out of the tyranny of the past. Dr. Berne adds, 'It is well known that people speak differently under varying conditions . . . careful observation of patients has led to the discovery that there are three basic ways that an individual may exist at any time. These are called ego states. An ego state includes the way a person is thinking, feeling or behaving at any one time. The three ego states available to any person are called the Parent, the Adult, and the Child.

---

[6]Thomas A. Harris, M.D., *I'm OK—You're OK*. Harper and Row, Publishers, New York, 1969.

Regardless of how old a person is (except in the case of a very young infant), he exists in one of the three ego states. . . . The three ego states are referred to as the structure of the personality and diagnosis of the ego states is called structural analysis. This is usually the first part of a transactional analysis. The action begins when two people get together. Every individual has [within him] a Parent, an Adult and Child ego state. . . . A transaction is a stimulus from one person and a related response from another.' "

Dr. Harris adds, "Early in his work on the development of Transactional Analysis Dr. Berne observed that as you watch and listen to people you can see them change before your eyes. A 35-year-old lawyer Berne was treating said, 'I'm not really a lawyer, I'm just a little boy.' Away from the psychiatrist's office he was, in fact, a successful lawyer, but in treatment he felt and acted like a little boy. Sometimes during the hour he would ask, 'Are you talking to the lawyer or the little boy?' Both Berne and his patient became intrigued at the existence and appearance of these two real people or states of being and began talking about them as the 'Adult' and the 'Child.' The treatment centered around separating the two. Later, another state began to become apparent as a state distinct from 'Adult' and 'Child.' This was the 'Parent' and was identified by behavior which was a reproduction of what the patient saw and heard his parents do when he was a little boy. Continual observation now supports the assumption that these three states exist in all people.

"In the Parent are recorded all the admonitions and rules and laws that the child heard from his parents and saw in their living. They range all the way from the earliest parental communication, the tone of voice, facial expression, cuddling or non-cuddling to the more elaborate verbal rules and regulations espoused by the parents as the little person became able to understand words."

A person may unconsciously, in his relationship with

others, mimic the treatment he experienced from his own parents: a stern tone of voice, an attempt to dominate others, or a sitting in judgment on the actions of another.

Dr. Harris continues, "On the other hand a person may react as a Child, not as a Parent. When a person is in the grip of feeling we say his Child has taken over. When his anger dominates his reason, we say his Child is in command."

For instance, a Child reacts to a situation (now as a grown-up person) such as: "This is mine. You can't have it," or "I'm going to tell my mama on you." Or, "If you don't like what I do I'm going to take my toys and go home." Similar childish reactions, such as whining, pouting, crying, or screaming to get attention, are definite examples of the Child in control of the grown-up person. Normally, the child himself *should* begin to grow up and emerge, not as a child with childish reactions nor a mouthpiece for parental admonition which he often copies in his play with other children, but he should gradually grow into an adult with stable, poised, adult reactions. Many people make this normal transition. Many do not. Sometimes, under stress, even "normal" adults may revert to the states of Child or Parent.

Dr. Harris concludes, "The boundaries between Parent, Adult, and Child are fragile, sometimes indistinct and vulnerable to those incoming signals which tend to recreate situations we experienced in the helpless, dependent days of childhood. However, though we cannot erase the recording, we can choose to turn it off.

"The goal of Transactional Analysis is to make every person in treatment an expert in analyzing his own transactions. In my opinion individuals get well faster in group treatment using Transactional Analysis than in the traditional one-to-one treatment relationship. By 'get well' I mean achieving the goal stated, one of which is the alleviation of the present problem symptoms; for example, marriage breaking up, fatigue, headache, job failure. And the other is to learn to use the Parent, Adult, and Child accurately and effectively. Getting well (in this sense) is a means of freeing up one's Adult from the trouble-making influences and demands of Parent and Child. 'Freed Adults' are not upset by transitory mental disturbances. The Adult viewpoint is, 'I am important — You are important. I am a person — You are a person. I'm OK — You're OK.' This helps to make a good family person a good citizen."

The Adult point of view continuously maintained indicates that balance has been achieved in the "I'm OK — You're OK" position. The goal of Transactional Analysis is self-understanding, helping you to become an emancipated adult, enabling you to have freedom of choice and the ability to change negative attitudes into positive ones. This newly acquired pattern can result in happier, more effective living, not only with others, but with yourself. Thus, if aroused feeling begins to be apparent, it is a sign that the Child is responding. By counting to ten and using restraint before reacting, you can shift gears from the Child to the Adult position. Immediate relief may come, as you start to react to a stimulus, from asking yourself the question, "Who is coming on?" and then doing something about it.

If you wish to know more about this method of therapy, you will find a complete and interesting explanation in the book, *I'm OK — You're OK.* If, after reading it, you feel the need of further help in solving your problems by this method, you may write to The International Transactional Analysis Association, 3155 College Avenue, Berkeley, California, 94704, for the location of a group in your area.

The body should act as a *whole unit,* integrated into a smoothly running engine. Mind, body, and spirit should work together harmoniously without friction. The result is greater contentment, peace of mind and body. This should be one's goal.

John, mentioned in Chapter 1, used much of the psychological help described in this section to remove subconscious resistance to his own healing. He purged his negative mental states in order to clean his slate before starting afresh with physical therapies to repair his body.

He began by substituting positive, constructive thoughts of his physical condition for negative ones, since he began to realize his illness was tied in with negative emotions and thinking. As he did so, his tension began to dissolve. He made a picture of the way he wanted to be. He wrote it out, item by item, on a want list. Twice daily, once in the daytime, the other just prior to sleep, in a state of complete relaxation, he visualized his goal and suffused it with the feeling of the good health he wished to acquire. He gave autosuggestion to his subconscious at these times and often during the day for added reinforcement.

We can all learn to bring our subconscious under control to *help* us, rather than fight us, in our goal to achieve a healthier, happier state of being. *Warning*: visualization, commands, feelings, and autosuggestions must be used for good, not evil purposes, where others are concerned. Otherwise the process will boomerang. The wish for revenge or harm you may be trying to perpetrate upon others will be unleashed upon *you* with untold fury! This is the inexorable law of giving and receiving. Though it may not come at once, it eventually comes full circle. It never fails. So use your newly found knowledge for good for yourself and others and you will reap exactly what you sow. There is no compromise.

Once the re-education of your mind, conscious and subconscious, is under way, then it is time to put in order the next department of your being: your body. The following section deals with fascinating, unusual, and helpful therapies which can speed physical healing.

PART TWO

Unusual Therapies
for Physical Health

7 *"United We Stand: Divided We Fall"*

Each of us is a composite of body, mind, and spirit. These states are so closely interwoven that it is impossible to draw a boundary line between them. What affects one, affects all, and each state affects the other. This is where John made his mistake; he thought the care of the physical body was the *only* avenue to health. He learned the hard way that *all* approaches, blended together, are necessary.

You will find in this section various physical therapies for improvement of your health. You may select one or more or use them all. Nutrition, which is a basic need for everyone's body, is a *must;* the others may be optional. So long as you blend the *physical* with the proper use of the *mind,* as we have already studied in the first section, you are creating unity or integration so that your mind is not pulling one way and your body another. They are working as a team headed in the same direction: health. "A house divided against itself cannot stand." If you use a physical therapy to try to get well and at the same time think and fear and visualize illness, your team of body-and-mind are canceling each other's progress and you remain rooted to the spot.

I began this book with a discussion of the power of the mind only because I had to begin somewhere, but we have by no means left it. Because its cooperation with the physical state is so necessary and the two cannot logically be separated, you will find the subject cropping up from time to time as we investigate the other equally important techniques. I am saving the best — the spiritual, with ESP and other exciting subjects — for the last. (No fair peeking yet. For permanent results it is important to take a step at a time in order to be on solid ground before advancing to the next stage.) Meanwhile, do not be surprised to find references to ESP in this section, too.

Incidentally, the therapies which make up this section have all been found to *work*, or I would not have included them. They may be new to you but they have been tested by experienced researchers with many people. The first one concerns energy. Where do we get it? How can we increase it? How can we use it to improve our health?

Joseph J .Weed[1] says, "Our physical energy comes to us from what we eat and drink and from the air we breathe. . . . Everything we can see, feel, smell, hear or taste is a form of vibrating energy. . . . We live in a great sea of vibrating energy. . . . A hundred years ago this idea was very difficult for people to accept but today we know, and all our scientists agree, that physical matter is made up of atoms which are in turn composed of electrons and protons and neutrons, all in violent motion, in other words particles of energy moving at incredibly high speeds."

We can, if we have the know-how, harness this sea of energy which surrounds us and put it to good use in our bodies. As just one example, plants capture it, and we, in turn, can use the plants as food to introduce it into our bodies. There are other ways to tap and transform this energy so that we can use it physically. It will not sound so "far out" when you stop to think that this unseen energy has already been used for other purposes now considered common: telegraph, radio, TV, solar heating and cooling systems; infrared rays for heating, cooking, and photography in total darkness; x rays for photographing the in-

---

[1]Joseph J. Weed, *Wisdom of the Mystic Masters*. Parker Publishing Company, West Nyack, New York, 1968.

terior of the body; as well as electricity to produce heat, light, and power. Although universal energy employed for such means cannot be *seen* by the naked human eye, the power is there just the same. It can even be used for remote control to open a garage door, guide a missile, or, with a little gadget held in the hand without the use of connecting wires, to operate a TV from across the room. One man has monitored, from the ground, every organ in the bodies of the astronauts during a moon flight! (I have his detailed report before me.) Apparently almost anything is now possible.

There is no mystery about this concept of using universal energy. It is not mystical. It is not religious, though some religions are based upon it because Jesus, a great psychologist, used the method. Actually, we know now that the concept is merely common physics, many of the laws of which we learned in high school.

Dr. Frederick W. Bailes[2] says, "This power activates everything in the universe. Since it holds together the atoms and keeps every blade of vegetation growing; since it controls the action of the sun which keeps this planet alive; since it digests our food and keeps our hearts pumping; since it controls the nerves so we can see, hear, and move, would it not be a good idea to spend time in finding all we can about it in order to achieve greater cooperation with it?

"The human body is the greatest example of the working of this universal intelligence that the world has ever seen. This intelligence, whose work we watch in the body, is the same mind that knows perfectly how to heal the structure which it has built. In 280 days it builds a complicated organism of belts, pulleys, hinges, trap doors, with kitchen, pantry, dining room, complete hot water system, air conditioned to keep the temperature always at 98.6° and even wired for sound. It knows how to build these cells out of

<hr>

[2]Frederick W. Bailes, M.D., *Your Mind Can Heal You.* Dodd, Mead & Co., New York, 1941, 9th Printing.

nothing; it certainly knows how to rebuild new cells when something has happened to sicken the old ones. Our part is to set before it the perfect plan to follow in rebuilding.

"Another example of the intelligent working of Universal Power is seen in a cut finger. . . . No man lives who knows how to grow one new cell to heal a wound. In the case of the cut finger, the new cells are built up from the bottom of the wound under the protection of the scab. If one should pull the scab away before the entire rebuilding is complete, the cut will bleed again and the whole process will have to be repeated, formation of clot, scab, etc. so that the repair can be completed according to the plan of spirit. . . . If universal intelligence can do this, it can do anything we want it to; besides it does all this silently, easily, effortlessly and without any fuss. The power flowing into a sick body can heal any situation."

Dr. Bailes concludes, "It is clearly evident that a healing principle exists in the universe operating independently of any medication used by man. A bird in the forest, breaking a wing or a leg, is healed after a lapse of time. The torn hide of a jungle animal heals without outside intervention. Yet there is an intense rivalry among the various schools of healing on the human plane, each insisting that his is the only method and that all others should be barred from practice. In spite of the diverse systems of treatment, it is evident that *there must be something outside of these systems that contributed to the return of health to the patient.* So we must find the real cause of healing . . . there must be a deep underlying principle of healing beneath all of them; this principle is not the exclusive property of any of them."

In other words, no one has the monopoly on healing. Everyone has access to it. Any honest doctor, regardless of his specialty, will admit that it is not he but nature who does the healing. The doctor may be a channel and set the stage by various methods for healing, but in the long run, it is the Universal Power which does the work. One group of authors[3] states: "The symptoms developed will naturally vary with the psychological type of the individual. Also, such factors as debility, sunlight, sleep, exercise and vitamins play their recognized part and hence at times purely physical treatment such as change of diet, a course of medicine, physiotherapy, or an osteopathic or chiropractic adjustment will relieve the physical symptoms of psychosomatic disease."

While Dr. Bailes was a student at a large London hospital, he closely observed the mental factors which were a factor in the recovery of patients. He noticed there were certain thought patterns which invariably produced certain body reactions. Trained in the sciences, he realized there must be a law operating and later he proved conclusively that both sickness and health find their origin in corresponding mental states. He also found there is a definite technique of setting this mental law in action which will result in physical health.

He says, "The secret in healing lies in man's ability *to consciously unite with the universal intelligence and to draw upon it for the removal of diseased thought patterns and the substitution of a health pattern.* This is far easier to do than most people imagine. Millions of men and women have done it already and have eliminated sickness from their experience. I have seen it done every day of my life by those with whom I have been brought in contact.

"When we understand that the universal mind fills the universe, we can picture it as a great surrounding ocean in which we are submerged and upon which we draw. . . . It has no power of choice, *but must be directed into action.* It is highly intelligent; it has all the knowledge of the uni-

---

[3]A chapter from *The Mystery of Healing,* by the Theosophical Research Center, Theosophical Publishing House, London, Ltd. 1958. (A Quest Book, revised edition, 1968, Theosophical Publishing House, a department of the Theosophical Society of America, Wheaton, Ill.). This book is the work of N. Beddow Bayly, M.R.C.S., L.R.C.P., Laurence J. Bendit, M.A., M.D., Mrs. Phoebe D. Bendit, H. Tudor Edmunds, M.B., B.S., and Mrs. Adelaide Gardner, B.A.

verse within it, but it does not reason. It knows only one thing—this is, *to move in the direction to which it* is directed."

Judge Troward[4] adds, "What the individual does is to *give direction to something which is unlimited,* to call into action a force infinitely greater than his own, which, because it is in itself impersonal though intelligent, will receive the impress of his personality and therefore make its influence felt."

Dr. Bailes sums it up: "We are using a power we do not fully understand, but we have learned one thing about it: *it flows in the direction which man's mind indicates.* To the person who thus lifts himself into the higher levels of thought and life, a new world comes. A person who has had a diagnosis should drop his diagnosis, ignore the prognosis, and turn away from his terror and say to himself, 'I know that all of the life of the universe streams through my body at this moment; it knows nothing of such things as incurable conditions. I know that the only thing that hinders my complete restoration now is my own blindness to truth.' The secret of healing lies in *unification with cosmic intelligence.* There is a definite law of mental healing which can be applied by anyone."

Before learning how to operate this law, William Wolff,[5] writing about the same concept, known as Concept Therapy, provides us with further hints: "Concept Therapy begins its instruction with the unknown power, the source of all created things and ultimately of all ideas and concepts. Concept Therapy begins with the creation of the world. . . . The entire material universe is constructed of small particles of matter called electrons and from the electrons the world was created.

---

[4]Judge Troward, *The Edinburgh Lectures on Mental Science.* Robert M. McBride & Co., 1924.
[5]William Wolff, *Psychic Self-Improvement with Concept Therapy.* Grosset & Dunlap, New York, 1968.

"The first law taught by Concept Therapists is the Law of Perpetual Transmutation of Radiant Energy: this law explains the truth that everything in the material universe, all that we see, hear, touch, taste or smell, our emotions and our thoughts are simply manifestations of energy. Those specializing in the field of physics tell us science has learned that we can't create energy and we can't destroy energy. *Just change it . . . we can change energy at will"* (emphasis mine).

This raises two questions: how can we draw upon this energy, and after we once get it, how can we change it into what we want? There is a definite method for absorbing the universal energy, which I will explain shortly. After you once have indrawn it, then you can, by thought and visualization, turn it over to the subconscious to direct it into any purpose you desire. In other words, just as a power plant acts as a transformer for this unseen energy into heat, power and light, and delivers it by conduit or wires in the form needed to the place where it is required, you can act as a transformer too. Once you have acquired the energy you can turn it over to the subconscious with instructions by thought, feeling, visualization, and suggestions (the language it understands) and the subconscious then takes over the job assigned to it and prepares it for delivery. This method is slightly different from the techniques previously discussed. The subconscious *can* accomplish the same and without the added use of the energizing power, but the results are greater and often quicker if the two are combined. For example, you can get a light by using a candle or an old-fashioned kerosene lamp. But you can get a *greater* light if you hook up a proper light fixture with electrical power!

Joseph J. Weed, mentioned earlier, describes how the power of universal energy must be used to be successful. This power is vibrating energy, he says. It can be tapped by thought, harnessed by thought, and directed into whatever channels you wish. It can be used to build a thought form to create some goal which you desire. Mr. Weed[6] writes, "Every thought form has a tendency to reproduce itself in the physical world as an action, an event, or a physical thing. A weak and tenuous thought form will disintegrate long before this 'out-picturing' can take place. But one powerfully endowed will usually result in a physical manifestation in a relatively short time. . . . Some thoughts are too weak, some too complicated to ever reach the physical stage, but a clear thought repeated again and again is almost certain to create a replica of itself sooner or later. . . . The most important factor in bringing a thought into physical manifestation is the clarity of the visualization that accompanies it."

Here, at last, is the method of acquiring universal energy. The technique is taken from my book, *Get Well Naturally*, and is called the Star Exercise: "In the quiet privacy of your room, stand tall with feet apart, and hands outstretched to the sides. Your left palm should face up, your right palm down. This places you in a star position. Now say aloud, or silently, 'Universal Life Energy is flowing through me. I feel it now.'

"If you remain relaxed you will soon feel a tingle in your finger tips or hands. This is the power flowing into you. It is as simple to tap as flicking on the light switch to get illumination. If you don't feel it the first day, don't over-try. Wait until the next day and try again. As you learn to relax, you will be able to feel the power more readily. In due time it won't be necessary to stand in the star position at all. You can merely make the affirmation silently, wherever you are and you will feel the power begin to flow."

If you want energy, you need go no further. You've got it! A friend of mine who had become severely depleted told me that he wasn't even strong enough to stand up. So he lay flat on the bed, in the Star position, and said the

---

[6]Joseph Weed, *ibid.*

affirmation over and over, for varying lengths of time, until he had accumulated enough energy to get up. Eventually, as he stored it without using it all as fast as he acquired it, his supply increased, as in a reservoir, and he gradually needed less time to become re-energized.

This formula did not originate with me. It has appeared worldwide, in countless books, and apparently was originated by the late Baron Eugene Fersen. He wrote that you can use the Star Exercise for accomplishing *anything*. Now listen closely for the next step: Baron Fersen advised tapping the power *before* requesting it be used for money, housing, or health. It can also be used when you are frightened or depressed, as well as to gather strength for any task which faces you. It comes more quickly, and becomes stronger, the oftener you use it.

So, once you have indrawn a supply of this unseen energy, the next step is to *transform it into whatever you need* by turning the blueprint for its desired use over to the subconscious. State exactly what you wish this power to produce.

Dr. Bailes[7] gives an analogy: "The subconscious mind knows exactly how to lay down cell after cell in a million fingernails and make each one perfect as it is doing at this moment. The subconscious mind is a part of infinite mind. There is no limit set by infinite mind. Man can go as far as he wishes, or stay where he is. The only limiting factor is man himself.

"The body thinks; that which the body thinks it becomes . . . to change a physical condition one must change the thought. *It consists of the conscious unification of oneself with Universal Intelligence.*"

According to the Concept Therapists, the vibratory power which is now generating within you after you have tapped it, can, like electricity, be transmitted from one object to another or from one human to another or to your

---

[7]Frederick W. Bailes, *ibid.*

subconscious through the medium of the electron. Concept Therapy states, "Vibratory control of the body, mind, or soul of a person for the restoration of human equilibrium of health is possible. It may be exercised through the medium of the resonant electric waves of the brain cells. It can also be combined with visualization.

"We get what we *image*, not necessarily what we deserve. . . . Concept Therapy teaches that *if you hold one image to the exclusion of all other thoughts for 33-1/3 seconds, it will succeed in sinking into the subconscious and in due time it will manifest into your life* (emphasis mine).

"It is also a physiological fact (as well as psychological) that feeling also tends to concentrate the mind. A thought-feeling combination helps a greater degree of image manifestation. After you have created a detailed mental picture of not only what you want *but how you would feel* after you actually received what you want, then it is necessary to take the first physical steps toward your objective. Remember this, movement must accompany thought and feeling . . . you must have some kind of a plan of action that you believe will lead to the accomplishment of your image."

The Rosicrucians believe that the longer you can hold onto the visualized picture without changing it, the faster the results.

Dr. Bailes gives us assurance of its effect upon health: "The body is completely replaced every few years, but the mind remains continuous. Mind molds the body. A 'treatment' is a definite movement of thought in a specific direction to accomplish a specific result.

"This is the intelligent power to which man has access because he is one with universal Mind. That tremendous Power is available for his use, but it will not be called into use until he himself calls it. When he understands and accepts the fact that the same power which holds the universe in action is ready to hold his body free from sickness, then

he can know that there are no incurable diseases, only incurable people, incurable because they remain blind to their
potential healing.

"One single thought is enough to change a life. One
clear idea steadily followed is sufficient to remake your
physical condition. Therefore you should hold steadily to
your new beliefs."

So the steps for using and transforming the universal
energy become clear:

1. Use the Star Exercise to draw the energy into your
   body.
2. Make a clear picture of *what* you want it to do.
3. Add a strong feeling of happiness, or satisfaction
   of how you will feel after it is accomplished.
4. Use suggestion for added force. In order to concentrate or focus the power, say aloud or silently, "I
   ask that this universal life energy be directed to . . ."
   adding the words to accomplish whatever you wish,
   such as health, supply, money, etc.

You must NOT interfere by giving directions or any
thought as to HOW it is to be accomplished. Otherwise
you will only delay the final manifestation process. Once
you have taken the steps outlined, forget the whole thing.
Put it completely out of your mind until your next "session."
I have been amazed, again and again, at the unexpected
ways in which the subconscious has produced results.

John told me how he was led to his eventual recovery
by this method. No one had been able to pinpoint the exact
problem tension had produced in his body. General measures had brought general improvement once the tension
was removed, but some disturbing symptoms still remained.
For one thing, his heart would race, hippity-hop, at the
slightest provocation. Yet tests showed that his heart was
in sound condition. Finally he got tired of his racing heart,
and one day, after drawing in the power, he said with fer-

vor, "I ask to be shown the underlying cause of these palpi-
tations!" He not only said it with gusto, he added intense
feeling that he wanted to know the answer, and soon!

Soon afterward, a friend, a minister, called him and
said, "I have the strong feeling that your problem is caused,
pure and simply, by anxiety."

John thought this over and decided it was wrong; he
was no longer suffering from anxiety. His relative had been
removed from his care so the need for anxiety had passed.
Still later, another friend was discussing her symptoms
which had been similar to John's. She mentioned that a
substance which she had been taking had been prescribed
by her nutritional physician to help her adrenal glands,
which are the first to reflect shock, worry, tension. The remark was made casually, but somehow the word "adrenals"
came through that conversation to John like a beacon light!
And, in every bit of technical reading John picked up, the
word "adrenals" seemed to stand out on the page. John told
me wryly, "I was pretty dense. I still didn't get the message."

One morning he awoke with the intense desire to read
everything he could find about the adrenals. To his amaze-
ment he found he had acquired every single symptom of
adrenal disturbance, including a fast heartbeat! The explanation was given that though shock or worry can temporarily
trigger the adrenals, if stress continued over a long period
of time, they *remained upset,* even though the initial shock
or worry or anxiety had passed. So at last, in a response to a
strong deeply felt request, the cause of his trouble had been
given him by his subconscious. With the help of a nutritional physician, he began to include the necessary natural substances for repairing and restoring the adrenals to normal
and his condition took a great step forward. It had taken
at least three thrusts by his poor, valiant subconscious, each
from a different source, before John at last recognized the
clue he was seeking.

Once you make your request, be alert for information beamed to you. Meanwhile, watch yourself like a hawk so that between sessions you do not give yourself counter-suggestions (which will cancel out the original) or unconsciously picture what you do *not* want. Also, don't give up too soon. Time, as well as clear-cut pictures, and *intensity* of thought are required for most changes. I have learned that when I really want something *hard* and I put a lot of "oomph" into it, the desired result comes much faster than when I am wishy-washy about the whole thing. Others report that the greater the change required, the more energy is needed to produce that change.

The next chapter contains another method of re-educating the body in order to improve health and tells of people who used the method with success.

CHAPTER 8 *Talking to Yourself*

There seems to be a belief floating around that if you talk aloud to yourself it is a sign you are off your rocker. This is a generalization which can become ridiculous. An elderly woman I know, who like many elderly people lives alone and seldom has anyone to talk to, says it is of great comfort to talk to herself. It helps her to formulate her thinking, as well as to hear the sound of a human voice. Thought can often become vague and fuzzy. The spoken word, as we will see in the chapter on sound, has real potential for power. We have already seen how one can talk, silently or aloud, to the subconscious. In this chaper you will learn that you can talk to other parts of the body too, with good results.

Skip Eldridge, who was introduced in Part I, says, "Our bodies are composed of billions of cells. Each cell is an entity, which has a specific job to do as a part of its 'community.' Its community may be an organ or tissue—the liver, skin, the blood, or a bone. The cell may be a strong, helpful, and valuable member of the community; or it may be weak, malformed, and unhealthy, contributing little or nothing to the general welfare. The health of the entire body is the sum-total of its cells."

If you have an ailment, *your body is trying to tell you something.* If you will find where that ailment is located,

[1]Catherine Ponder, *The Healing Secret of The Ages.* Parker Publishing Co., West Nyack, N. Y., 1964.

you may uncover a clue as to why you have that particular disturbance. Knowing the cause is half the battle. You can then begin to take steps to eliminate the ailment.

Reverend Catherine Ponder[1] states that various centers of the body are related to various disturbances. For example, the centers involving the conscious mind are located in the head area: the center of the forehead between the eyes, the base of the brain in the back of the neck, and the throat. She says that health problems in the forehead, brain, ears, eyes, nose, or throat can often be traced to negative thinking, and can, in turn, be relieved by using conscious, constructive thoughts for treating these areas.

The upper part of the body, she continues, includes centers at the heart, the solar plexus, and the navel; there are also body centers located in the organs of elimination in the lower back, and in the genital organs. Reverend Ponder points out that when you have physical ailments in the heart and abdominal region, it may often be traced back to old hurts, prejudices, resentments, bitter emotions, and past memories. She says, "People who have heart trouble, female disorders, kidney trouble, stomach trouble, and various elimination problems are usually carrying deep subconscious resentments toward people and experiences of the past, which must be cleared out before permanent health can be restored in the abdominal region of the body."

Catherine Ponder presents another fascinating concept: the relationship of the right and the left side of the body. She states that the right side of the body is masculine and symbolizes wisdom; whereas the left side of the body is feminine and symbolizes love. She conjectures that if ailments have affected one side of the body, say in an arm, a leg, an eye, an ear, whether they are chronic or accidental ailments, the cause could be rooted in a resentment toward someone of the masculine or feminine sex, depending upon which side these repeated health problems occur. It might be the resentment to a father, brother, or husband (if these ailments insist on attacking the right side of the body); or if they attack the left side, it might be due to the domination of a mother or some other woman who has had an aggressive or disturbing effect on one's life. This is a highly intriguing idea and may provide a clue to the cause of many a disturbance.

Just as a part of the body tries to talk to you by sending out distress signals, so can you talk to a particular part of the body to help relieve its distress. Yogi Ramacharaka[2] explains why this method of healing can succeed, and he tells how to do it. He says, "The cells of our body are built into organs, parts, tissue, muscle, etc., and form what is known as cell communities in which their minds seem to combine. In the case of the liver, for instance, the millions of cells composing that organ have a community mind which may be called the 'liver mind' and which acts as an 'entity,' subject always to the control of the subconscious. This is most important to remember . . . this principle [of healing] depends upon the fact that these organs, through their minds, are amenable to mental control and direction. . . . Organs, heart and even cells of the body have a 'mind' in them. This 'mind' in the cell, cell groups, nerve centers, ganglia, etc., respond to a strong thought impression from the outside, particularly when the thought is heavily charged with universal energy. The parts are thus reached directly rather than through the subconscious, as is the case of thoughts and visualization used alone."

Yogi Ramacharaka assures us that, if correctly used, this method of healing is simple, direct, and wonderfully effective. The theory, he says, is that speaking firmly to the afflicted part overcomes a rebelliousness in the "mind" of the part and forces it to resume its normal function. The part then begins to re-establish normal conditions and the diseased condition begins to vanish until health returns.

---

[2]Yogi Ramacharaka, *The Science of Psychic Healing.* Yoga Publication Society, Box 148, Des Plaines, Illinois 60016, 1934.

You may use this technique though you may be under the care of a doctor. Ramacharaka tells how to do it: "Speak positively, either by uttering the actual words, or speaking them mentally, something like this: 'Now, (naming the part) you are behaving badly. You are acting like a spoiled child. You know better and I expect you to do better. You must, and will, do better and act right. You must bring about normal and healthy conditions. You have charge of these organs and I expect you to do the work properly that infinite mind gave you to do.'"

Ramacharaka adds, "Point out to the 'mind' of the part just what you expect it to do and you will be surprised at how readily the cell minds obey. The rebellious mind as a part acts like a child who is pouty, cross or out of sorts, which must be coaxed, scolded, led or loved into right action, as the case seems to require. The idea of love . . . of course should be behind it all, just as in the case of handling a child. The cell mind is essentially an undeveloped childlike mind and if you remember this you will be able to apply this treatment to the best advantage.

"You can also use your hands by placing them on the area to attract the attention of the mind in the cells and the parts, just as we attract the attention of a man by clapping him on the shoulder. Awake the attention of the cell mind and you will find that your orders are intently listened to."

Here is an example of a woman who used this method with success. Myrtle Fillmore and her husband, Charles Fillmore, founders of Unity, had both suffered from serious illness before being healed, an experience which led them to the founding of this worldwide religion. Myrtle Fillmore received a diagnosis of tuberculosis and was given six months to live. She describes her own experience.[3] Mrs. Fillmore said, "Life has to be guided by intelligence in making all forms. The same law works in the body. Life is simply

---

[3]James Dillet Freeman, *The Household of Faith*. Unity School of Christianity, Lee's Summit, Mo., 1951.

a form of energy and has to be guided and directed in man's body by his intelligence. How do we communicate with intelligence? By thinking and talking, of course. Then it flashed upon me that I might talk to the life in every part of my body and have it do just what I wanted. I began to teach my body, and got marvelous results.

"I told the life in my liver that it was not torpid or inert, but full of vigor and energy. I told the life in my stomach that it was not weak or inefficient but energetic, strong and intelligent. I told the life in my abdomen that it was no longer infested with ignorant thoughts or disease . . . but that it was all a-thrill with the sweet, pure, wholesome energy of God. I told my limbs that they were active and strong.

"I went to all the life centers in my body and spoke words of truth to them—words of strength and power. I asked their forgiveness for the foolish, ignorant course that I had pursued in the past when I had condemned them and called them weak, inefficient, and diseased. I did not become discouraged at their being slow to wake up, but kept right on, both silently and aloud, declaring the words of Truth until the organs responded."

Myrtle Fillmore's health immediately began to improve, and within two years she was completely well and lived another 40 years, well and happy, instead of dying at the end of the six months which had been previously allotted her. Her husband, who had been a chronic invalid for 25 years, was slow to accept this concept of healing. But when he did, a diseased hip, a shriveled leg, a deaf ear, and a weak eye all responded to the healing. Mr. Fillmore concluded, "I am satisfied that here is proof of the law that the mind built the body and can restore it."[4]

Dorothy Wynn Smith, and her husband, Melvin O.

---

[4]Charles Fillmore, *Atom Smashing Power of the Mind.* Unity School of Christianity, Lee's Summit, Mo., as reported by: Catherine Ponder, *The Healing Secret of the Ages.* Prentice-Hall, Inc., Englewood Cliffs, New Jersey, 1962.

Smith, internationally renowned as teachers in religious and ESP circles, have long recommended the technique of talking to parts of the body to achieve health. Dorothy Smith told me, "Whenever anything is amiss in your body, sit down and talk to whatever part is giving you trouble: your liver, your heart, or whatever. Tell it that it is a part of Universal Intelligence and that you want it to unite with this intelligence and get back into balance. The imbalance may be due to a fault of yours, something you may or may not have done, but the healing formula is always the same." Dorothy says that this method has worked for her, and she has seen it work for literally thousands of others.

Joanna, a friend of mine, has used this method for many years. She learned about it originally from a family doctor. At the time she suffered from a nervous stomach. With little provocation she would upchuck again and again and nothing could seem to stop it except injections of drugs. Soon it became clear that the drugs were causing more trouble than her stomach. Her physician decided some other method of calming her stomach must be found. Finally he said to her, "Try this: put your hand on your stomach and tell it to calm down and perform normally."

She followed his advice and was surprised that it worked. Drugs were no longer necessary. Joanna told me, "I had more success when I talked to my stomach *before* it began to act up, or at least at the earliest sign that an upset was imminent. If I waited until the upchucking had begun violently, it seemed that neither was I able to give directions nor was the stomach able to listen to them."

Joanna also has a long history of back trouble, due to a serious injury. At the slightest exertion the spinal column alignment goes out of place and she suffers great pain. An osteopathic physician can give her an adjustment and restore the alignment to normal, but often the vertebra pops out of place during the weekend when the doctor is out of town, or at other times when he is attending to house calls and cannot be reached.

So Joanna has reverted to her old technique of talking again, not to her stomach, which has recovered, but to her back. She says, "While I am vacuuming or doing some other necessary chore which involves my back, *before* it causes trouble, I say, 'Back, you are strong. You are getting stronger all the time and are going to be equal to any need I have for you.'" She says not only does this work for her back, but she told me how the system also provided a speedy relief from heart trouble.

In addition to her other ailments, largely due to prolonged emotional stress, Joanna's heart suddenly began to cause her trouble. She went to a nutritional physician, an expert on hearts, and he gave her certain nutrients for repairing her heart. He warned her, however, that the repair process would take time. Meanwhile her heart symptoms continued and there were times when she felt she would not make it. Often, for instance, as she leaned over, she experienced frightening symptoms. Other times, on unusual exertion, her heart symptoms would suddenly reappear. So she decided it was time to start talking to her heart. She would put her hand on her heart and say, "Now, Heart, listen to me! I am sympathetic with your problems to keep my body going. You have worked long and faithfully and I do appreciate your efforts, but don't stop now! Nutritional help is on the way. Meanwhile I need greater cooperation from you than ever. I want you to be strong and equal to all my physical needs. I want you to become normal. Get on the job, Heart. Do your job better than ever!"

Again she stated that results were better if she began *before* or at least at the first sign of a symptom rather than waiting for it to become severe. Her heart responded and the trouble cleared long *before* the nutritional program had had the required time to do its work. Perhaps the heart took advantage of the nutritional help and put it to work faster, who knows? At any rate the doctor was amazed at the speed of her progress. Joanna, who has now used the technique for three different ailments with excellent results, was not surprised at all.

She did offer these additional suggestions that she has learned are necessary for success: Never think of the offending body part as ill. Don't say, "I have a bad back, or stomach, or heart." Think of it as WELL. And when that part of the body does improve, give it lavish praise! Like a child, it will respond faster. In other words, "Nothing succeeds like success."

The information in this chapter contained an interesting twist for John. He used the method for his heart, placing his hand on the heart region and telling his heart to slow down. It obeyed, temporarily, but the effect was never permanent. It was this fact that finally pushed him to the point of demanding to know the cause of his trouble, and his subconscious came up with the information about the adrenal glands. These glands, as I explained before, after prolonged punishment had reached the hair-trigger stage and had developed the habit of excreting adrenalin at the slightest excuse of anxiety, nervousness, or stress. This in turn overactivated his heart which would beat like a trip hammer. Once he learned that the cause lay in his overstimulated adrenals, not in the heart itself, he began to talk to the adrenal glands and he reports that the improvement in his heart was amazing.

John did not seem to have need for all the other therapies mentioned in this section, partly because he was already using some of them, particularly nutrition, a subject in which he is an expert. He did, however, derive great help from the information in the next chapter. You may find, as so many have, help in the chapters which follow. Meanwhile, you will not hear more about John until Section Three. At that time I will tell you how he hit the jackpot and achieved complete healing.

CHAPTER **9** *Breathing in Health*

It is possible to live without food for weeks, without water for days (as evidenced by those lost in the desert and on sea-going expeditions); however, it is not possible to live but for a few seconds without air. Air, of course, contains oxygen, which is needed by the body in order to survive, but air is also a carrier of other substances, some contaminating, such as chemicals, pesticides, fallout, and smog; some beneficial. Many people go to the mountains, the desert, or to the sea-shore, or take an ocean voyage to "breathe" the mountain, desert, or sea air, and their health seems to improve. Both positive and negative ions have been discovered in the winds blowing down the slopes in certain mountainous terrains in Europe, with varying effects upon human energy. Most of us take, or did take, air for granted until the air pollution problem developed. Now clean air is so rare, the Japanese are bottling and selling it!

Once, long ago, when I was in a California beauty salon having my hair done, I heard an astounding statement. The salon owner said, "I believe the time will come when we will be able to take into our bodies what we need by merely breathing it from the air." In addition to hearing this statement in such an unlikely place as a beauty salon, its startling idea made quite an impact on me. I have never forgotten it. Now it appears that it may contain some truth. Different groups, both physical and metaphysical, believe that we can, by eating and breathing properly, *absorb* energy essences for stimulating, calming, or healing the body, as the need may be. The naturopaths believe that "vital force" can be extracted from natural plants and substances which have stored it, and it can be taken into our bodies by means of certain foods and beverages. Whether it is realized or not, this is, at least partially, the foundation principle of nutrition.[1]

Yoga calls this same vital or life force "prana." They teach that it can be accumulated and stored in the body by certain breathing techniques. The Hawaiian kahunas call it "mana" and consider it highly important for their successful method of healing. The Rosicrucians call it "psychic energy." They believe that an insufficient supply produces disease, whereas when drawn in by means of the breath it can be released to all parts of the body, removing congestions and obstructions and promoting health. I will give you the highlights so you can try each of these different methods of using the same principle. Although the concept is similar to the use of the "universal life force or energy" which we have already studied as the Star Exercise, you may find the formulas used by these various groups convincing and helpful. Certainly many healings have been attributed to each of them.

Our breathing, since it is controlled by the subconscious, of course, continues automatically night and day without our doing anything consciously about it. So, we are inclined to take breathing, like air, for granted. We are also inclined to thoughtlessly abuse the act of breathing. Dr. Edna Lister, mentioned in Section One, tells us that feeling

[1]Linda Clark, *Get Well Naturally* (Paperback edition). Arco Publishing Co., 219 Park Ave. South, New York 10003.

weak or old means that the body has been drained of universal energy; that it can be replenished by deliberate, and constant, deep breathing. She explains, "The whole body is starved a little at a time as our breathing becomes shallower and shallower. The real feeling of energy and youthfulness comes from the permeation of every cell in the body by this means.

"Breathe deeply and declare that you are now transforming universal energy into physical energy for every need in the restoration and revitalization of your body."

I have not met Dr. Lister, but I know some of her adult students. In spite of a history of near blindness plus an accidental injury to her vocal cords which threatened to leave her voiceless, her students tell me that she acquired perfect vision, a normal speaking voice, unlimited vitality, and was still going strong until she passed on in her late 80's.

Dr. Lister's use of the breath is one secret of her physical success. She said, "Train yourself to take time out to breathe every hour on the hour, and in between times, if you have need of extra strength when something unexpected happens. From somewhere comes a surging up of strength to answer the call for help."

Dr. Lister felt that the average shallow breath is *not* enough. It should be "deep and high" involving the entire lower, middle, and upper diaphragm.

The Kahunas of Hawaii are described by Max Freedom Long,[2] who is probably the best-known researcher on the subject. Long reports that Baron Eugene Fersen, the originator of the Star Exercise, used the same universal life force or energy principle which the Kahunas called "mana." The Kahunas were undeniably successful in getting answers to their prayers. One of their first steps was to breathe in a surcharge of mana. They then combined it with a clear pic-

[2]Max Freedom Long, *The Secret Science Behind Miracles*, Kosmon Press, Los Angeles, Calif. 90006, 1948. See also, *The Secret Science at Work*, Huna Research Publications, P. O. Box 2867, Hollywood Station, Los Angeles, Calif. 90028, 1953.

ture of what they wanted, and with a few other steps they considered necessary apparently got instant or nearly instant results.

Some sects visualize the vital force as a bright light. The Kahunas used the symbol of water to represent mana. Long says, "When they wished to accumulate a surcharge, they breathed deeply and visualized mana rising like water rises in a fountain, higher and higher until it overflows. The body is pictured as the fountain and the water as mana."

There are various formulas for breathing. They not only vary slightly according to the group or sect which uses them; they also differ according to what you wish them to accomplish. Trying to remember them all is confusing. I suggest that after reading this chapter, you decide what your needs are and choose the formulas that appeal to you. Copy them on a card and keep them where you can find them quickly. If you are a man, tuck them into your billfold. If you are a woman, put them in your purse, or in a safe place on your bedside table.

Lobsang Rampa,[3] a Tibetan Lama, tells what he learned from his teacher: "We should learn to breathe slowly and deeply. We should make sure that all the stale air is removed from our lungs. If we breathe only with the top of our lungs, that air which is at the bottom becomes staler and staler. The better our air supply is, the better our brainpower is, for we cannot live without oxygen and the brain is the first thing to be starved of oxygen. If our brain is deprived of the minimum amount of oxygen, we feel tired and sleepy; we become slow in our motions and we find it difficult to think. A regular breathing pattern soothes ruffled emotions. If you are feeling thoroughly bad-tempered, or out of sorts, take a deep breath instead, the deepest breath you can manage and hold it for a few seconds. Then let it out slowly for a few seconds. Do that a few times and you will find you

---

[3]T. Lobsang Rampa, *Doctor From Lhasa*, Bantam Books, 1968. See also: *The Rampa Story*, Bantam Books, 1968. (Both in paperback).

calm down more quickly than you thought possible.

"Draw in a breath slowly, steadily, and think, as is truly the case, that you are inhaling life and vitality itself. Here is the method: Try to expel as much air as you possibly can. Then over some ten seconds of time completely fill your lungs, throw out your chest, take in as much air as you can, and then cram in a little more. When you have got in as much as you can possibly hold, hold it for five seconds, then slowly let out the air, so slowly that you take seven seconds to get rid of the air within you. Exhale completely, force your muscles inward to squeeze out as much air as you can, then start all over again. It might be a good idea if you do this half a dozen times. You will find that your frustrations and your bad mood have gone.

"If you are going for an interview, take some deep breaths. You will find that your racing pulse will race no more. It will steady down and you will find that you are more confident, have less to worry about. As you breathe, think in rhythm with the breathing, 'Peace. Peace. Peace.' If you think 'Peace,' you will have peace. If you think ease, you will have ease. If you think relaxation, you will have relaxation. If people would devote ten minutes out of every twenty-four hours to this, the doctors would go bankrupt, for they would not have nearly so much illness to deal with."

The Lama warned not to experiment with breathing, because to do so is dangerous. You can become intoxicated through incorrect breathing or breathing too quickly. Never experiment with different ratios of breathing without a competent teacher; the directions given here, according to the Lama, are safe and healthy and harmless.

Lobsang Rampa concludes, "Breathing to a particular pattern is the main secret of many Tibetan phenomena. . . . Have you ever tried to lift a heavy object when your lungs were empty of air? Try it and you will discover it to be almost impossible. Then fill your lungs as much as you can, hold your breath, and lift with ease. Or you may be frightened or angry. Take a deep breath, as deep as you can, and hold it for ten seconds, then exhale slowly. Repeat three times at least and you will find that your heartbeat has slowed up and you will feel calm. These are things which can be tried by anyone at all without harm."[4]

The Yoga methods of breathing have much to offer, particularly if taught and supervised by a reliable and well-trained teacher. Richard Hittleman, one of the most highly respected Yoga teachers, writers, and lecturers, has been seen on his television programs from coast to coast in the United States. He, too, can be relied upon for giving safe, sound, and helpful advice. He says,[5] "If your breathing is short and rapid, your mind will work nervously, agitatedly. If your breathing is erratic, your mind must be disturbed and anxious. But if your breathing is long, slow, smooth, and even, the wildly racing mechanical nature of your mind will become tranquil and peaceful.

"The life-force can be controlled and directed with very positive results. It is possible to consciously direct the life-force from one point in the organism where it has been stored, to another point, for purposes of alleviating pain, illness, and other negative conditions. This is also a wonderful technique to use for quick recharging. . . .

"Remember that you can direct the life-force to any area of the body. If your shoulder requires attention, you would transfer your fingertips from the solar plexus to the shoulder and so forth. This is the fundamental practice in yoga, to raise the vibrations of an afflicted area of the organism and help to restore it to normal functioning. It is used specifically; as a strong refresher and revitalizer of the mind and body; a quick recharge for the storage battery of the organism; to relieve pain and discomforts; to promote relaxation, especially from emotional and nervous

[4]T. Lobsang Rampa, *The Third Eye.* Ballantine Books, New York, 1964. Paperback.
[5]Richard Hittleman, *Guide to Yoga Meditation.* Bantam Books, New York, 1969. Paperback.

tension. It has also proved to be an excellent method for overcoming insomnia. . . ."

Yogi Ramacharaka[6] gives further valuable help:

Healing Yourself

"Lie flat on the floor or bed, completely relaxed, with hands resting lightly over the solar plexus (the pit of the stomach where the ribs begin to separate). Breathe rhythmically. After the rhythm is fully established, visualize each inhalation as drawing in an increased supply of prana or vital energy from the universal supply to be taken up by the nervous system and stored in the solar plexus. At each exhalation image the prana or vital energy being distributed all over the body, to every organ and part, to every muscle, cell, and atom, to every artery and vein, from the top of your head to the soles of your feet; invigorating, strengthening and stimulating every nerve, recharging every nerve center, sending energy, force and strength all over the system. Try to form a mental picture of the inrushing prana coming in through the lungs and being taken up at once by the solar plexus, then with the exhaling effort, being sent to all parts of the system down to the finger tips and down to the toes. Simply commanding that which you wish to produce and then making a mental picture of it is all that is necessary.

Recharging Yourself

"If you feel that your vital energy is at a low ebb and you need to build up and store a new supply quickly, the best plan is to place the feet close together, side by side, and lock the fingers of both hands. This closes the circuit and prevents any escape of prana through the extremities. Then breathe rhythmically a few times and you will feel the effects of the recharging."

Some yoga teachers suggest that prana be visualized

---

[6]Yogi Ramacharaka, *The Science of Psychic Healing*. Yoga Publication Society, Box 148, Des Plaines, Ill. 60016.

and directed into the various "chakras," which are sensitive control or psychic centers for the various parts of the body. The theory is that by focusing the prana, visualized as a light, as entering the body via these particular points, the prana can be sent to various glands which control the body.

I discussed this subject with Richard Hittleman and he told me he was greatly opposed to the chakra method since it could be dynamite! For this reason, he said, he had not included the location of the chakras in his books since, *unless one was supervised and protected by a teacher,* a pupil might run into physical, mental, or emotional danger by opening and influencing the chakras without knowing what he was doing or how to control possible explosive results. Respecting Richard Hittleman, as I do, and knowing that he knows what he is talking about, I pass the warning on to you. Other experts agree with him.

The Rosicrucians, on the other hand, have a safe method which can accomplish the same ends without the need of a teacher standing by for protection. This method, according to Joseph J. Weed,[7] is to visualize a bright white light, like snow scintillating in the sunlight, and then to mentally direct it into your body area through the segment of the spine which is related to that particular area. You will find a chart on page 108 to help you locate the segment or vertebra that influences each area of the body. You can thus direct the healing energy, visualized as the white light, as entering through the proper "door" and thence to the area you wish to treat.

Mr. Weed tells of an example of healing achieved by this method. While he was walking in the woods with his dog, the dog accidentally ran into a dead branch which broke off in his eye. It apparently was causing excruciating pain and was beginning to bleed. Mr. Weed took the dog in his lap, yanked the sharp piece of wood from the dog's

[7]Joseph J. Weed, *Wisdom of the Mystic Masters.* Parker Publishing Company, West Nyack, New York, 1968.

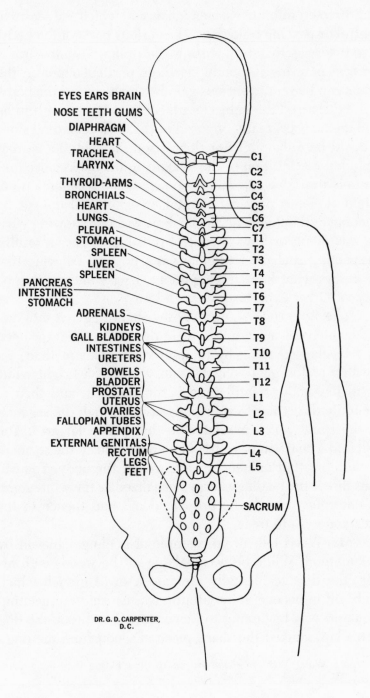

EYES EARS BRAIN
NOSE TEETH GUMS
DIAPHRAGM
HEART
TRACHEA
LARYNX
THYROID-ARMS
BRONCHIALS
HEART
LUNGS
PLEURA
STOMACH
SPLEEN
LIVER
SPLEEN
PANCREAS
INTESTINES
STOMACH
ADRENALS
KIDNEYS
GALL BLADDER
INTESTINES
URETERS
BOWELS
BLADDER
PROSTATE
UTERUS
OVARIES
FALLOPIAN TUBES
APPENDIX
EXTERNAL GENITALS
RECTUM
LEGS
FEET

C1
C2
C3
C4
C5
C6
C7
T1
T2
T3
T4
T5
T6
T7
T8
T9
T10
T11
T12
L1
L2
L3
L4
L5

SACRUM

DR. G. D. CARPENTER,
D. C.

eye, then visualized the energy flowing from the back of the head into the eye to heal it. After ten minutes or so, the wound, which had been large, was beginning to close and the bleeding had stopped. The dog walked beside him contentedly for nearly an hour before they reached home. At that time the wound had been reduced to a mere pinpoint and the next day showed no trace of injury or even a scar.

Mr. Weed's book, based on Rosicrucian principles, is filled with helpful information anyone can use. It also tells of two breathing treatments: one to neutralize a negative condition in the body, the other to neutralize an overpositive condition such as an infection or cold.

For overcoming or balancing a negative or chronic condition, Mr. Weed advises sitting with your feet separated and flat on the floor, knees separated and the first two fingers and the thumb of one hand touching the thumb and fingers of the other hand in the form of a triangle. Relax, breathe deeply, hold the breath for seven counts, then release it. Repeat this seven times. If it needs repetition, wait for two hours between these breathing treatments.

For neutralizing an overpositive condition, Mr. Weed says to sit as before, but this time, your feet should touch each other and the tip of each finger of one hand should touch the tip of each finger of the other hand. Hold the hands somewhat as if in a prayer position in front of your chest. Take a deep breath, exhale completely, emptying all the air out of your lungs. While it is *out*, hold and slowly count to five. Then breathe naturally five or six times, and repeat until you have done the exercise five times. He says, "Three of these treatments an hour or two apart should be adequate."

It may take from two to six hours to see the results of these exercises. If you do not know which treatment to use, Mr. Weed assures us it does not matter, "The wonderful part of these treatments is that if you err and use the positive where the negative is called for, or vice versa, there are no harmful effects."

Dr. Lister concludes, "Even though the physical body has reached a stage of decline, it can be brought back. Wanting it with all the mind and heart and inbreathing of light from the source becomes energy. This energy soon melts and dissolves and absorbs any crystallization of the outer cells, replacing the old ones with newly created ones."

I believe you will agree that we are exploring some exciting fields. But this isn't all! In the next chapter you will learn another surprisingly simple method of using energy manually to get rid of many ailments.

10 *Contact Healing*

According to some investigators, the body is divided into invisible physical zones, running up and down in parallel lines from head to foot. These zone lines are quite close together — as close, for example, as toes or fingers are to each other. The zone lines are something like latitudinal and longitudinal lines on the map of the earth, although the body lines, also invisible, are all vertical, not horizontal.

Somewhere on every one of these lines is located the contact to a nerve, organ or gland. The theory is, and it is not only an exciting theory, but an accomplished fact in thousands of cases, that if there is disturbance somewhere in the body it will register on one of these zones. There is a simple method of relieving this disturbance. No harm can come from it, and those who have used it report that a great deal of good can result. If, by checking the road map of these body zones, you find a sore spot when you press on it, it means, according to the investigators, that something is wrong with some area lying on that body pathway. The fact that there *is* a sore spot (which shouldn't exist if the area is in a healthy condition) is a sign that there is either congestion or an energy leak. Those who have taught or used the method of simple treatment to reverse the condition report remarkable results with such disturbances as sinusitis, eye strain, asthma, duodenal and stomach ulcers, high blood pressure, gall bladder disfunction, heart trouble, digestive problems, bursitis, thyroid imbalance, and many other disorders. This technique is not offered as a "cure" for anything; rather it is a means of helping nature relieve a disturbance so that the body can help heal itself.

The earliest form of this therapy was discovered thousands of years ago by the Chinese. It consists of inserting a needle, as fine as a hair, in a spot somewhere on the zone line of a gland, organ, or area which is causing trouble. Although the needle insertion sounds formidable, it is usually painless and many amazing results have occurred from its use. The method is known as acupuncture, and although it is belittled by some American doctors, I know doctors who use the method, and they and their patients swear by it. Aldous Huxley stated in his foreword to a book on acupuncture, written by a London physician,[1] "That a needle stuck into one's foot should improve the functioning of one's liver is obviously incredible. . . . It makes no sense. Therefore we say it can't happen. The only trouble with this argument is that as a matter of empirical fact it does happen."

Even the *Journal of the American Medical Association* wrote, "Acupuncture has for the millennia constituted the mainstay of traditional Chinese medicine. In recent years it has by decree become part of the medical practice in the People's Republic of China. It has maintained its popularity without compulsion in Japan, and most surprisingly, it has taken a firm foothold in such medically enlightened countries as France and Germany."

Acupuncture is obviously not a do-it-yourself treatment; I mention it merely because it apparently acts on the same zone lines involved in the simple do-it-yourself method I will soon explain. A more recent method than acupuncture, which is based on the same principle, is called "zone therapy."

In books on zone therapy there is usually a map of the bottom of the feet showing where the zone lines end, and

[1]M. B. Felixmann, *Acupuncture*. Random House, New York, 1963.

revealing the exact areas which correspond to the parts of the body. Even without this chart you could probably find your own troubles just by probing the bottom of your foot. Wherever you find and bear down on a sensitive spot, believe me, you will know it! Zone therapy teaches that if you firmly press or even massage or knead these spots with your finger tip for a minute or more, you help to loosen crystalline deposits which have formed at the nerve endings, and the electrical impulse of the nerves can be restored.

F. M. Houston, D.C.,[2] has been working with a similar but different method with great success. He uses the zonal areas not on the bottom of the feet but on the head and body. He has been doing research and testing with this method for thirteen years and has taught the method in classes all over the United States. He has gradually discovered 88 different points on the head or body which relate to different trouble spots in the body. His charts show where these painful spots can be located on a zone line and what they mean when you find them.

He says, once you have located a tender spot, "Put the end of your finger on the painful spot and just hold it there. Do not move it, or you will move off of the zone which needs help. Just hold your contact, pressing fairly firmly, then see if you can feel what is going on inside your body. As soon as you close the energy leak, the polarity is reversed and the energy flows back into the part of the body which was losing it. You will feel a warmth build up in the organ you are treating (its location is identified in the chart), and this warmth indicates that regeneration and repair are beginning to take place. When there is no longer any tenderness at the contact point you can feel assured that the regeneration is complete."

The diagrams show exactly where the energy leaves

[2]F. M. Houston, D.C., *Contact Healing*. Self-published, revised edition, 1972, price $25.00, available only from Dr. Houston, P. O. Box 51, Highway 80, Guatay, Calif. 92031.

the body, thus where to stop the energy leak. This reversal of symptoms does not usually take place in one treatment. Dr. Houston explains, "None of these nerve centers will ever be tender or painful unless something is in a state of disease or imbalance. The more toxic the body is, the more nerve centers you will find in trouble. Also the more tender the specific spot, the more that part of the body needs help. In some chronic cases where the nerves are very weak, it may take several treatments in order to stimulate them alive again to the point that they will begin doing the job they were intended to do.

"I know of no illness or condition that Contact Healing does not help immeasurably. In over 30 years of working with sick people I have never seen a therapy that so consistently gave results. In many cases the healing was so fast it seemed like a miracle."

The following head charts list most of the areas where body ailments can be treated by pressing your finger tip firmly on them. The charts were contributed by Dr. Houston. I recommend Dr. Houston's book for all-over body treatment. In addition to the head charts given here, in his book there is a map of the entire body with the appropriate contact points for treating.

However, experiment with the head charts. If you find a sore spot and do not know what it affects, treat it anyway! Contact healing is completely safe. You may use it with or without other treatment from your doctor. After all, your body belongs to you and there is no law stating that you cannot use any treatment you wish, providing it is safe.

I try to use this pressure therapy every day since I believe it is good for prevention as well as reversal of physical complaints. I find that after a few minutes of pressure on a sore spot, a relaxing warmth does occur in the area which needs help. And if you will continue the technique daily, consistently, I am sure you will discover, as I have, that the soreness lessens and finally disappears altogether. You need

Contact Healing

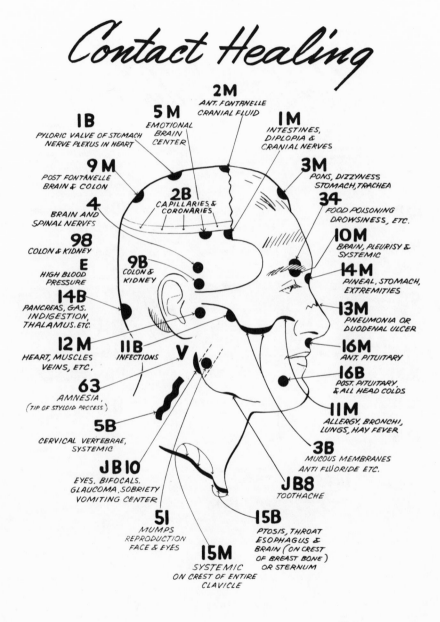

2M ANT. FONTANELLE CRANIAL FLUID

1B PYLORIC VALVE OF STOMACH NERVE PLEXUS IN HEART

5M EMOTIONAL BRAIN CENTER

1M INTESTINES, DIPLOPIA & CRANIAL NERVES

9M POST FONTANELLE BRAIN & COLON

3M PONS, DIZZYNESS STOMACH, TRACHEA

2B CAPILLARIES & CORONARIES

34 FOOD POISONING DROWSINESS, ETC.

4 BRAIN AND SPINAL NERVES

10M BRAIN, PLEURISY & SYSTEMIC

98 COLON & KIDNEY

9B COLON & KIDNEY

14M PINEAL, STOMACH, EXTREMITIES

E HIGH BLOOD PRESSURE

13M PNEUMONIA OR DUODENAL ULCER

14B PANCREAS, GAS. INDIGESTION, THALAMUS. ETC.

12M HEART, MUSCLES VEINS, ETC.

11B INFECTIONS

V

16M ANT. PITUITARY

16B POST. PITUITARY, & ALL HEAD COLDS

63 AMNESIA, (TIP OF STYLOID PROCESS)

11M ALLERGY, BRONCHI, LUNGS, HAY FEVER

5B CERVICAL VERTEBRAE, SYSTEMIC

3B MUCOUS MEMBRANES ANTI FLUORIDE ETC.

JB10 EYES, BIFOCALS. GLAUCOMA, SOBRIETY VOMITING CENTER

JB8 TOOTHACHE

51 MUMPS REPRODUCTION FACE & EYES

15B PTOSIS, THROAT ESOPHAGUS & BRAIN (ON CREST OF BREAST BONE) OR STERNUM

15M SYSTEMIC ON CREST OF ENTIRE CLAVICLE

Contact Healing

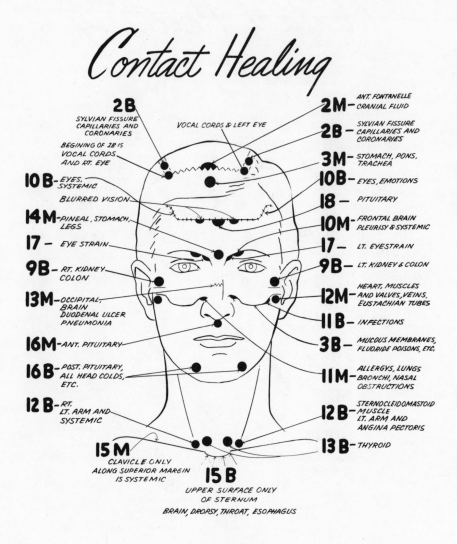

2B SYLVIAN FISSURE CAPILLARIES AND CORONARIES

BEGINING OF 2B IS VOCAL CORDS AND RT. EYE

VOCAL CORDS & LEFT EYE

2M – ANT. FONTANELLE CRANIAL FLUID

2B – SYLVIAN FISSURE CAPILLARIES AND CORONARIES

3M – STOMACH, PONS, TRACHEA

10B – EYES, EMOTIONS

10B – EYES, SYSTEMIC

BLURRED VISION

18 – PITUITARY

14M – PINEAL, STOMACH, LEGS

10M – FRONTAL BRAIN PLEURISY & SYSTEMIC

17 – EYE STRAIN

17 – LT. EYESTRAIN

9B – RT. KIDNEY COLON

9B – LT. KIDNEY & COLON

13M – OCCIPITAL, BRAIN DUODENAL ULCER PNEUMONIA

12M – HEART, MUSCLES AND VALVES, VEINS. EUSTACHIAN TUBES

11B – INFECTIONS

16M – ANT. PITUITARY

3B – MUCOUS MEMBRANES, FLUORIDE POISONS, ETC.

16B – POST. PITUITARY, ALL HEAD COLDS, ETC.

11M – ALLERGYS, LUNGS BRONCHI, NASAL OBSTRUCTIONS

12B – RT. LT. ARM AND SYSTEMIC

12B – STERNOCLEIDOMASTOID MUSCLE LT. ARM AND ANGINA PECTORIS

15M
CLAVICLE ONLY ALONG SUPERIOR MARGIN IS SYSTEMIC

13B – THYROID

15B
UPPER SURFACE ONLY OF STERNUM
BRAIN, DROPSY, THROAT, ESOPHAGUS

© REV. DR. F.M. HOUSTON

not make a martyr of yourself and press so hard you cannot bear the pain. Use only as firm a pressure with your finger tips on the contact point as you can comfortably endure. Hold it for several minutes until the discomfort seems to ease.

Sometimes it is hard to find time to apply this simple technique. Yet many of us waste many minutes during the day doing something far less important and rewarding. If you are waiting for someone in the car, or if you stop to get second wind from your work (where you will be unobserved) you can use those minutes to good advantage. If you prefer to go to a specialist such as Dr. Houston, and pay for the service, that is up to you. Because I am so busy, the only time I can be sure of finding time for my own pressure therapy is in the bath tub. This is a natural for me. If you are a shower-taker, then you will have to find another time and place. Most of us procrastinate in doing the easy as well as the free things in life. So find a time, a place to escape to for a few minutes, and get going! It is the easiest, cheapest, and one of the most rewarding helpful therapies I know.

CHAPTER **11** *Speak Up!*

Everything on earth emits radiation: rocks and minerals, plants, medicine, foodstuffs. Even people radiate certain wavelength frequencies which can be measured by instruments. I have already mentioned the scientist who monitored a moon flight and measured the emanations of the various organs of the astronauts while they were in orbit. He accomplished this using a sensitive instrument, operating it from the ground!

The late Dr. Oscar Brunler discovered that brain waves can be measured and that the direction in which the individual uses his brain or thinking power can become creative or destructive, positive or negative, as he chooses. He developed a special instrument to measure brain wavelengths. His wife, Grace Brunler, M.D., is carrying on this research in both England and America, where she has served as psychologist, psychiatrist, and lecturer for lay institutions, universities, and clinics.

Any student of high school physics already knows that sound, too, creates vibration which can make an impact on various kinds of matter. For instance, it can cause particles of sand to arrange themselves in patterns. Clarence E. Bennett[1] explains, "Vibrations in plates and bars may produce

---

[1] Clarence E. Bennett, *Physics Without Mathematics*. Barnes & Noble, New York, 1970 (paperback, College Outline Series).

118

standing wave patterns of unusual complexity, which can be readily observed by sprinkling fine sand upon them as they vibrate. The sand piles up at the node and disperses in the vicinity of loops. Such designs on sand or in vibrating plates are called 'Chladani Figures.'"

One of the greatest examples of the effect of sound waves is the fall of the wall of Jericho (Joshua 6). According to God's instruction, men of war marched around the city of Jericho for six days. They were accompanied by seven priests who were blowing on seven trumpets of rams' horns. On the seventh day they encircled the city seven times, the priests gave a loud blast on the rams' horns and as Joshua had directed them, the people then shouted together; and the wall fell flat. This mighty power of sound is impressive. Another example is the well-known experiment in which an opera singer with a vibrant voice has shattered a drinking glass by the tones which he emitted.

Such effects are, of course, due to the use of *audible* sound. There are also many effects of *inaudible* sound. The word "inaudible" does not mean that there is no sound at all; it means that it is inaudible to *man*. Insects, birds, and animals, including dogs, horses, and bats, can hear sounds of higher frequencies that man cannot hear. The "silent" dog whistle is one example.

Another type of "inaudible" sound is ultrasound. Ultrasonic frequencies begin where normal human hearing ends. Ultrasound can be used for such things as homogenizing milk by killing many bacteria in the milk, and for giving a smooth and permanent mixture to mayonnaise, peanut butter, face cream, paint, and chemicals. Ultrasound can also be used for physical and diagnostic purposes. Theodore Burland[2] compares ultrasound with x rays, which have a different wavelength frequency. Mr. Burland says, "X rays damage some living cells no matter how judiciously they are

---

[2]Theodore Burland, "Medical Miracles with Ultra Sound," *Family Circle,* October 1966.

applied. . . . Unlike x rays, ultrasound waves do not zip through flesh and other soft tissue at the speed of light. Ultrasound waves are conducted by the watery fluid (lymph) which makes up all soft tissues, thus the slightest subtle change in the tissue density brought on by disease or other physical condition change can be detected by ultrasound though it [the condition], may be invisible to x rays."

Ultrasound can therefore be used to make photographs of a body condition and it is also becoming an important surgical tool. In addition, the sound waves of ultrasound are now being used to clean watches and clocks, and as a measuring device which can detect the depths of the ocean.

Among other things, ultrasound is also used in physical therapy to relieve such ailments as aches and pains and stiffness. This method has existed since it was first introduced in Germany about thirty years ago. According to Mr. Burland, "Dr. David I. Abramsen, professor and Head of Physical Medicine and Rehabilitation at the University of Illinois Medical Center, states that much of the ultrasound's benefits come from a physical vibration of the tissues. This 'micromassage,' as some doctors call it, shakes harmful or foreign substances out of the tissue and sends them on their way. This is why, Dr. Abramsen says, ultrasound works well in bursitis; it loosens and mobilizes the tiny deposits of calcium which cause pain. Similar actions make ultrasound useful in softening scar tissue and in reducing nerve tissue growths. . . ."

However, ultrasonic therapy *must* be handled by a well-trained technician. Otherwise, if one is exposed to it too long, serious damage may occur. One expert in this field told me of a case in which ultrasound was continued too long during a leg treatment and actually cut through the leg itself. I have heard from professionals, of cases of death or life-long effects of injury resulting from over-use of ultrasonic therapy. I have a friend who became a permanent invalid with continuous excruciating pain as a result of ultra-sound treatment. Too much of anything may be question-able. Even too-loud music has proved dangerous in some cases: Dr. David M. Lipscomb, Director of Audiology, Clini-cal Services at the University of Tennessee, reported that pop music at full blast can cause damage to the ears. Cell de-struction was found in the unprotected right ear of a guinea pig subjected to approximately 90 hours of rock-and-roll music. As a result cells were "displaced, collapsed, or totally missing. The animal's left ear, protected by a plug, was undamaged."

The type of music produces varying effects, too. In a series of carefully controlled experiments at Temple Buell College in Denver, plants exposed to prolonged rock music first leaned away from the loud speaker, then finally col-lapsed and died, whereas those subject to semiclassical mus-ic leaned toward the loud speaker and flourished. In 1966 Cleve Backster recorded emotional reactions in plants by using a lie detector. Comparable tests carried on at a Swiss University by Dr. Edwin Kapphan in Zurich also showed that plants experience emotional reactions similar to those in humans. Dr. Kapphan used a sensitive machine, some-what like a skin galvanometer, and learned that a nail stuck into a growing tomato produced a reading on the instru-ment not unlike the response of a man who reacts to a shock caused by extreme anxiety and even fear of death.

Dr. Kapphan concluded, "We must develop a better communication with plants if we are to understand and use them to mankind's fullest advantage. We must also learn to be kind to them." Perhaps this explains why people who love plants are known to have a "green thumb" and can en-courage more flourishing growth from their plants.

A friend who lives in my community told me how she influenced her plants with sound to grow better, by talking *aloud* to them. After one unsuccessful garden year, she talked her plants into producing a better yield the second year. This gave her the courage to try to grow melons, which people find are not successful in our area. Nevertheless, my friend planted the melon seeds, then talked daily, in a firm, loving voice, to the little plants as they came up. She told them what people were saying about growing melons in our area and cautioned the plants to pay no attention. She said, "I want you to grow, keep growing, and produce melons! I appreciate your efforts, and I want you to come up with some melons." They did! She is the only one in this locality who has been a successful melon grower.

She used the same method on bugs. One day when she went out to her vegetable garden (a small portion of two acres) she saw chewed leaves everywhere. Being an organic gardener she refused to use dangerous pesticides. So she talked to the bugs instead. She said aloud and with emphasis, "Now listen, bugs. Stop chewing my vegetable plants! There are plenty of other things on these two acres for you to chew. Eat them, but keep away from these vegetables!" They obeyed and she reports that she had the fewest bugs of any time in her entire gardening experience.

She also applies this method to her own ailments. I will share this with you at the end of this chapter.

Garden plants are known to also react to music. An Indian botanist, Dr. T. C. N. Singh, reports that tapioca and sweet potatoes subjected to music yielded 40 per cent more than control plants. Rice plants yielded 50 per cent more when exposed to classical music; tobacco yielded 50 per cent more as a result of violin music. Photographs are available of corn which had been treated with music as compared with untreated corn.

George E. Smith,[3] a botanist, reasoning that sound waves are a form of energy planted four plots. On one plot Mr. Smith beamed a musical score to the corn plants. To another plot he beamed a continuous high note. A third

[3]*Popular Mechanics*, May 1963.

plot received a continuous low note, and a fourth plot
heard no music at all. These are the results:

	Number of Ears of Corn	Bushels per acre
Silent plot	269	171.3
Musical plot	287	186.1
High-note plot	300	197.8
Low-note plot	328	200.9

Mr. Smith's experiments indicate that musical energy
does affect plant cells. He also points out that it is a matter
of record that sound waves can also destroy cells. Perhaps
the most interesting result of his experiments was that when
all of the corn was exposed to the multiple sounds of music,
the corn borer moth was scared off in the exact pathway in
which the sound was turned on.

Music affects animals too. In Minneapolis, workers at
a research farm of a feed division of a poultry manufacturing
company turned on disc jockeys so that thousands of hens
could sit all day and listen to everything that came out of
the radio. This proved to be a tranquilizer for the high-
strung hens and resulted in better egg production.

The effect of music on mental and emotional response
in humans is already known. John E. Gibson[4] writes, "Music can step up a person's mental performance and actually
increase his ability to think, reason and remember. In New
York University studies this was found to be the case, and
in studies at Louisiana State University a study exposing
students to classical jazz and rock-and-roll music or no music
at all, the result was that the students made the lowest score
on performance when rock-and-roll was played."

Mr. Gibson makes this surprising statement, "A stimulating type of popular music alleviated fear and anxiety
better than calm music or even silence, according to a study
by a team of psychiatrists." Psychological studies on other
men and women who were in extremely worried and anx-

[4]*Family Weekly,* October 4, 1970.

ious states also revealed that depressed people responded favorably to lively and exciting music. More interesting still, studies at a university in Germany found that music which gets on your nerves and thus disturbs or irritates you can definitely *give* you an ulcer; whereas music you enjoy can help prevent ulcers! Researchers have learned that every patient, especially the mentally ill, responds differently to a tune whether it is mildly exciting or joyous. Some will cry when they hear a happy melody.

Frances Paperte, a former star of the Chicago Lyric Opera, organized the Music Research Foundation to explore the scientific benefits of music therapy. As a result of her work, researchers now have a music bank in which they catalog musical numbers to be prescribed according to the individual needs of each patient. Seventy-four per cent of the patients subjected to music therapy showed definite improvement when exactly the right music was played. According to Miss Paperte, "Music has played a large part in the eventual discharge of a great number of patients from mental institutions. In many cases, only thirteen music sessions constituted the course of the treatment."

The effect of sound on physical health is a comparatively new field. Ultrasound has already been described as influencing the human body. One researcher[5] has stated, "It has been found by experiment that certain specific sounds affect certain parts of the body; a different sound vibration for each part and for each purpose of treatment which may be used, for instance, to encourage cell formation, to repair damaged tissues, to treat diseased bone, muscle, skin, etc. Therapeutic sound can be recorded on tape, ready for use whenever required."

There are also therapeutic sounds on records which have been used in literally thousands of cases of certain types of physical disturbances with good success. This form of therapy was developed by the late Christian A. Volf,

[5]Sonic Therapeutics Ltd., Raleigh Park Road, Oxford, England.

Ph.D., a native of Copenhagen, Denmark, and a resident of the United States. The manner in which he discovered that sound can be used for certain types of health therapy came as a surprise to him.

Dr. Volf was the inventor of internationally used police, fire, and city alert sirens. (There is one atop the Eiffel Tower in Paris, others in major cities of the United States.) One day Dr. Volf was holding one of his siren models in his hand, when suddenly and unexpectedly it went off. The sound was terrifying and until he could turn it off, he felt it vibrate throughout his entire body. Temporarily it left him shaken, but afterwards he felt better than he had for years. Apparently, that sound *had acted as a therapeutic stimulus to his entire body.* How, he wondered, could sound be applied to help certain specific body conditions?

As an acoustical physicist, he had already conducted extensive research on defective hearing (an interest arising from having been deaf himself for one year at the age of eleven) and had served as consultant to several well-known American acoustical companies. Sound in any form was his major interest. He had also tested the hearing of many patients by the sound pressure method and had established sound pressure tolerance tests. He was aware of research done years ago by the French investigators who had suggested that sound stimulation might help deafness. Itard[6] an eminent otologist (hearing specialist) of Paris, had said, "Musical tones must of themselves serve as an agent to restimulate the defective action of the auditory nerve and awaken its functioning possibilities. Sound vibration is the most valuable stimulation for the ear and a reawakening of the auditory sense cannot be accomplished without its application. We may employ musical apparatus producing intense tones; we may apply the sonorous tones of a bell in intense or mild degree to stimulate the auditory nerve. In deaf-mutes where complete deafness does not

[6]Itard, *Traite des Maladies del'Orielle et de L'audition,* Vol. I. Paris 1921.

exist, all tone accessories must be consistently and persist-
ently applied."

So Christian Volf first decided to apply the sound
method to deafness; later he extended it to other ailments.
He put the sounds mentioned by Itard on records and "prescribed" certain records for certain types of hearing loss in
order to stimulate the part of the ear which had become
dormant. He found that this sound therapy could often improve hearing to the point that in some cases no hearing
aid would be necessary; or it might raise the threshold of
the hearing of those people who had been unable to use a
hearing aid. As a result, after this sound-stimulation treatment, many people could use a hearing aid for the first time.

Dr. Volf knew there were different types of deafness.
Nerve deafness, indicated by a hearing loss exclusively in
the high register, indicates auditory nerve damage and his
sound therapy did not help this type. Sound should also
travel through the body (many otologists call this "bone
conduction"), but in some people this type of sound transmission through the body has become diminished so that
a hearing aid built to take advantage of this method of de-
livering sound to the ear does not work for them. However,
for this type of loss, Dr. Volf found that sound therapy could
improve bone-conduction (Dr. Volf called it lymph-con-
duction) hearing even if it did not completely restore it.
He reasoned that the proper sound vibrations (the wrong
ones might be damaging, hence the "prescription" for the
right kind of sound for each person) could condition the
body to conduct sound more efficiently.

But there is still another approach to hearing: conduction of sound by air waves. Hearing aids can bring sound
by this method even to those who have nerve deafness or
diminished bone (lymph) conduction, and this type of
hearing aid is now considered preferable for most people.
Meanwhile, except for nerve deafness, Dr. Volf's sound
records, as established by before-and-after audiometric

graphs obtained from hearing tests, showed improvement in numerous cases of deafness. Nine recordings contained synthetic sound limited to an octave or combination of octaves. The prescribed record was used for five minutes daily and could be used at home by attaching earphones to a record player and piping the sound directly into the ears of the patient.

For his humanitarian work, particularly to the hard of hearing, Dr. Volf was later awarded the American Grand Priory of the Sovereign, Military and Hospitaler Order of Saint Lazarus of Jerusalem. He also received the 1949 Award of Merit presented by the New York Museum of Science and Industry for outstanding scientific achievement for the relief of those suffering impaired hearing. In addition, 21 nations have bestowed honors upon him.

I feel fortunate in having known Dr. Volf. One of the fascinating things he told me is that feathers of birds, such as peacock and turkey feathers or even an Indian headdress, can act as a sound gatherer. He said, "Watch a peacock; each feather will individually wave according to a specific sound frequency. Thus feathers can actually become a hearing aid."

After Dr. Volf had successfully treated hundreds of cases of impaired hearing through sound therapy, his work took an exciting turn. Diagnosis of hearing loss has been routinely made by otologists through the use of tuning forks by placing the stem of a vibrating tuning fork on the forehead, the top of the head, or behind the ears. These tuning fork tests led Dr. Volf to a new and exciting method of detecting other disturbances.

One day, while experimenting, he applied the fork to the knee of a patient. Instead of the sound traveling to the ear, as it should, the sound stopped short in the appendix area without traveling further. Surprised, Dr. Volf asked his patient if he had noted any disturbance there. The patient admitted he had. Dr. Volf sent the patient to a physician, who found, indeed, that there was inflammation of the appendix. Then came a further revelation. To test the well-known theory of how sound travels, he had already tried the tuning fork approach to sand on a wooden table. He had scattered sand on the wood and noted that the sound vibrations of the tuning forks, each of a different wavelength, some with lower tones, some with higher ones, *always* created their own distinctive patterns in the sand. The effect of the sound of each tuning fork would cause the sand to shift into these characteristic patterns, and the pattern was always the same for each tuning fork. One day, however, on a different table, Dr. Volf found, for the first time in his experience, that the principle refused to work. Looking for an explanation, his glance fell upon a knot in the wood. Apparently it was obstructing the usual pathway of the sound vibrations. In other words, the knot had blocked the usual travel of the sound. Would a similar "block" or congestion or disturbance in the body mean that something was wrong at the site where the sound stopped, as in the case of the appendix?

With great excitement, Dr. Volf began to try the tuning fork placement on various parts of the body, with other patients. Time after time, somewhere in the body, the sound would hit a "block" and travel no further. At that point of blockage, medical diagnosis would confirm a disturbed or diseased state. It looked as if Dr. Volf had hit upon a painless, simple method of diagnosis, without the necessity of exploratory surgery. Better yet, it could alert a patient to a condition which might have escaped detection or not yet been noticed. But the most exciting part was still to come. Dr. Volf wondered if sound were beamed via the ear, through a record player and earphones, as used in deafness to stimulate and increase circulation to the hearing areas, would it also massage and eliminate an ailment in some other part of the body? He set to work to find out.

He finally established various disturbances that the

tuning forks could locate. In addition to the diseased appendix he found that diagnosis could be made with tuning forks of five different types of headaches, bed wetting, some types of kidney disease, epilepsy, congenital syphilis, tuberculosis, word blindness, word deafness and reading difficulties, hypo- (not hyper-) thyroidism, aphasia (a defect or loss of ability to speak, write, or comprehend due to injury or disease of the brain center), schizophrenia, kleptomania, fear neurosis (in connection with reading), depression, and sinusitis. He then used combinations of his original sound recordings to treat some of these ailments. He found that headaches could be alleviated by use of therapeutic sound recordings as could bed wetting, word blindness, word deafness, hypothyroidism, aphasia, kleptomania, fear neurosis, depression and sinusitis. Schizophrenia could be helped to a degree.

The sinus record has a series of sounds of a specific frequency which seem to stimulate the sinus area. Dr. Volf said, "The sound acts as an internal massage. It vibrates the bony structure, stimulates blood circulation, and starts the sinuses draining. Listening to the sound through earphones should clear up this condition within 30 days." Dr. Volf named his method "The Acoustic Reflex Theory."

I have read letter after letter giving testimonials of the success of the Volf treatment (one of these was from Aldous Huxley). I have seen bound volumes of 10,000 case histories of people for whom Dr. Volf's sound diagnosis and treatment have been used successfully. I have witnessed the good effect of the method used with a bed wetting child (it stopped with no other treatment). Another child, according to her mother, was always "disorganized" — she never could find her shoes, her school books, or put her thoughts in order (the sound reversed this condition rapidly). I have known of an overactive child who could not be admitted to school. After sound therapy he quieted down so that he could attend school, became calm, manageable, cooperative, and able to take up his studies. I have seen a newspaper write-up of a famed child actor on the Lassie TV show whose reading difficulties were eliminated by the Volf sound treatment.

You will wonder at this point where you can get these sound therapy records. You can't. Your government won't allow their use. The history of medicine is replete with examples of refusal to accept something new, no matter how safe and inexpensive. The methods are eventually accepted, but it often takes centuries. Instead of grasping eagerly at the opportunities to help mankind, the medical monopoly not only greets such well-tested therapies with grim silence (or refuses to test them as in the case of safe, natural cancer cures) but often persecutes the originator because his method may be a financial threat to the monopoly. Dr. Volf was ordered to stop using his sound therapy in the U.S.; he was charged with practicing medicine without a license (the usual method employed by government agencies); and his records were destroyed! Yet in Austria a clinic treating up to 1,000 patients a day is using Dr. Volf's therapy on those patients where its use is indicated, and in Denmark there is a private clinic treating school children, who have reading difficulties, with this sound therapy. So Dr. Volf died, an unfulfilled genius with the ability to help many people in the United States.

Other researchers have found out that this type of therapy has merit. In England there is a similar method of using audio-sound waves by means of tapes instead of records, to locate and treat muscular, skeletal, peripheral, and nervous conditions, as well as such disorders as arthritis, fibrositis, bursitis, lumbago, charley horse and many others. Mobility has even been restored to "frozen" hip joints. The respected organization which employs this sound method has had its share of persecution, too. Certainly, it would not be allowed to give treatment outside of England. So we must look for other means of using sound.

If it were not for scientific laboratory tests proving that the effect of sound is not a figment of the imagination, one might shrug off the whole bit as being "all in the mind." One of the most exciting accounts I have ever read is about the visible proof of *how* sound works: John H. Heller, M.D., supplies proof which should be history making! Dr. Heller is a graduate of Yale and Western Reserve University Schools of Medicine, with postgraduate training at Cornell and Bellevue hospitals; consultant for the U.S. Atomic Energy Commission, Navy nuclear submarines and Air Force manned satellites; as well as founder and director of the New England Institute for Medical Research in Ridgefield, Connecticut. Dr. Heller and his group decided to expand work started many years ago by German and Swedish scientists who observed how sound vibration or energy could affect inert particles of matter; they went a step further and observed the effect on live organisms.

Dr. Heller writes,[7] "We constructed a piece of electronics apparatus that would give us the ability to pulse our energy and to pick up many different wavelengths or frequencies to study. . . . We noted that if we put certain bacteria in our radio frequency field, they would line up nose-to-tail in long chains. It was an eerie sight to look through a microscope and see thousands of bacteria in their normal random arrangement, and then turn on a radio frequency field and suddenly see them line up into dozens of chains. . . . As soon as the force field was turned off, the bacteria would gradually return to their normal random distribution."

The experiment was repeated with one-celled organisms, including the paramecium and the amoeba. Dr. Heller explained, "Normally these organisms swim randomly about in all directions. When we turned on the force field, it was as though a minute invisible hand had affected each

---

[7]John H. Heller, M.D., *Of Mice, Men and Molecules.* Charles Scribner's Sons, New York, 1960.

one of them. Their random swimming ceased immediately, and they began to swim back and forth in straight parallel lines. Furthermore, they were unable to leave this rigid back-and-forth pattern as long as the radio frequency field was turned on. . . . The radio frequency field prevented them from doing so. The instant the field was turned off, however, they immediately returned to their normal swimming pattern, rushing about in all   . . . To our complete astonishment . . . when we changed the frequency, the 'animals' changed their directions. Sure enough, at one frequency the 'animals' went back and forth in one direction, and at a higher frequency they wheeled about to pick up a new back-and-forth direction at right angles to the path they had been traveling before." (There are pictures of this phenomenon in Dr. Heller's book.)

What does this mean? It means that matter can be influenced to do what one wants it to do, providing sufficient and the right type of energy and direction are supplied! The Kahunas (and some Indian tribes) could change the weather. With incantations they could make rain and they could also stop it; they could also heal and produce other miracles. So, using sound in the form of the spoken word can influence matter.

Catherine Ponder[8] says, "Every time you speak, you cause the atoms of your body to tremble and change their place. Not only do you cause the atoms of your own body to change their position, but as you mentally raise or lower the rate of your own vibrations, you also affect the bodies of other people with whom you come in contact, just as they do you."

She explains why, after being with negative-speaking people, you feel tired, depressed and run down; but after associating with positive-speaking, happy people, you feel uplifted, even exhilarated. She says, "Every word brings

[8]Catherine Ponder, *The Healing Secret of the Ages.* Parker Publishing Company, West Nyack, New York, 1967.

forth after its kind — first in mind, then in body, and later in the affairs of the individual."

Eleanore Thedick[9] writes, "When you say, 'I am tired,'" you increase the condition. If you would overcome the condition, you must not allow such words to pass your lips. You must say, instead, 'I am well, I am healed, I am strong.' Watch carefully and avoid the negative words that creep into your conversation. Idle words delay and impede your progress.

"Speak words of hope, faith, courage and love and your words will return to you with blessings multiplied. Clear out of your mind all negative thoughts: of fear, worry, or doubt and replace them with positive thoughts. Every positive word spoken affects the life of the one who is speaking the word. The Bible says, 'By thy words art thou justified and by thy words thou art condemned.'"

Joseph J. Weed[10] writing about the methods of the Rosicrucians, also states that we can influence animate or inanimate matter by simply talking to it. He says, "You not only speak to it, but you simultaneously exert an aura of energy to reinforce your will. The words are entirely subordinate to the focused thought reinforced by energy." In other words, energy combined with spoken words is apparently an unbeatable combination for influencing matter.

Concept Therapists believe, and practice with success, the principle that the spoken word can mobilize the molecules and the atoms of matter, just as Dr. John Heller mobilized his one-cell organisms with radio waves. Here is a true illustration: A small child whose face was covered with warts was treated again and again. One day, to the mother's surprise, she saw her child outside surrounded by a group of playmates. The playmates had joined hands in a circle

---

[9]Eleanore Thedick, *Jewels of Truth and Rays of Color.* The Seeker's Quest, P. O. 9543, San Jose, Calif. 95117. 1970.

[10]Joseph J. Weed, *Wisdom of the Mystic Masters.* Parker Publishing Company, West Nyack, New York, 1968.

around the child and were going round and round, chanting, "Warts go away! Warts go away!" Before long the warts did go away and never returned.

Reverend Laura Kemp Anderson is a minister of The First Divine Science Church in San Diego, California. She has exceptional healing ability. Her method is to "speak the word." She uses sound in the form of an affirmation, and gets excellent results. I have known her to "speak the word," even on the telephone, to someone suffering from an excruciating headache and within a few minutes the headache disappeared. In more stubborn ailments, it may take longer and it may take repetition on her part, but even so, the results are truly amazing. She has helped me and members of my family many times. She may say something like this: "You are now being freed from any disturbance. Your condition is clearing and being healed *now*."

Some religious groups of the East use a mantram (the Rosicrucians state that any uttered sound which is used to influence a response in humans is called a "mantram" or "mantra"). It can be powerful if enough concentration is put behind it. Lobsang Rampa[11] explains why: "Man is composed of molecules in motion. The brain generates electricity of its own. Let us consider again this matter of vibrations, for vibration is the essence of life upon this earth. . . . An illustration of vibration is the violinist; as he takes his violin he can by playing a single note for some seconds cause vibrations to build up in a wine glass with the result that the glass will shatter with a surprisingly loud explosion. If one can say the words, *Om Mani Padmi Hum* (a Near East mantram) in a certain way and keep on saying it for a few minutes, one can build up a vibration of quite fantastic strength."

Lobsang Rampa tells how to use the mantra: "It is very important to speak or send a message to the subconscious in the form of incantations or mantra, a means of subjugat-

[11]T. Lobsang Rampa, *The Rampa Story*. Bantam Books, New York, 1968.

ing the subconscious. By repeating the mantra, the conscious mind, only one-tenth of us, is able to send an imperative order to the subconscious. You should repeat this mantra (or affirmation) in groups of three. Having stated your mantra once, the subconscious is not at all alerted. The second time the same words are stated, and they must be stated identically, the subconscious begins to take notice. At the third affirmation the subconscious wonders what it is all about and is fully receptive to our mantra, and the mantra is received and stored. Supposing you say your three affirmations in the morning, at midday, again in the afternoon, and again before you retire and go to sleep. It is knocking in a nail; one goal is not enough, you have to keep administering blows until the nail is in the wood to the depth desired. This is not a new device, by any means. It is as old as humanity itself.

"I also wish to impress upon you that you must keep your affirmations to yourself and not let anyone else know about them, for if other skeptical people know about them, they will laugh at you and perhaps put doubt in your mind."

This brings us to the exciting little book called *Toning*, by Laurel Elizabeth Keyes.[12] Mrs. Keyes discovered toning by accident and after she began to use it, she said she asked a woman who was clairvoyant to watch her while she did her toning. She sought the aid of this woman who had diagnosed such ailments as inflammations, ulcers, and tumors, which were later confirmed by medical x rays and tests. The woman described that the tone which Mrs. Keyes discovered and was using in a certain way, appeared as a force which began to swirl in the area of the reproductive organs, then seemed to draw magnetic forces up from the earth through the feet and legs and finally rise in a spiral of light to the throat area. And as it passed out of the body, it appeared to cleanse the entire body and release tensions in

---

[12]Laurel Elizabeth Keyes, *Toning*. 2168 South Lafayette St., Denver, Colorado 80210.

congested areas. The clairvoyant reported that the body had an appearance of balance, like an engine which had been overhauled and all parts were working together once more. Although chronic conditions were not immediately healed, Mrs. Keyes found that each toning session had a beneficial effect. It seemed to stimulate the healthy cells and tissues so that they could overcome the diseased ones. She also found that she could direct the tone into the various areas of the body.

Mrs. Keyes' book tells how to tone. She says, "Let your body speak. Let the body groan. It may be an audible, deep sigh, but it is a feeling of release. . . . All of the hurts, physical and emotional, which you have received, are buried in the subconscious memory and groaning offers a release for them. Once the door is open, repressed feelings of your entire life may begin to flow out.

"The toning session may last for five or twenty-five minutes, but finally the body is satisfied with what it feels is a perfect one. . . . There will be a deep, contented sigh following that note. This is your signal that there is peace in your nature and what you wish to have the subconscious do for you may be introduced to it. . . .

"One may use the notes A, B, C, and the vowels, a-o-u-e on the note you choose. You may use a tuning fork or a piano to supply a pitch. However, when one has a pain somewhere in the body, he begins toning as low as his voice can reach and slowly raises the pitch. He will find that there is a tone which resonates with the pain and relieves the tension. . . . Toning is always done on the exhaling breath. If one tones softly for 15 or 30 minutes on the note that one feels comfortable in using, many report that pain has been greatly relieved or eliminated."

Many people have reported the interesting results of toning. One woman said that she wouldn't think of facing her day without toning and to her it is more important than putting on her shoes or eating her breakfast. A man states that he always toned in his car as he drove to work, and felt much better because of it. *Toning* gives many case histories of healing various disturbances. Toning can be done for other people, even for animals. Mrs. Keyes says, "We are not doing a miraculous thing in toning; we're simply relaxing the person or ourselves into a natural state of health. Toning may only be the removal of whatever obstruction has crept into the person's 'field.'"

Mrs. Keyes says, "I know from my own experience and the experience of others that toning always makes you feel better. It is something you can do to make any situation or experience better. The first thing in the morning upon rising you can sigh or groan if you feel like it, and then start to choose one vowel, Ō-ē-oo-ah, beginning on the lowest note you can sing easily, then climb upward from one note to another until you find one that seems to 'pull you together.' Let the tone ride on the exhaling breath as loudly or as softly as you feel inclined until you feel a release or relief."

If you prefer, you may choose a comfortable note and use the Ō followed by M-M-M-M which becomes the Far East ŌM. Try each of these sounds on each pitch and climb up the scale until you find something that feels good to you. The sound and the pitch will find a haven somewhere in your body which will be an answering response to a need and you may "tone" this loudly or very, very softly. You may do it a few seconds or as long as it feels good. When it no longer feels good, stop.

In addition to healing, sound can also help you achieve a specific desire in your life. Suppose, for example, you wanted a new car (perhaps a second-hand one but at least new to you). You *could* send a *thought* to your subconscious such as, "Find me the right car which I can afford." If the thought were strong enough and sent often enough, your subconscious would no doubt eventually obey. But as a second step, you could speed up the process by first taking in (and visualizing) the *universal life energy* flowing through you, then directing it by thinking, "I direct this power to find me the right car."

If you added a third and fourth step and *visualized* yourself driving the car and looking happy and *feeling* happy in it, you would have added both visualization and feeling which would motivate the subconscious to work even harder and faster to do your bidding. But if, on top of all these ingredients, you add a fifth and final step substituting *the spoken word* for a thought, you would have indeed created an irresistible force! This is because sound, as proved in Dr. Heller's experiments, actually mobilizes the molecules of energy to make them march in the direction you want them to. So if you speak the words aloud firmly, with energy, instead of just thinking them, results should be greatest of all!

Lobsang Rampa[13] reminds us that to be sure the spoken word gets through to your subconscious, the statement should be repeated *three times.* He says, "We have to repeat ourselves in order to make sure that the message gets through. . . . Speak as you would speak through a long-distance telephone line. Speak with absolute clarity and actually think of what you are saying. Use simple language making sure that your requests are always positive and never negative. . . . Give your command or make your request three times, saying exactly the same thing."

Rampa likens the process of repetition to a woman trying to get the attention of her husband who has hidden behind the morning paper at breakfast. She will make a statement. (No response from her husband.) She repeats the statement. (Still no response.) She repeats it the third time and her husband finally puts down his paper and gives her his complete attention. So, says Rampa, your subconscious behaves in a similar manner. However, even speaking once, but repeating it at intervals daily has brought good results.

[13]T. Lobsang Rampa, *ibid.*

My friend, whom I mentioned earlier, who used the spoken word to grow melons and discourage bugs, applied the spoken word to her body to get rid of ailments. She began with an arthritic finger. She looked at it one day and said, aloud, "Now, this has gone on long enough. I want you to get well and stay well! I will give you one week — and I mean *one week* — to get help from my body in any way necessary to get well. GET WELL!" Within a week the finger was well.

She adds that if she wakes up in the morning with signs of a cold, she says to her body in loud commanding tones, "Now, look here; what can you accomplish by acting like this? Do you really want to experience the unpleasantness and the suffering of a cold? Of course not! You and I don't have time to be bothered. Stop this foolishness and go away! GET WELL!"

She tells me that by using this method she has not had a lasting ailment of any kind for seven years. As she described her technique, speaking the words aloud with force and vigor, I could just see the germs and bacteria marching out of her body, like Dr. Heller's experiment.

So speak up! Sound really works.

12 *The Effect of Light on Health*

Good health is dependent upon exposure to light, pro viding it is in the right amount and comes from the right sources. Look at plants. When they are exposed to natural sunlight they grow strong, upright, develop intense color and are healthy. If plants or young seedlings are placed on the window sill, they will lean toward the light. A sunflower growing in the garden does the same thing: it literally follows the sun, hence its name.

Artificial lighting, particularly flourescents, has been found disturbing, even damaging to plants, animals, and people.[1] Even worse, if you put a plant in the dark, unless it is temporarily hibernating, you stop its growth. Darkness leads to loss of color and stamina, and eventually death. Life of the living organism depends upon light. People respond in a similar manner.

Dr. Margaret Cleaves, writing on the subject of light energy, explains why! "Sunlight charges the nervous system. Its action upon the millions of nerve terminals in the skin causes the electrical currents to arise in them which stimulate the individual to greater energy and activity in the summer. Under the influence of light, the skin also releases a substance called the 'light hormone.' This substance

---

[1]Dr. John N. Ott, *My Ivory Cellar*. Revised Edition, Devin-Adair Co., Old Greenwich, Conn. 1972.

is carried by the blood and increases the functional capacity of the muscles and sense organs. A person exposed to light hears, sees, and acts better than one who is in the dark."

This does not condone unlimited exposure to sunlight. Too much sun, particularly the intense rays during midday, can actually create health problems. Animals which can choose their sunning hours will avoid the midday hours of sun, seeking the shade. People who overdo sun worshipping in order to acquire a suntan pay the price of early aging of their skin and, in some cases, skin cancer.

Light contains, and can be divided into, colors. Each color has been found to have a certain wavelength of energy. When selected colors are beamed at the body, or even to certain parts of the body which are below par, the color energy has been known to stimulate the depleted cell, tissue, or organ and raise its rate of vibration in order to help it heal itself. Color therapy is not new. Pythagoras used colors for healing five hundred years before Christ. Color therapy is presently considered useless by most members of the medical profession, at least in the United States, but there are some who believe that it is the "coming" method of diagnosis and healing of the future. Color therapy is slower acting and does not mask symptoms or serve as a crutch as drugs do. There are substantiated reports of the healing effects of color on mind and body. I have written about it elsewhere.[2]

Light is one source of vital force and it exerts a tremendous influence in many ways on all types of life. In addition to exposure to natural sunlight, there are other ways to absorb light safely. Since it is entirely possible that physical health and energy can be proportionate to the amount of light which enters the body, to step up our own energy, we can use all sources of light, whether it is acquired by

[2]Linda Clark, *Color Healing.* Devin-Adair Co., Old Greenwich, Conn., 1972.

means of exposure to light itself, thought, correct breath-ing, or pure water and food.

One of the best methods for increasing energy, as well as repairing and maintaining health, is to use the type of food which contains stored light. Such food is naturally grown, not synthetic, and contains elements derived from the sun, air, and rich, naturally treated soil. These elements are, in turn, transferred to the plant food and then to the person who eats (or drinks) them. This form of nourishment is known as nutrition. Its use for health is thoroughly explained in many books, including three of my own.[3]

Yogi Ramacharaka, cited earlier, states, "Prana is that principle of life which is found in the air, water, and food from which the *living organism* absorbs it to use it in the work of the body. Man may and does use this force every moment of his life. Man absorbs his supply of vital force from the food he eats, the water he drinks, and largely from the air he breathes. He also has a mental source of energy where he draws to himself energy from the great reservoirs of universal power. This vital energy is stored up in the brain and great nerve centers of the body from which it is drawn to supply the constantly arising needs of the system. It is distributed over the wires of the nervous system to all parts of the body. In fact, every nerve is constantly charged with vital force which is replenished when exhausted. Every nerve is a 'live wire' through which the flow of vital force proceeds. And more than this, every cell of the body, no matter where it is located or what work it is doing, contains more or less vital energies at all times.

"A strong healthy person is one who is charged with a goodly supply of vital force, which travels to all parts of the body refreshing, stimulating and producing activity and energy.

---

[3]Linda Clark, *Stay Young Longer*, Pyramid Publications, New York; *Get Well Naturally*, ARCO Publishing Co., New York; *Secrets of Health and Beauty*, Pyramid Publications, New York. All in paperback at health stores.

"A restoration of normal conditions resulting from improved nutrition, and proper thought, will gradually bring about a return to normal functioning, and matters may be very much expedited by orders given directly to the cell groups. It is astonishing how soon order and discipline may be restored in this way."

Richard Hittleman[4] gives his opinion of the effect of correct nutrition: "It is the diet of the yogi which provides the perfect natural alternative to a diet of adulterated foods. The science of yoga, offering a program of natural development for body, mind and spirit, considers nutrition of paramount importance and has evolved through the centuries a philosophy of eating which today deserves the most serious attention of every American. . . . The entire practice of Hatha Yoga is concerned with: 1. Gaining access to the storehouse of prana [another name for life force, universal energy, or light] already existent within the organism, but which lies dormant, asleep, waiting to be aroused; 2. Introducing an abundance of prana into the organism from external sources. The techniques for accomplishing both these objectives come from a major source of prana: food, which is of such great importance.

"Which are the life-force foods? Natural foods — primarily those which *grow*: vegetables, herbs, fruits, nuts, greens, legumes, and certain dairy products. . . . The crux of the matter is this: what you eat can either impart great life force, vitality, help to regenerate the body, regulate your weight, have a profoundly positive effect on your mind and emotions or can sap life force, add excess weight, cause premature aging, be a contributing factor in many illnesses, and greatly lower the vibrations of the entire organism."

Which specific foods store light most efficiently? Dr. George A. Wilson[5] answers, "The rays of the sun appear to

[4]Richard Hittleman, *Yoga Natural Foods Cookbook*. Bantam Books, New York, 1970. Paperback.
[5]George A. Wilson, D.C., D.Sc., F.C., *A New Slant to Diet*. January 1950. (Out of print.)

give more life elements to vegetables in which they have a more direct action. My research shows that the following foods are particularly high in light energy value: alfalfa, asparagus, red beet leaves, carrot leaves, celery stalks and leaves, dandelion greens, endive, kale, lettuce, mustard greens, parsley, spinach, turnip leaves and watercress, which is especially high."

Dr. Wilson continues, "The . . . foods which grow in the sunshine but on which the sun rays have less direct action, therefore have slightly less light energy value, include: artichokes (Jerusalem), green beans, broccoli, white and red cabbage, cauliflower, cucumbers, eggplant, Irish moss, leeks, lentils, okra, green peas, green and red peppers, pimientos, pumpkin, rice bran (refined), winter squash, tomatoes, whole grain flours and soy flour. Fruits, similar to this latter category of vegetables (less direct sunray action)include apples, apricots, bananas, cranberries, grapefruit, lemons, oranges, peaches, prunes and persimmons."

Root vegetables, though nutritious, according to Dr. Wilson's research, register lower light energy because they grow in the ground, though some light is no doubt transferred to the roots via the tops which are exposed to the sun. McCollum, the late nutrition expert, ranked leafy vegetables high in the list of protective foods. He considered them the more complete in many food elements.

The stored supply of light or vital force in the body is constantly used up and must be as constantly replenished, or it will gradually run out, leading eventually to loss of energy and health, conditions synonymous with aging. This explains why scientists now tell us that aging begins at birth. It need not, if the supply of vital force is constantly re-supplied, especially through the foods which are "charged" with light or vital force. The feeling of "lift" created by ersatz foods, including coffee, sugar, and alcohol, is temporary, similar to whipping a tired horse.

Yogi Ramacharaka says, "The actual work of repair,

replacement, change, digestion, assimilation, elimination (of correct food) is performed by the subconscious mind. This wondrous work of the body is carried on on this plane of mind without our knowledge. The intelligent work of the cells, cell groups, ganglia, organ intelligences, etc., is under the superintendence of this mind.

"But the subconscious *must* have the correct nutritional substances to work with. There can be no lasting perfect results without proper nutrition, and there can be no successful nutritional results without proper assimilation."

If plants and people absorb and store light, why don't we see it shining from them, as we see it shining from a firefly? Some people can. Most people, however, do not have finely enough tuned vision, any more than they possess the ability to hear the high frequency sound of the "silent" dog whistle. We are fast uncovering knowledge today that previously we dared not dream of. Just because you do not see light or color emanations from various forms of nature such as trees, flowers, growing vegetables and fruits, don't assume there is none. Yale University has measured the emanations of trees with a sensitive instrument which registers the intensity a foot or more away from the tree. It cannot be *seen*, any more than electricity can be seen, but it can be *measured*, so it does exist!

But other emanations can be *seen*. Dr. John Ott's[6] microscopic time-lapse photographs clearly showed the streaming of protoplasm from the cells of a living leaf or plant.

The wavelengths emitted by all forms of nature are often called an aura. Now there is scientific confirmation that human auras also exist. Dr. R. A. Faraday[7] stated, "It has been shown that man has a built-in ability to react to various types of energy. He responds in varying degrees to

[6]Dr. John N. Ott, *My Ivory Cellar*. Twentieth Century Press, Chicago, 1958.
[7]Newsletter of the Radionic Magnetic Center, Oxford, England, Autumn, 1970.

light and color, sound and music, electricity and magnetism, heat and chemical energy, atomic radiation and even thought. In other words, just as a microphone transduces sound energy into electrical energy, so is the human being a biological transducer of all the energies."

So, the existence of the human aura has now passed the stage of guess work. It, too, can be seen under some circumstances and definitely measured by instruments.

Actually, the human aura is really not a new idea. This is indicated by pictures from early civilizations including Egypt, India, Greece, and Rome. It has long been known, particularly since the early 1900's, when Dr. Walter Kilner of St. Thomas' Hospital in London was able to measure the aura through glass screens colored with a certain type of dye, through which one could actually see the human aura. Dr. Kilner discovered that this aura extended around the body as far as six to eight inches and contained definite colors and could be influenced by fatigue or disease, in which case the size and the color in the aura were altered.[8]

One Russian research team has developed an instrument that detects and records the human aura, the auras of animals, and even of insects. They discovered that this aura is a complex electric field around the body and they hope in the future to use this auric information picked up by the device to diagnose illness. Furthermore, the Soviet scientists reported that thought, which produces muscular reactions, can be detected and measured in the "electrical aura" as they call it. They feel that this aura, or force field, may be the source of communication between animals, fish, and insects.[9]

The researchers also found that outside conditions (in addition to thoughts generated internally) could affect the force field or "electrical aura." The negative thoughts of

[8]Dr. Walter J. Kilner, B.A., M.B., Cantabile, *The Human Aura*, University Books, New Hyde Park, New York, 1965.
[9]Sheila Ostrander and Lynn Schroeder, *Psychic Discoveries Behind the Iron Curtain*. Prentice-Hall, Inc., Englewood Cliffs, N. J. 1970.

other people definitely interfered with telepathic activity in some of the cases tested; whereas when these same people were surrounded by friendly individuals who were open-minded, the experiments took much less time and were much more clear-cut.

The Russian research team, Valentina Kirlian and her husband Samyon Kirlian, have photographed the aura in color. They discovered all colors: blue, green, gold, and violet in all living things. The color photographs prove that these colors emanate from the human body; that there is an envelope of color which surrounds the body. Glowing color and sparks and flashes and small explosions, all in color, are noted as coming from the hands as well as other parts of the body when placed in a field of high frequency electrical currents. Disturbances within the body, or even within a plant, have been reflected in these color photographs and seem to mirror or even predict an illness long before it actually takes place. Still more exciting, the photographs show the difference in the radiation coming from a healthy person's fingertips as compared with that coming from the fingertips of the same person after he has become tired and overstrained. It appears that the tired body "leaks" more energy than a rested one. The Kirlians' photography coincided with the findings of Dr. Walter Kilner, who also had found that ill health, fatigue, and depression were all recorded in the aura, leading to a new method of diagnosis of illness. The Kirlian photographs have captured emanations, not only from the body as a whole, but from its various parts. And the patterns of the emanations from each part are different! For instance, the Kirlian photographs show emanations from the human chest which make one type of pattern, and luminescence from fingertips which makes another. Series of pictures taken from a plant leaf also reveal flares, glows, twinkles, colors, all of which fade as the leaf dies. The aura is also described in a fascinating book, *The Boy Who Saw True.*[10]

---

[10]*The Boy Who Saw True,* anon., ed. by Cyril Scott, Neville Spearman, London, 1953.

Edgar Cayce once told me his own story about auras. (It is also recorded in a booklet.)[11] He said that he had always noticed auras around others as routinely as most people notice their clothes. He had assumed that everyone else saw auras too, until he found out differently. One day he was in a city department store, on an upper floor where men's wear was displayed. He had finished his shopping and rang for the elevator. Just as it stopped, and the elevator boy opened the door to reveal a full load of people, a bright red sweater on a counter suddenly caught Edgar Cayce's eye. He decided to examine the sweater and signaled for the elevator to go on down without him. As the elevator door closed, he suddenly realized that something was wrong with the occupants of that elevator. He could not see a single aura! Seconds later the elevator crashed and every occupant was killed.

As the Cayce booklet on auras explains, "Apparently the aura reflects the vibrations of the soul. When a person is marked for death, the soul begins to withdraw and the aura naturally fades."

Lobsang Rampa remarks,[12] "Everyone with any perception or sensitivity at all can *sense* an aura, even when he does not actually see it. How many times have you been instantly attracted or instantly repelled by a person when you've not even spoken to him? Unconscious perception of the aura explains one's likes and dislikes.

"All people used to be able to see the aura, but through abuses of various kinds, they lost the power. . . . It is necessary that the colors match each other before two people can be compatible. There is often the case when a husband and wife will be very compatible in one or two directions and completely incompatible in others. That is because the particular wave form of one aura only touches the wave form of the partner's aura at certain definite points and on

---

[11]Edgar Cayce, *Auras*. A.R.E. Press, Virginia Beach, Va. 1945.
[12]T. Lobsang Rampa, *The Rampa Story*. Bantam Books, New York, 1968.

those points there is complete agreement and complete compatibility . . . whereas those who are incompatible have colors that clash.

"In some people the etheric covering extends for about an eighth of an inch around every part of the body, even around each individual strand of hair. In other people it may extend for some inches but not often more than six inches. The etheric aura can be used to measure the vitality of a person. It changes considerably in intensity with the health. If a person has done a hard day's work, then the etheric will be very close to the skin, but after a good rest it will extend perhaps for inches. It follows the exact contours of the body.

"Since the aura is made up of colors, it is a fact that one can influence one's health by wearing clothing of certain colors. If you wear a color which is at divergence with your aura, then you will undoubtedly be ill at ease or self-conscious. Or you may even be indisposed until you take that unsuitable color off. You may find that a particular color in a room irritates you or soothes you. *Colors, after all, are merely different names for vibrations.*"

(It was Edgar Cayce's opinion, as he told me, that one's favorite color is usually the major color of one's aura.)

Lobsang Rampa concludes, "All of us can, if we want to, raise our thoughts to a high level, and so help our auras. . . . A good deed brightens one's outlook by brightening one's auric colors. A bad deed makes us feel 'blue' or puts us in a 'black' mood. Good deeds, helping others, make us see the world through 'rose-tinted spectacles.'"

Lobsang Rampa predicts that the day will come when the doctor will not bother to ask the patient any questions about his ailment. Instead he will take out a special camera and photograph the aura of the patient. Within minutes, this nonclairvoyant, medical practitioner will have a color photograph of his patient's aura to study, as a psychiatrist studies the brain wave recordings of a mentally ill person.

Says Mr. Rampa, "The general practitioner, having compared the color photograph with the standard charts, will write down a course of ultrasonic and color spectrum treatments which will repair the deficiencies of the patient's aura. . . .

"The aura can tell the whole medical history of a person by determining what is *missing* from the aura, and by replacing the deficiencies by special radiations, people can be cured of illness."

PART THREE:

Help from Spiritual ESP

CHAPTER **13** *Enter ESP*

The veil between the seen and the unseen is becoming thinner and thinner. For centuries a few people have reported having visions, feeling unseen presences, experiencing intuitive hunches or premonitory dreams, and witnessing loved ones who appeared to them at the time of, or even after, death. But these happenings, and countless others, were kept more or less hush-hush because those who experienced them were afraid of being considered peculiar. It was just not "done" to talk about such things publicly. Now this is all changed. So many people are having extrasensory perception experiences (without the aid of psychedelic drugs)that it is almost becoming the rule, rather than the exception. It is now old hat to talk about such things. There is so much interest in the subject that the circulation of magazines which deal with it is booming. ESP has apparently come of age!

Those die-hards who still believe such things are pure fantasy, had better "put up or shut up." Research into telepathy, clairvoyance, and other psychic phenomena, has now officially become respectable. The American Association for the Advancement of Science can no longer ignore such happenings. They now have to face up to the fact that just because some people do not see or cannot explain something, does not mean it does not exist. The AAAS sponsored a symposium in 1970 in which psychiatrists and psychologists began to try to find out how human beings and even

animals sometimes seem to possess powers that operate beyond the normal senses. And well they may! To find sane
and sensible reports of the experiences of humans, one need
only to turn the pages of such fascinating magazines as *Fate*.
But if you are still not ready to accept these reports of human experiences with ESP at face value, then you will have
to make your peace with reports about animals, who cannot be said to be using their imagination in experiencing
such phenomena. Here are three examples, taken from the
news:

The Return of Smokey, the Cat

One recent dispatch reports the return home in Wor-
cestershire, England, of Smokey the cat. He had been gone
six years. He disappeared one spring evening in 1965. One
evening, six years later, he walked in, drank a little milk and
curled up on his favorite chair and went to sleep. There are
no explanations offered. (Associated Press, 1971)

The Return of Salty, the Dog

In Detroit, a black-and-white dog, wet, tired, and dirty,
with bleeding paws and near starvation, found her way
home after walking nearly 300 miles to a place she had never
been before.

"Salty is home for good now," said her owner. "She
really impressed us. We're not going to let her go again."

Salty's owner, who lives in an upper flat with her 6-
year-old daughter and some cats, gave the 21-month-old
mongrel to a family in August 1970 before moving away.

"My place is so small that I thought it wasn't fair to
keep her here. I thought she needed some place to run
around."

The new family kept Salty until she delivered a litter
of puppies, then gave her to another family in Cheboygan,
Michigan, 272 miles northwest of Detroit.

For three days, Salty stayed in a fenced yard at her new

Cheboygan home. Then "she dug her way out."

The Cheboygan owners said Salty ran away December 14. Eighteen days later on New Year's Day, 1971, she was outside her real owner's new home, which she had never seen.

A snowy expanse of woods, fields, lakes, streams, roads, and towns stretches for 272 miles between Cheboygan and Detroit.

"I had gone downstairs to take out the trash and there she was," her owner said. "She knocked me down and started licking my face and kissing me. She was wet and tired and so dirty that it was difficult to tell what color she was. Her paws were bleeding and she was starving."

What enables an animal to find its way home to familiar territory is uncertain. Salmon return to the streams in which they were born to spawn and die after living in the open sea. Some turtles traverse thousands of miles of open sea to reach a particular breeding ground. Homing pigeons regularly accomplish similar feats. But Salty returned to her family in *un*familiar territory! (United Press, 1971)

The Swallows Return to Capistrano

"From the plains of the Patagonia, across the jungles of Brazil, over the great Amazon and Orinoco rivers, past the Panama Canal, above arid Mexican deserts, the swallows returned right on schedule to San Juan Capistrano.

"More than 400 persons flocked to the old missions to watch them return from a winter in South America. About 25 birds winged in shortly after 7 a.m. and more followed on the day of their traditional return.

"They came in and went to their old nests. They'll be coming in all day," said Gloria McDowell, coordinator of the annual three-day celebration in this Southern California town of 1600 persons.

"The four bells of the crumbling mission pealed a greeting to the birds. Some people say the length and angle of the sun shadows stir an inner sense in the grayish brown, split-tailed swallows that starts them on their journey north to Capistrano. The birds will head south from their mud nests there on October 23." (Associated Press)

Such true stories as these should leave your minds wide open to other unexplainable phenomena such as the presence of beings who are all around us, ready and willing to help us if we will only acknowledge them and ask their help. It is only recently that I have been introduced to the fascinating world of angels. Whether you are ready or not to accept them, you can at least read the experiences of those who have met and seen them. They are probably akin to the fairies and "little people," so well known but not limited to the Irish. But the angels, if you care to learn about them, really have something to offer and can help you make your life easier, happier, and more exciting, according to those who are aware of them. I did special research for several years to bring this information to you and I do believe you have a treat in store. To my surprise, I found that angels are fun!

CHAPTER 14 *Angels Are Fun!*

For those who already know about angels, the title of this chapter may seem somewhat irreverent. Not so! Instead of looking upon angels with awe, or a "thou shalt not touch" attitude of over-reverence, there is every indication, at least according to what I have learned, that angels are friendly, charming creatures who want us to consider them as daily helpers, not to be held at arm's length and called on, if at all, in emergencies or on special occasions only. After you have read about them here and found that you have unsuspected allies at your beck and call, I think you will find them both helpful and enchanting. But let me sound that warning again: just because you may not be able to see angels is no reason for assuming that they do not exist. Many people *have* seen them under all sorts of conditions, usually because such people possess higher powers of perception.

T. Lobsang Rampa[1] writes, "It is people laughing and throwing doubt which has stopped success in many cases, including that of seeing the angels, which people used to do easily." He adds, "Probably everyone knows that a cat can see things which humans cannot. This is because a cat's perceptions are higher than ours."

My own Siamese cat apparently sees "something" when he lies on the bed beside me at night while I read. A friend tells me that his calico cat also stares fixedly at something above his head, while his owner, too, is reading.

[1] T. Lobsang Rampa, *The Rampa Story*. Bantam Books, New York, 1968.

Both of us hope that these "somethings" are angels. The cats seem interested, friendly, not frightened, so we assume the beings, if they are really there and which we unfortunately cannot see, are kindly entities. At least we hope they are angels hovering around to help us.

One book[2] states, "An angel is a messenger from heavenly spheres. Angels are God's messengers sent to help man through spiritual experiences. Certain grave and important events in man's life are always attended by angels. . . . Guardian angels, heavenly visitors, do not function at the same level or in the same way as human beings, even though they come into close contact with them.

"Some of you have queer things happen to you when you say, 'What an extraordinary experience! By chance I went somewhere . . . or by chance I picked up a book, or by chance someone spoke to me.' These simple happenings which have brought an enormous change into your life, did not come by chance but as a result of guidance by your guardian angel. You have not only a human companion or guide in the unseen world, but also a guardian angel who comes from supernal states and has you in his or her care.

"Of course, man has been given free will. Every time he responds to a higher, a good, a spiritual impulse he is helped by his guardian angel. No effort that you make to reach high to respond to that higher influence is ever wasted . . . but it must be by his own decision by his own free will. It lies with man to accept or reject. The guardian angel helps the soul when it desires to be helped."

Apparently there are other types of angels in addition to guardian angels. I had not even thought about angels, much less accepted the concept, until very recently. Then when I was introduced to the idea, it changed my whole outlook. The first person who awakened my interest in the possibilities of everyday help from the angels was Dorie

---

[2]*Wisdom of White Eagle*, The White Eagle Publishing Trust, Liss, Hampshire, England, 1965.

D'Angelo, a friend who is spiritually knowledgeable, but also very practical. She is a professional woman and has a great deal of responsibility with very little time to do her professional work and take care of her home and family. She said to me one day, "You know, I don't know what I would do without the angels."

I was somewhat surprised. And then she added, "I use angels as secretaries. Every chore that I don't know how to get done, or when to do it, I just turn over to the angels. I say, 'Would you please take care of this for me?'" And she told me that the angels have never let her down. She gave an amusing incident as proof.

One night she had guests for dinner and they stayed late. There was not time to do the dishes before bedtime and when she got up the next morning it was all she could do to get breakfast for her family and get off to work. She gazed at the dishes piled high in the kitchen with despair, but she simply did not have time to do them. So she asked, "Angels, will you please see that these dishes are done for me by the time I come home?" She returned late in the afternoon and sure enough the kitchen was sparkling clean; not a dirty dish was in sight.

I was telling this story later to a friend who also knows Dorie, and she smiled knowingly. She asked me, "Do you know who really did those dishes?"

I answered, "No. I must admit I have often wondered."

She said, "Well, a friend of mine and I had an urge to stop by one afternoon at Dorie's house and when we walked into the house we were staggered by the piles of dirty dishes. Why we were urged to go there, because it *was* an inner urge, we didn't know. But while we were there we decided to clean up the kitchen because Dorie had done so much for us and others, and she had so little time to spare on her own extracurricular duties."

This does not mean that the angels may always perform a miracle which is as unexplainable. But when they are asked for help, they do provide it in unexpected and often charming ways.

Children apparently see angels more easily than adults. Perhaps they are not as likely to sit in judgment or screen out experiences they do not understand, as adults do. Many a young child has been known to have an unseen companion. Linda Lee, one of my granddaughters, when she was around four years old, insisted she had a friend named "Corky." Corky played with Linda Lee, and ate at the family table (though, of course, no one else saw her). Now that Linda Lee is in her teens, I asked her if she remembered Corky. She gave a shy smile and said, "Yes. But I am afraid I made her up." I don't believe a word of it! I think Corky was real and some adult may have talked Linda Lee into believing she wasn't. Maybe Corky was a fairy, one of the "little people" or an angel. Who knows!

A young man told me that when he was a child his mother, a very stern woman, would come in after he had gone to bed and demand to know to whom he was talking. He answered, "Why, to the angels, of course!" She admonished him in no uncertain terms that there were no such beings as angels; that if she heard him even mention them again she would punish him severely. From then on he kept the angels to himself, he said, until they finally disappeared. If they did exist, a mother like that would frighten them off, no doubt, or at least frighten the child from continuing to believe in them.

There is a delightful little book which supplies proof that some children do see angels. This booklet about a true experience of first-graders is one of the choicest gems on the subject of angels I have been privileged to discover. (See reference list, Page 176.)

A friend of mine, a Ph.D. and former member of the faculty of a university, wrote the book's foreword after interviewing the children and the teacher. It seems that angels had visited the six-year-old children in the first grade of a private school in Los Angeles County, California.

Mrs. Baker, the teacher, stated, "It was about a month before the close of school, just after the long big tests; we had just finished our devotional exercises that morning when all at once the children cried out: 'Teacher! Teacher! Angels! Angels! Lots and lots of angels!' "

Mrs. Baker says, "Of the 31 children in my class all but three could see the angels and talk with them. The angels said they had come because we had sent so much love up to them." Many details of this wonderful happening poured from Mrs. Baker's lips. Fairies had come with the angels, and after the first day, angels and fairies continued to come every day until the close of the school year. Jesus, Mary, and the Archangel Michael apparently also visited them.

Mrs. Baker, although she tells this story, did not see or hear the angels herself. The explanation is given that children are more simple and pure and open-minded than most adults who have learned to close their minds against anything they cannot see. Nevertheless Mrs. Baker felt grateful that she had been able to teach her students the principles which opened the doors to the angels so that they came into her first-grade classroom.

Some adults have been lucky enough to see angels too. S. Ralph Harlow, a retired professor of religion and biblical literature at Smith College, and an ordained minister of the Congregational church, is author of more than ten books. Dr. Harlow tells in one book, *A Life After Death*,[3] of the time that he and his wife were walking through the woods in Massachusetts. First they heard a murmur of muted voices in the distance, but saw nothing. And then suddenly angels came into view.

He writes, "There about ten feet above us and slightly to our left was a floating group of spirits — of angels — of glorious, beautiful creatures that glowed with spiritual

[3]S. Ralph Harlow, *A Life After Death*. Doubleday & Co., Inc., Garden City, New York, 1961.

beauty. We stopped and stared as they passed above us. There were six of them. Young, beautiful women dressed in flowing white garments and engaged in earnest conversation. If they were aware of our existence they gave no indication of it. Their faces were perfectly clear to us, and one woman slightly older than the rest was especially beautiful. Her dark hair was pulled back in what today we would call a 'pony tail' and although I cannot say it was bound at the back of her head, it appeared to be. She was talking intently to a younger spirit whose back was toward us and who was looking up into the face of the woman who was talking."

Dr. Harlow and his wife could not understand the words of these angels. The sound was something like hearing people talking outside of a house with all the windows and doors shut. Dr. Harlow continues: "They seemed to float past us, and their graceful motions seemed natural — as gentle and peaceful as the morning itself. As they passed, their conversation grew fainter and fainter until it faded out entirely and we stood transfixed on the spot, still holding hands, instilled with the vision before our eyes. It would be an understatement to say that we were astounded. Then we looked at each other, each wondering if the other had also seen." But each confirmed the description of the other. They had both seen the angels!

Although it seems true that on some occasions angels may appear unsummoned, it is also apparently true that if one wants help it is usually necessary to call them to your aid. The reason is that it is said that the angels are anxious to help but that they are not allowed, as their part in a high hierarchy, to interfere with free will. So they stand ready, willing and hopeful that you will call on them. And when you do, they are delighted to come to your aid, according to the many reports of those who have received their services.

Grace Cooke[4] writes, "Once you have opened your heart to admit the companionship and guidance of the angels, *you will never be left without their help.*"

I, personally, can testify to the fact that now I have been introduced to, and have called upon the angels, I am nudged and helped and guided all day long. Sometimes it is a very important reminder that I receive; sometimes it is a minor one, but all are helpful. For instance, I may be reminded to turn off a light, or a burner on the stove, or a garden sprinkler (in California at what seems like a dollar a drop, running water is really a problem). There are other noticeable angelic helps galore, from morning until night. Other people who use the services of the angels say the same thing. One business woman tells me that a crowded schedule sometimes is more than she can manage so she asks her angels at the beginning of the day, "Please arrange my appointments for today to be smooth and uncrowded." And, like magic, her schedule seems to clear itself. If two people insist on coming at once, one will suddenly cancel an appointment which makes room for the other. And so it goes. The angels are charming, willing, helpful, and wonderful companions and helpers. As I have said before, angels are so much fun!

How do angels work? One book contains a thoroughly documented study of angels. The author, Dr. Pochin Mould, is a Catholic convert, a geologist, as well as a graduate, a research fellow, and a Ph.D. of Edinburgh University. (See reference list, page 176.)

The following are excerpts from the book: "The angels are very numerous. They act as messengers of God and sometimes carry out His specific decrees. God can make His will known to man either directly or by means of an angel messenger. Every man is given a guardian angel at birth,

---

[4]Grace Cooke, *Meditation.* The White Eagle Publishing Trust, Liss, Hampshire, England, 1965.

but this guardianship takes on a new and more intimate character after an individual is baptized. It is also commonly held that there are other angels appointed as guardians of nations, cities and even parishes. The good angels fight alongside the human . . . in the cosmic struggle against the Devil and his angels." (There are also dark angels, who have fallen from grace, and may be in league with the devil—L. C.)

"Each angel has his own unique intellectual status . . . both angels and devils are better informed than we about the course of future events.

"One angel can speak to another, and a higher one enlighten a lower, but each retains his free will and no higher angel can compel the will of a lower one. True, the higher angel can make truth known to the lower, can show the situation more fully, but the effect is only that of persuasion and the second angel's will is not bound by such an illumination. Only God can effectively move the will of an angel or of man. There is no limit for one angel's reception of messages from another . . . the battle between the good angels against the devil and his angels is on all the time."

Why should God not act directly upon men; why should there be a need for angel help at all?

Dr. Pochin Mould answers, "Man has a free will and is free to use it; an angel can indeed suggest and persuade. . . . They mediate God's help and guidance and instruction to us; they are powerful friends to help us at all times and in all places.

"The guardian angel both assists our minds showing us truth and what we should do, and also protects us against attacks by the devil, our own passions, or any other threatening danger."

Flower A. Newhouse has written several delightful books listed in the references on angels (on page 176). She has dedicated her life to researching, studying, and learning as much as possible about angels in order to acquaint others with their wonderful potential; to bring the understanding of the angels and their work to the people they are trying to reach and help.

Researchers agree that the angels have their own hierarchy or kingdom, from the lesser to the higher levels of importance, somewhat like our departments of government. An angel can apparently gain in spiritual stature and growth by doing good works. As they do a good deed, or a series of good deeds, they eventually become eligible for elevation to higher realms. As mentioned earlier, angels can also fall from grace, become an instrument of Lucifer, or the devil, and thus become a dark or fallen angel. For this reason it is always necessary, when calling upon an angel for help, to designate that you wish the help of a *good* angel.

Researchers agree that angels have always been angels and that they have never lived on earth. There is disagreement on several other points, however. Most people believe, as artists have depicted them, that angels have wings. One of the few people I know who sees angels, says this is a myth, a figment of the imagination of the artist. She says angels do not have wings. Other points of disagreement include the number of guardian angels one has and their sex. One investigator states that guardian angels are always female; another believes they are always male; and still another says that the guardian angel for a man is female, and for a woman, male, in order to establish polarity. Some clairvoyants seem to see two guardian angels, whereas others believe there is just one. Except for these minor disagreements, those who have spent the better part of their lives learning about and reporting on angels (many of whom have higher frequency vision and can actually see them) agree on the important factors.

Ann Ree Colton, a minister and author, says, "There are many categories of angels. They include Agrarian, Archetypal, Celestial, Cherubims, Fertility, Flora (for plants and foliage), Guardian, (including personal, family, home, nation, race, tribal), Judgment, Luciferic, Luminosity, Mending, Ministering, Chastity, Hope, Pure Desiring, Pollinating, Procreation, Propagation, Recording, Species (for care of animals), Healing, Succoring, and Terrestrial, and Nature (also called Devas), among others. The angels stand third in line from the top; No. 1 being Jesus; No. 2, the greater beings and saints; No. 3, angels." (See chart, page 176.)

Flower Newhouse states, "The archangels are the head of the ranks of angels. The most familiar archangels in sacred literature are Michael, Gabriel, Raphael and Uriel. St. Michael . . . is particularly consecrated to cleansing persons, groups, or localities of discord and evil. The archangel Gabriel is usually portrayed as carrying a lily, an olive branch or a torch. Each is symbolical of the work he serves. . . . Sacred books emphasize this great being's faithful service to mankind.

"The archangel Raphael is an appointed treasurer of creative talents, whose work will be to reveal beauty through the arts. In addition, this great one has often been identified with healing missions. . . . The archangel Raphael also wields healing currents and initiates the healing angels in the use of curative rays. He does not work with individuals, but he directs spiritual beings into hospitals, institutions and homes where his healing beams are needed. The pilgrim's staff, a lyre or hands outstretched in healing, signify the blessing of the archangel Raphael.

"The archangel Uriel is the alchemist, imparting transforming ideas to those who, when ill, discouraged, or unsuccessful, need to realize how to achieve their goals constructively with renewed dedication. Uriel is also associated with the arts, particularly music.

"To be an angel of lesser or higher rank signifies a being who has achieved enlightenment and who is thenceforth capable of disseminating the light of God into all the regions and among all the lives God has created at levels less evolved than their own. The multiple divisions of the labors of angels are too numerous to mention."

There is an impressive reference book, called *Dictionary of Angels*. This book lists alphabetically, short, descriptive items of approximately 5,000 angels, their characteristics, duties and other pertinent material.

For practical purposes, although you *may* specify which category of angel you are calling on for help, it is apparently not necessary. If you just send out a call to a good angel to help with your problem, which you will no doubt state, the angel switchboard is said to get busy and summon the angel or angels you need to handle your particular problem.

Whether or not you believe in God does not seem to necessarily make any difference in connection with the angels and their work. Most people believe there is a good higher, universal power or divine intelligence of some sort which has created the world, including this earth and its inhabitants, and which keeps it in orbit and in order (unless man interferes). The name of the power is a matter of terminology. If you or your religion call this power by some other name, by all means substitute the name of your choice, providing it is synonymous with good, not evil. Otherwise you will be calling the powers of darkness to your aid, which can eventually destroy you and others. In quoting the findings of investigators I will use *their* terms. My name for this intelligence, and theirs, is God, but yours may be different. It is the concept, not the name, which counts. The concept is also timeless, and embraces many religions. You may also prefer to call the angels "helpers." Many people do.

Flower Newhouse explains, "Angel is the Greek word for a messenger, 'one sent,' and is used generally to indicate the 'ministering spirits' sent out as messengers of God. God does not require angels to assist him, but he employs their services for the sake of their own development. . . . The angels do not seek or want our homage, but only our love, trust and respectful cooperation in carrying out the will of God in ourselves on earth.

"There has always existed a belief in the kingdom of angels; numerous references to these great benefactors of mankind are to be found in almost all the sacred books of world religion. . . . Those races and religions which especially accepted the reality of angel visitants were the Egyptians, Greeks, Romans, Persians, the Mohammedans, Japanese Shintoists, Jewish Kabalists, the Hindus and the Maoris. We find much regarding them in Daniel, Isaiah, the Psalms, Revelation, and the Acts. The deep teachings in the Jewish Kabala accord the shining ones frequent and reverent mention." (There are 395 references to angels in the Bible.)

"Enlightened thinkers in past centuries believed in angels, either as a result of their intellectual conclusions, or because they had had experiences of contact with the bright messengers of higher dimensions. Some of the more profound of these thinkers were Protagoras, Tertullian, Homer, Thales, St. Thomas Aquinas, Jacob Boehme and Swedenborg. . . . Pluto made known Socrates' perception of devanic ministrations.

"In time of worship, crisis or even during an enjoyment of nature's beauties, a few persons have known a sudden rapturous enlightenment of one of the most inspiring realities of the eternal creator. They have come into contact with the kingdom of angels, a path of God's evolving life well represented in the sacred writings of all great religions and in the poetry and art of every advanced civilization.

"The ministering ones who surround us minutely are almost too numerous for description. We are in the presence of city, state, and national angels. Of the weather angels who affect us, there are the angels of calm, storm and wind. The electric angels are more difficult to perceive, but we are aware of their force affecting our planet. Despite the tumultuous and mercenary qualities which emanate from a great metropolis, far above its heavy aura a strong angel resides. The spiritual, cultural and artistic activities in a city respond to the quickening of such a presence. . . . No place is too material or too evil to repel the appointed ser-vitures of the divine will.

"Go to National Parks, not only to see the outer beauty which they hold, but also to sense the *inner presences* that guard and permeate these localities.

"There are many homes that have angels protecting them. There are many individuals who, when they walk into the countryside, are companioned by pure presences.

"Amongst the Nature Angels are many species. In learn-ing of the vivacious presences who pervade the outdoors, ours is the joy of inviting them into our gardens. Where they are recognized and appreciated, gardens become more healthy and luxuriant. Ordinarily, these devas do not enter busy cities."

Mrs. Newhouse tells of the time she and some friends were sitting outdoors in the country trying to enjoy the pleasures of nature. Unfortunately the wind was blowing a gale and was interfering with the occasion. Mrs. New-house stood the wind as long as she could, then she asked the "wind angel" to stop it, then and there! In seconds the wind died down completely for the remainder of the day.

Religious Angels frequent churches and bring encour-agement to the worshipers, also raising the vibrations of the church itself.

But, the angels with whom we are most likely to be in contact, whether we are aware of them or not, are Guardian Angels.

Mrs. Newhouse says, "Guardian Angels are truly like patient older sisters who uphold and direct us, and admin-ister correction or encouragement whenever necessary.

"A Guardian Angel stands at our right side. A Guard-ian Angel is of great importance to our higher progress. . . . As time advances the Guardian Angel refrains more and more from counseling but still remains as a protectorate."

Mrs. Newhouse tells the following story: "A Catholic nun who was travelling by train, suddenly decided to get off at a station before she reached her destination. Another train was not due until morning, but even so the nun was adamant in leaving the first train. Within an hour, news reached the station where she was waiting that the train from which she had embarked had suffered a terrible accident and many people were injured and killed. When the nun was asked why she had let her train go on without her, she replied, 'My Guardian Angel told me to get off.'"

Mrs. Newhouse says, "The Guardian Angel remains with the human being longer than any other angel presence of any type whatever. . . . Guardians exert so much influence over the lives, progress, and destinies of individuals that without such help, human beings would seldom achieve sustained spiritual interests or possess courage for making advancement.

"Nominally unfolding persons have their battles between the lower and higher forces within themselves, and they are aided and given self-revelation at such times through the angels.

"When humans face testing and tragedy they should remember the angels who are always standing ready to lend their celestial assistance, comfort, and counsel.

"Angels execute their tasks with creative joy, resourcefulness and colorful movement beyond anything comparable to human labors on earth. No drudgery infects their efforts. *They work with joy of creating.* Fatigue and impatience never enter their states. Usually after a duty is once assumed it is acted upon tirelessly until its end is accomplished.

"We realize then that the angelic kingdom served mankind faithfully and selflessly long before men became aware and appreciative of the shining ones who are useful to them."

If you wish to learn more about angels, Flower New-house's books are extremely valuable.

Ellen G. White, the beloved leader of the Seventh Day Adventists, included the subject of angels in many of her writings.[5] She said, "We need to understand better than we do the mission of the angels. It would be well to remember that every true child of God has the cooperation of heavenly beings. Invisible armies of light and power attend the meek and lowly ones who believe and claim the promises of God.

"Today, as verily as in the days of the apostles, heavenly messengers are passing the length and breadth of the land, seeking to comfort the sorrowing, to protect the impenitent, to win the hearts of men to Christ. We cannot see them personally; nevertheless they are with us, guiding, directing, protecting.

"His [God's] angels are appointed to watch over us and if we put ourselves under His guardianship, then in time of danger they will be at our right hand. When unconsciously we are in danger of exerting a wrong influence, the angels will be by our side, prompting us to a better course, choosing our words for us, and influencing our actions."

Agnes Sanford writes[6] "Abraham saw an angel and heard his voice. . . . I am quite sure that more people can see angels today than in Abraham's day, and I could fill many chapters with stories about them."

One of her stories concerned missionaries in the Outback in Australia who were attacked by the Aborigines riding on horses. The missionaries were waiting to be killed, when suddenly the horses reared with terror and carried the attackers away. Later, when the Aborigines were converted, the missionaries asked for an explanation. The chief asked, "Did you not see the shining ones? The horses saw them first, then we saw them, and were much afraid."

[5]Ellen G. White, *Gems of Thought*, compiled by R. A. Lovell, P. O. Box 274, Loma Linda, California 92354.
[6]Agnes Sanford, *The Healing Power of the Bible*. J. B. Lippincott Co., Philadelphia and New York, 1969.

Another story told by Agnes Sanford is about a child who was playing with the handle of the car door as the mother drove on a California freeway. The door flew open and the child was catapulted across three traffic lanes where cars were traveling at high speed. Yet no car was damaged and the child was not hurt. Later the child asked his mother, "Did you see them?" When the mother asked what he meant, he replied, "All the angels who stopped the traffic!"

I have discovered that if I have prayed or asked an angel to do something, and a delay occurs, I know that the angel apparently is at work accomplishing the task but needs a little more time. I live in the country and invariably when I go into town to shop it is very difficult to find a parking place. So as I enter the congested area I ask the angels to find me a parking place. Sometimes, living in California, according to California law, I must stop time after time to let a pedestrian pass in front of the car. But on occasions it seems as if more pedestrians turn up than usual. Often I may be temporarily obstructed by a car which is parking or unparking, or by a truck or some other problem. I used to become very impatient with these delays. And then I discovered that sure enough when I got to the area in which I wanted to shop, there was always a parking place waiting. Often a car pulled out just as I arrived, and if I had not been delayed by these so-called nuisance obstacles, I would not have had that parking place! So now, I just relax, turn the whole thing over to the angels and everything works out fine.

Three of my friends actually see angels. A fourth friend, Rev. Dorothy Wynn Smith, an internationally known clairvoyant who sees those who have passed on very clearly, says that though she used to see angels, when she was a child, she no longer sees them. Even so, every time she flies and every time a plane is threatened with serious air disturbances, Dorothy immediately calls upon the angels to protect the plane and quiet the weather. She says it always works.

Eleanore Thedick, a teacher of spiritual concepts as well as an author, sees angels. She says, "Always *invite* the angels to help you. Don't invoke, don't beseech and don't beg. Just mention your specific problem and if you don't know which angel to call upon, the right one will come.

"But," she warns, "always ask them to work on the problem *according to the will of God,* otherwise you may be interfering with a divine plan or not get definitive results."

Mrs. Thedick believes that working with angels is an "Open Sesame." She also believes that when you talk to the angels you should make it simple. She suggests that you say, "Dear angels, I need your help. I ask for it."

Then, after asking for the help of the angels, she advises, "Get out of the way. Don't jog their elbows. Let them do things in their own way. And always remember to thank them, before and after they have responded to your request."

Patty Settles is another friend who sees angels. She works with them to help departing souls cross over to the other side. She also uses their services for daily living. I asked Patty if she had always seen angels.

She answered, "No, I have not always seen angels. I did not know anything at all about anything beyond the human realm of living until I was 40 years old and then I began slowly and painfully to learn about all the things new-age children come into being with today, equipped with almost a complete and full knowledge. I began seeing angels when I began contemplating and composing prayers in church. The prayer would appear like a picture and sometimes an angel would appear in the picture. In other words, I would sort of read what was in the picture and the prayer that came out when I spoke it would be very beautiful. Innumerable times people would come up to me and say, 'What a beautiful prayer.' At that time I couldn't tell them that I was just reading what I saw in the air, so to speak. Then as

I began to clear my own self from fears and some of the lesser feelings that humans frequently carry around, I began to sense that there were light beings or beings that had a very wonderful feeling about them when they were close. Eventually I not only sensed them but I began to see them.

"I have been working now since I was 40 years old and I am now 53, so I have been seeing progressively more and more, and into higher realms. Each day brings new experiences. This is a new age. It is completely different from any other age in the history of man and many are given instant ability to see angels as well as guides and teachers that we were not allowed to see before. Also, there are bands of angels which are forming to work in this new age.

"Among other types of angels there are cherub-type angels and they sort of go along with love and joy. If somebody is very happy, cherubs seem to hover in the air and they also seem to be around tiny children. There was one woman with a most beautiful smile, whom I didn't know personally but I had seen her frequently at meetings. One time I was guided to go over to her and just tell her how beautiful she was with all those pink cherubs around her head. She looked at me with great surprise and said, 'You know, I have often wondered what the babies and tiny children were looking at. I just love tiny children and babies and they would always look above my head or to the right of me or to the left of me and I always wondered why they did this.'

"I said, 'Well, I guess it was because you were radiating love and these dear little cherubs are there sending out the love force!'

"I have also seen these cherubs around babies in their cribs when the babies were content and happy and I have seen them during Christmas time around the tops of the trees. Angels come in great numbers at Christmas and Easter.

"There are also angels and other celestial beings that

do their work mainly at the hospitals. They appear and give the person energy and courage to go over to the other side; they actually help them over."

I asked Patty Settles about guardian angels. She answered, "Your guardian angel does operate automatically sometimes when you are in danger and you may not be aware of it. If sometimes you feel that you are almost literally snatched from the jaws of death, or if a policeman is coming and the spirit does not want you to be involved in a lot of technicalities of the law at that time, it will alert you by some physical method, by pulling your shoulder back, or stopping you physically from going through a red light, or something similar in order to help avoid some cataclysmic happening. A helper may do this to keep you free sometimes when you would ordinarily be involved in something that would take your time. But if you do not use this as a learning process, and over-rely on your guardian angel to keep you out of all these scrapes which you should handle for yourself, you will have to sit back and allow these things to happen to you. And for those of you who are allowing your angel to drive your car when you do not concentrate on your driving, may I inform you right now that this will not be allowed for a very long period in this new age!"

Patty concludes, "Angels never in any way coerce. They may place things around you or in your path for you to see. They might bring a physical teacher to contact you in order to help you evolve spiritually, but they will in no way force you to do anything. And in this new age one of the great laws is ask. And listen. Then *do*.

"When someone is very upset and asks for help, occasionally he will sense an angel who will be there. In a high emotional state a person is sometimes able to sense and see beyond the human level."

I have already mentioned Ann Ree Colton, who with the help of Jonathan Murro is a spiritual teacher and author who ministers to a group known as Niscience, in Glendale,

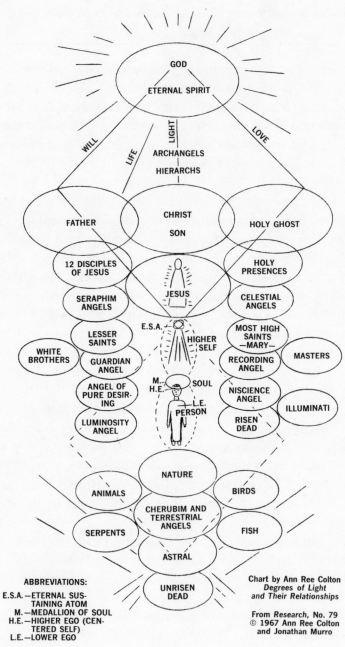

ABBREVIATIONS:

E.S.A.—ETERNAL SUS-
TAINING ATOM
M.—MEDALLION OF SOUL
H.E.—HIGHER EGO (CEN-
TERED SELF)
L.E.—LOWER EGO

Chart by Ann Ree Colton
*Degrees of Light
and Their Relationships*

From *Research*, No. 79
© 1967 Ann Ree Colton
and Jonathan Murro

California—a group which includes members all over the world. Ann Ree, as she is called by her devoted followers, teaches angelic ministry. She, too, sees angels as well as the higher celestial beings, many of whom have guided her in writing her many helpful and highly spiritual books.

One time Ann Ree was sitting behind a crying baby in a theatre. The mother could not get the baby to stop crying, so Ann Ree silently asked an angel to come and quiet the child. Within an incredibly short time the child relaxed and went to sleep.

There are many references to angels in Ann Ree Colton's lectures and books. Once, as she closed one of her lectures, she said to the audience, "And now that you have tried everything else to solve your problems, how about trying the angels?"

I leave the question with you. It is a good one. We will meet the angels in a later chapter in connection with healing.

Publications About Angels
Baker, M.
And Then the Angels Came to the First Grade Children. Summit Lighthouse Inc., P. O. Box 1155, Washington, D. C. 20013 or Box A, Colorado Springs, Colorado 80901, 1964.
Colton, Ann Ree
Men in White Apparel. A book of revelations about death and the life after death.
The Human Spirit. Spiritual techniques for dedicated healers.
The Soul and the Ethic. Healing suggestions and affirmations.
Ethical ESP. A book to awaken the unspeakable riches to be gained through spiritual illumination.
All published by ARC Publishing Co., Post Office Box 1138, Glendale, California 91209.
Davidson, Gustav
Dictionary of Angels. The Free Press, Crowell-Collier and Macmillan Co., 866 Third Avenue, New York, 1967.
Mould, Pochin, D.C.
Angels and God. Devin-Adair Company, Old Greenwich, Conn. 1963.

Newhouse, Flower A.

Natives of Eternity. Lawrence G. Newhouse, Publisher, Vista, California, 1950.

Rediscovering the Angels. Lawrence G. Newhouse, Publisher, Vista, California, 1950.

The Kingdom of the Shining Ones. Christward Publications, Vista, California, 1955.

Thedick, Eleanore

Light on Your Problems.

The Christ Highway.

Jewels of Truth and Rays of Color. All published by Seekers Quest, Christ Ministry Foundation, P. O. Box 9543, San Jose, California 95117.

CHAPTER **15** *How to Get Well*

When a person is chronically or continuously ill, he may not know why. There is *always* a reason. The body works as a whole unit. If any one department is out of balance, it can throw the entire body out of focus healthwise. Dr. Aubrey T. Westlake,[1] of England, writes, "One deals with a sick person, a person out of balance, out of harmony, physically, mentally, emotionally, spiritually. The object of therapy is to restore that person to a harmonious functioning *as a whole.*"

The problem is to find the *cause* so you will know which therapy to use. Similar physical symptoms can result from a variety of disturbances in the physical, mental, emotional, and spiritual categories, so you cannot always judge by or treat the symptoms alone. You must find out what is causing your illness; then, instead of fumbling around in the dark and using the wrong methods, you can use the right therapy in order to get well.

The first step is to check your *physical* condition. There are several ways to do this. First, if you have confidence in a medical doctor, by all means seek his help. Next, since nutrition is now acknowledged as a new science, there is evidence that a person may be ill because his body is suffering from a deficiency of certain dietary elements. The

---

[1]Aubrey Westlake, B.A., M.B., B.Chir. *MRCS, LRCP, The Pattern of Health*. Devin-Adair Co., Old Greenwich, Conn., 1961.

179

competent doctors of the future will add this new knowledge to their kit of tools. They will not merely prescribe a
drug to mask a symptom, or cut out an organ because it is
not working. They will check to find out which element, of
the many of which the body is built, is in short supply. These
deficiencies can lead to a host of symptoms, in fact are probably the major cause of disease. When the missing substances needed for repair are supplied to the body, then the
body often proceeds to cure itself. Unfortunately, today's
physicians, for the most part, tend to condemn or make fun
of this approach to health. The reason is very simple: they
have not been taught the nutritional concept in medical
school. They don't understand it, thus don't accept it. There
are a few nutritional doctors but they have had to teach
themselves this art. They are so successful in getting people
well without drugs, without surgery, without pain, that they
are swamped and even are becoming forced to turn patients
away. Giant medical organizations that thrive on surgical
and other severe measures, and giant drug companies which
are kept financially alive by drug sales, understandably are
fighting this simple, logical, comparatively inexpensive, nutritional method of preventing illness and maintaining
health. However, both approaches may be necessary. It is
obvious that if a splinter lodges in the body, it must be removed surgically to prevent further complications. There
may be other more serious obstacles which need to be removed. But this should not be an excuse for wholesale surgery, which is often the rule, rather than the exception. The
natural methods should be given a fair trial first. They have
saved many a life.

There are drugs which can also save lives, but even
they, because of their extreme action, should be used only
in exceptionally serious situations. Drugs, indiscriminately
used, have been found to mask, rather than cure, a symptom
and taken continuously and indiscriminately can cause more
illnesses than they cure. If only we could use the method

adopted by the early Chinese doctors: pay a doctor to keep us well and not pay him when we get sick.

Nutrition is nature's method of keeping people well. If you can find a nutritional M.D. (they are extremely rare) by all means seek his help. He will have added the science of nutrition to his other therapies so that you can benefit from his method of treating the body as a whole. Another type of doctor worth your while seeking is a homeopathic M.D. These physicians, in spite of unfair criticism, can work miracles quickly and cheaply.

If you do not have confidence in a regular doctor, or cannot find a homeopathic or nutritional M.D. (please do not write to me for help since I do not have this information), then I suggest that you go to a health store, get every book you can find about nutrition, and learn how to help yourself. Adelle Davis, the pioneer in the nutritional field, as well as Catharyn Elwood, Carlton Fredericks, I, and many others, have devoted many years in searching for this helpful information for you. You will find our books, usually in paperback, in the health stores or through book stores. You will also find in the health stores the nutritional substances we have mentioned which have helped others get well and stay well. Such stores are not panaceas, of course, but they do specialize in natural foods free from preservatives, additives, and other pollutants which have made so many people sick in the first place. Through intelligent reading (which, incidentally, you should find enjoyable) and intelligent application of what you have learned, like millions of others, you can help yourself, if necessary.

In addition to checking the type of "fuel" you put into your body, check to see that you are digesting these nutritional substances properly. I have explained the subject thoroughly in one of my books.[2] You can eat the best diet in the world, but if you are not digesting it, you are not reaping its benefits.

---

[2]Linda Clark, *Secrets of Health and Beauty*. Pyramid Publications, New York, 1970. Paperback edition.

Next, check your circulation. If it is sluggish, though you are eating an excellent diet, your circulation may not be distributing it to some or all parts of your body needing repair. If your circulation is not efficient, there are certain safe supplements described in the books I have mentioned which help. An easier way is to step up your exercise. Someone has advised that if you exercise or walk to the point of perspiration each day, you have accomplished your goal. Exercise should not be sudden or too vigorous. Choose what you like: sit-ups, swimming, gardening, bowling. Walking is the simplest. Jogging is not for everyone. And look to deep breathing to be sure you are eliminating poisons through your lungs. Many people forget to breathe, due to tension.

But please believe me when I say that more people are getting well, and staying well, through nutrition alone, than through any other method used today. Everyone can expect to improve his well-being in some way, if not all the way, by using the nutritional approach. I, and many others, have witnessed too many people who recovered their health via the nutritional route, in spite of jealous critics, to chalk it up to "being all in the mind." If we can keep dogs and cats and horses in perfect health because we have learned to feed them what their bodies need for health, then we can do the same for people. It is merely a matter of maintaining correct body chemistry, and it is high time that the doctors face up to and use it.

Our bodies were given to us to live in and it is our duty to treat them kindly. We keep our cars serviced to keep them in top condition; why not the most intricate of all machines, our bodies? So, check your physical condition first, use the necessary precautions, and you may not need to go any further to acquire perfect health.

Ann Ree Colton[3] writes, "There are seven methods of healing the physical body:

[3] Ann Ree Colton, *The Human Spirit.* ARC Publishing Co., P. O. Box 1138, Glendale, Calif. 91209, 1966.

1. Walking and exercise
   To rejuvenate the circulation in the blood stream
   To bring the respiratory system and muscular system into harmony
2. Massage, corrective therapy for the skeletal structure
3. Eating and food chemistry
   Through study and guidance one will discover his personal rhythms for eating and the foods best suited for his individual chemistry. He will seek vital foods.
   Devitalized, denatured, gross foods will be avoided.
   All foods from which the life germ has been removed will be offensive to his digestion and will imbalance the nutrition within the body.
4. Natural herbal medications
   Through natural herbal medications he will seek to energize and give vitality to his body.
5. Medicine and surgery
   Through medicine and surgery he will place his dependence upon the ethical diagnosis, physical ministrations, and skills of a qualified and dedicated physician.
6. Correction of the emotions and thoughts
   Through self-searching and the desire for self-discovery he will find the way to correct his immature emotions and thoughts.
7. The Mediative Healer
   His angels will direct him to a mediative (spiritual) healer who will open the door to the healing ministry of heaven."

Mrs. Colton concludes, "Neglect of the physical body results in ill health. Sickness inevitably occurs from accumulative interior ills of the negative emotions and thoughts. All defection from natural law protecting one's physical body produces illness. Such sicknesses appear first as emotional irritation and mental discontent."

Allow any physical changes you have made, including nutritional substances, plenty of time to work. Your illness probably did not develop overnight, and thus cannot be cured by these methods overnight. If your body has deteriorated due to a gradual accumulation of nutritional deficiencies, then it is going to take time for these substances, once again supplied to the body, to be rebuilt into the cells, tissues, organs where they belong. If after a fair trial by this method, perhaps for months or up to a year, you do not begin to see results, then, as I stated in Chapter 1 as in the case of John, it is time to look elsewhere for the cause of your trouble. It may be in the mind, in some way, interfering with the smooth running of your body machine. This may not necessarily be mental illness (which, by the way, often responds to nutritional therapy) but to something you are thinking or feeling to throw your body mechanism off balance.

Dr. Frederick Bailes[4] stated, "Jesus contended that sickness could be a result of disturbed inner mental states. He taught that when these mental states were corrected, the disease would disappear." Remember, Jesus was a Master psychiatrist.

Dr. Bailes added, "Health is natural, sickness is unnatural. Man provides his own obstructions to healing. Intelligence built the body with the intention of having it always function perfectly. Sickness is man's interference with this intention. Disordered mental states produce sickness because they break into and run counter to an eternally established law of universal harmony."

Negative thoughts and emotions attract negative conditions. Positive thoughts and emotions attract positive conditions. The result may not be immediate, but is like planting a seed; in due time, the seed sprouts and grows according to its kind.

---

[4]Frederick W. Bailes, M.D., *Your Mind Can Heal You.* Dodd, Mead & Co., New York, 1941.

Grace and Ivan Cooke[5] also comment on the effect of thought on health, "Good thought can create good health. Thought can heal, and thought of another kind can inflict pain and disease. Thoughts of suspicion, fear, and hate form the root of suffering. Thought can also hasten the coming of beauty, harmony, and brotherhood, and all else that man longs for. If you have a dear, cherished, but bad habit, the time will come when you must throw your habit away as a child throws away its rattle.

"Health is determined by whether the thoughts, feelings and emotions which comprise the subconscious are largely *health* thoughts or else *ill-health* thoughts. And here we come to the crux and the cause of things: what kind of thoughts do we entertain habitually about ourselves? Do we habitually install thoughts of well-being in the subconscious, hourly, daily, month in and month out, year in and year out? If so, then we are surely conditioning ourselves to healthy living. Or do we habitually think dolefully about our body? Does every ache and pain, creak and crackle, affect us with groaning apprehension? If so, then we are conditioning our body to a state of ill-health."

Dr. Bailes adds another warning: "Nothing kills the healing consciousness so easily as the habit of criticism. Criticism is a mild form of hate and sometimes it is not such a mild form either. It would be a wise move on the part of the beginner if he would take a stand that he would absolutely refrain from criticizing anyone no matter how much the criticism might appear to be justified."

I keep a copy of an old Indian prayer on my desk at all times. It reads, "Great spirit, grant that I may not criticize my neighbor until I have walked a mile in his moccasins." It makes me think twice before criticizing someone.

Chronic criticism and resentment are unsuspected

---

[5]Ivan and Grace Cooke, *Healing*. The White Eagle Publishing Trust, New lands, Liss, Hampshire, England, 1955.

causes of many illnesses. Many a case of arthritis has been traced to a prolonged feeling of resentment toward a situation or another person. I told the true story in my book, *Stay Young Longer*, of the woman who ran off with another man. Within 24 hours her husband had become a wheelchair patient, crippled with arthritis.

You can avoid illness caused by resentment or a critical attitude by the following method. R. Swinburne Clymer, M.D.,[6] explains, "If you will change your hatred into forgiveness, the beneficial results to yourself will be quickly noted, enabling you to overcome every obstacle placed in your path; your love and good will toward your enemies will act as an attracting power, drawing whatever good is in them. Moreover, your own resentment, changed into love, acts as a vivifying agency within yourself, and instead of inducing illness and mental depression with its sorrows, will give you health, love and life. Whereas hatred and resentment arouse poisonous conditions resulting in disease and illness; forgiveness and compassion are health-inspiring tonics that promote poise, peace and tranquility of body and mind. Admittedly, it may require a mighty effort to offer love and compassion in exchange for grudges, losses and malice, but the reward is proportionate to the effort, the gain is worth the price. By transmuting the destructive emotions to life-giving constructive forces, they return to us manifold for good."

So always bless, not damn, a person or a situation!

Harold Sherman agrees[7] that there is no doubt about the fact that wrong thinking can bring about illness whereas right thinking can encourage healing. He tells of his own case in which he felt greatly taken advantage of by an executive in a radio station for whom he had spent much time, effort and thought on a project for which he had been prom-

---

[6]R. Swinburne Clymer, M.D., *Making Health Certain.* Humanitarian Society, Quaker Town, Penna., 1914.

[7]Harold Sherman, *How to Make ESP Work For You.* Fawcett Crest Book, Fawcett Publications, Inc. Greenwich, Conn. 1964.

ised payment. But after the project was finished, he received nothing. As a result, he found himself in reduced financial circumstances, and faced a need to move to less expensive living quarters, since he had devoted all of his time to this work without receiving the promised money. Understandably he became embittered and resentful against this executive, who had not kept his promise. After some time, Harold Sherman suddenly realized that he had developed a growth in his throat. His doctor, after many tests, told him that it was an unusual type of ailment and he really didn't know what to do about it. After trying one substance, which did not prove permanently helpful, it appeared as if Harold Sherman's life was doomed by this fast-growing throat condition.

Finally, he realized, on self-analysis, that there was a link between his ailment and his feeling toward the man who had shortchanged him. He began to understand that undoubtedly his own state of mind had poisoned his mind, upset his body chemistry, and had created the disturbance. So, first he forgave the man, and then he began to make a picture of someone who might have the answer for healing his obscure ailment. He continued to make this picture clearly of someone bringing him this very necessary information, and in due time he was led to that very person: a man who had experienced the same disturbance in the tropics and knew exactly what to do about it. When he gave Harold Sherman the ingredients of the remedy, and Harold Sherman's doctor used it, the growth was cured. Harold Sherman says, "You cannot harbor destructive thought toward another without inviting possible destruction to yourself."

The fusion of thoughts and emotions is a powerful combination. Is there scientific proof of the effect of thought and emotion on the physical body? Yes, as you will see by the following examples.

According to Dr. Frederick Bailes, "Dr. W. B. Cannon's experiment at Harvard demonstrated the fact that feelings of love, consciously cultivated, brighten the eyes, improved the circulation and digestion and promoted a harmonious functioning of the eliminative system, whereas the opposite emotions of fear, envy, and hate affected the entire body in an opposite manner.

"Dr. Abraham Myerson of Boston told members of the American Psychopathological Association that stomach ulcers, asthma, skin disorders and heart trouble are frequently caused by mental upsets that continue over a period of time. He went on to say that adverse emotional states cut down on the production of red blood cells, thus leading to anemia; also that a great deal of so-called nervous indigestion is 'emotional indigestion.'"

A Russian team[8] found that their electroencephalogram (EEG) records were dramatically different when telepathy was accompanied by emotion. This was particularly true of negative emotions which led to those receiving telepathic thoughts experiencing unpleasant feelings in the body and pain in the head. However, when there was transmission of positive emotions, such as calmness and cheerfulness, the EEG became normal. Within minutes the unpleasant symptoms of the body disappeared and calmness and a feeling of soothing reaction replaced the negative emotions. This led to the conclusion that negative emotion has a negative effect on your body as well as your mind, whereas cheerful, positive, and constructive thoughts help the body to improve.

Another Russian researcher found that a device which records changes in the blood pressure could definitely indicate the influence by thoughts from another person.

Russian research also confirmed the finding that the number of white blood cells rose dramatically when the patient received suggestions of positive emotion, but after

[8]Sheila Ostrander and Lynn Schroeder, *Psychic Discoveries Behind the Iron Curtain,* Prentice-Hall, Inc., Englewood Cliffs, New Jersey, 1970.

negative emotion, the white cells decreased as dramatically. Remember that white blood cells are the body's main defense against disease, infection, and other physical disturbances.

Dr. Leonid L. Vasiliev conducted an experiment to see if he could mentally influence a person's body in order to make him sick or well. He beamed telepathic thoughts to a woman who had suffered from hysterical paralysis of her left side for some time. When strong repetitive suggestions were sent to this woman telepathically, she was able to move her paralyzed arm and leg.

So the effect of thought and emotion is now well established. Dr. Eric F. W. Powell[9] writes, "It is amazing what a positive state of mind can do. Nothing is good or bad, but thinking makes it so. There was a case of a weakly woman who had to spend much of her time in bed owing to ill health. She was, so she said, an ugly duckling, but she had the grace of possessing a spiritual understanding of life which was a great help to her. She was always trying to help others as far as her weakly constitution would permit, but felt she was doing but little to justify her existence.

"One day she thought that what she could not do of herself she could do through the power of God, so she imagined in her mind that her face was lit up with the kindness of the Master; that her hands were His hands, ready to dispense blessing; she was an instrument through which the power of the Divine would flow, insofar as she would *allow* that power to do so. This idea became a habit, with the astonishing result that she lost her physical weakness and became radiantly beautiful. . . . This is an example of the very truth of what has been said before. As we think in our hearts, so are we."

After exhausting the possibilities of physical, nutritional, and mental-emotional causes of illness, it is time to

[9]Eric F. W. Powell, Ph.D., M.D., *Lady Be Beautiful*. Health Science Press, Restington, Sussex, England, 1961.

turn to the spiritual category to see if you are lacking or "out of tune" in this department. If so, ill health could result.

In your efforts to get well, keep this important principle in mind. *The body is always striving toward health.* It needs your full cooperation in addition to using physical, nutritional and mental-emotional aid. You can also avail yourself of spiritual healing. The next chapter will show you how.

16 *The Art of Spiritual Healing*

Spiritual healers are increasing in number. You have seen many, no doubt, on TV or heard them on the radio or even read about them in books devoted to their works. Some healings are successful and permanent; others are not. A woman who is interested in all types of healing told me not long ago in a disillusioned tone of voice, "I have never witnessed a case of spiritual healing. I don't believe healing by prayer is possible."

I disagree with her because I have certainly seen any number of healings take place as a result of prayer, or other forms of spiritual healing. Sometimes the healing results from the efforts of a prayer group within a church, or a minister who has the gift of healing. Sometimes the healing takes place as a result of the efforts of an informal prayer group. Often a healing is brought about by a dedicated lay person with the healing gift, who prefers to avoid publicity.

Please do not write to me asking for names of spiritual healers; if I have not provided them, it is because they do not wish their names made public. I will, however, make a suggestion at the end of this chapter, should you wish to find a spiritual healer. You should find tips along the way too that you can use.

Meanwhile, let me share with you the healing methods of several people who have had amazing success. The first is Agnes Sanford, the wife of a minister of an orthodox church, who uses the healing light. She believes we can connect ourselves with universal or divine power as easily as we connect the vacuum cleaner with electric power: by plugging it in and turning it on. Naturally, if you don't plug it in, or if you don't turn on the switch, the vacuum won't work, on its own. She believes that too many of us try to do things on our own, rather than plugging into the greater power which motivates all life.

She writes,[1] "One must be careful not to take the responsibility of trying to do the healing himself. If he should, then this becomes magnetic healing, which is using the energy from the person's body. A far more satisfactory method is to use divine power. And in order to do so, it is necessary to ask that divine power to flow through you. You, like the electric wire, are merely a conductor. Or you can think of yourself as a channel or an open tube through which that power flows. Many people who have not been successful in achieving spiritual healing have discovered it was because they could not get themselves out of the way. One should take the point of view that it is God, not I, that 'doeth the work.'"

Agnes Sanford explains that when we make our connection with God (or Divine Power) via prayer, we can receive an increase of the flow of energy. Like many others, she has felt this power flowing through her hands. And when she has been asked by a patient how she turns on "God's Electricity" in her hands, she has answered, "I just forget everything else and think about God and know that He can do it. And He turns it on, and when He is through with it, He turns it off." This is a common experience among healers.

People have asked Agnes Sanford about her very successful technique of healing. She says, "There is Some-

---

[1]Agnes Sanford, *The Healing Light*. Macalester Park Publishing Co., St. Paul, Minn., 19th edition, 1955.

thing outside of yourself. Well, then, ask that Something to come into you, to help heal the condition. Then make a picture in your mind of that condition as *well,* and do this at least once a day, three times a day if it does not get tiresome. And do it at the same time every day."

Agnes Sanford, believes, like Myrtle Fillmore, that you should talk to your body; that you should tell the healing forces to get busy and mend the condition and then congratulate these forces and tell them they are doing a good job because, as she says, they won't work well unless you encourage them.

She sums up her method of healing as follows:

1. Choose the same time and the same place every day, relax and be comfortable.

2. Remind yourself that there is a power outside of you on which you are going to call.

3. Ask that power to come into your body.

4. Make a picture of the way you want your body to look and feel, concentrating on the part that most needs to be well. See it surrounded with God's light and then give thanks that it is being accomplished.

5. Be *sure* to ask that this be done in His name. (This is considered a necessary ingredient for successful healing.)

Here is a typical prayer, such as Mrs. Sanford gives, for a few assorted conditions:

"I give thanks that Thy life is now releasing tension in my legs and taking away all sickness."

"I give thanks that the shining of the Holy Spirit is restoring harmony and order to all the glands and organs of the pelvic region."

"I rejoice at this moment that Thy healing light is removing all pains in the spine and filling the back with more vigor and life."

"I rejoice that Thy perfect vision is restoring perfect vision to my eyes. . . ."

Prayers can be aimed at any part of the body.

Agnes Sanford adds: "If our minds are too confused by illness to follow our usual steps in prayer, let us compose one sentence of thanksgiving and repeat it over and over until the subconscious mind is full of it. This chosen affirmation should radiate the thought of health and as positive a statement as our questioning minds will accept."

She tells of a man who had suffered from a heart attack, and since emergency treatment was needed, while the doctor was coming, she said, "I talked informally to the heart, assuring it quietly that the power of God was at this moment re-creating it and that it need labor no longer. Finally I pictured the heart perfect, blessing it continually in the name of the Lord, and giving it thanks that it was being re-created in perfection. Soon I could hear the heart beats becoming more quiet and regular. . . . By the time the doctor came the patient had walked upstairs and gone comfortably to bed. The doctor could not believe it himself. . . . Had there been no one to administer that help, the man would have undoubtedly died."

Mrs. Sanford says, "Sometimes the sudden increase of life in the afflicted part causes temporarily an increase of pain, either at that moment or a few hours later. The healer should warn the patient of this, so that he will not be alarmed. He should assure the patient that it is a hopeful sign, as indeed it is. The patient should just bless the pain and put it in His hands, giving thanks that when it has finished what it is doing that it will go away."

Mrs. Sanford warns, however, that the healer must remember that the blood rushes to the spot on which he lays his hands and that should this be a blood clot or even a headache, one should not want to increase the blood flow to that spot. In this case, it is better to lay hands *near* the area rather than *on* it. Increasing the flow of blood to the head, for instance, could make the headache worse.

And don't forget to give thanks to God after a healing treatment because pride goeth before a fall. Do not take any credit, whatsoever, for any healing, because in the last analysis, you did not do it. God did.

Agnes Sanford was once called to pray for a mother suffering from excruciating pangs of childbirth. The woman had been in convulsions for 24 hours and when the doctor finally reached her and delivered the baby, he said there was no hope for either. Agnes prayed and imagined the light of God surrounding the mother and child. The mother's convulsions stopped, and the baby lived, although upon birth the baby was blue and cold—apparently dead.

Mrs. Sanford writes, "Now the veil is being torn away. Science has taken from us the smug excuse that we need not believe anything we cannot see. Who has ever seen an atom? Or an electron? Or even a DNA molecule? Who has ever seen pure energy or the actual flow of the vibration which makes electricity? . . . We cannot even see the wind, but we see it blowing the dead leaves before it.

"One of the reasons for our failure to heal may simply be that we have not understood that the light that heals is a real energy. . . . I have heard of scientific experiments showing a sort of light in the water after it has been blessed. . . . To my great delight science has now discovered that there *is* a little mind within the cells of the body that directs the cells as to what they should do. They call it the DNA molecule."

Agnes Sanford and many other healers use the method of laying on of hands. A Russian healer who uses a laying on of hands was subjected to the Kirlian photography. The photographs showed that during this healing process there was a complete change in the patterns of energy which emerged from his hands. "It was almost as if the energy pouring from his hands could focus like a laser beam. The Kirlian technique also showed variations in the pain that the patients were experiencing: bright intense colors for strong pain, pastel colors as pain diminished."[2]

[2]Sheila Ostrander and Lynn Schroeder, *Psychic Discoveries Behind the Iron Curtain*, Prentice-Hall, Inc., Englewood Cliffs, New Jersey, 1970.

The Cookes remind us that the laying on of hands is as old as the hills:[3] "A mother instinctively puts this method into practice when she runs to pick up her crying baby after a tumble, and rubs the place to make it well. She is then instinctively putting the method to work. In the same way we adults, when we suffer a blow on the head or a bang on the chin, instinctively try to rub the pain away with our hand, without bothering to reason this out. All we know is that by rubbing the pain it will lessen or disappear. Even palming suggested as eye strengthening by the Bates method is another example. A person sinks his eyes into the palms of his hands and leaves them there for some minutes. This is designed to rest the eyes and has proved more effective than any other method. Naturally, because the healing power of the hands is thus transferred to the weakened eyes. It should be recognized that this transferring of power from one to another is only an elementary form of healing that has been recognized down through the ages. It is a pouring in of magnetism from healer to patient. It is simple for anyone to put these statements to the test and thereby relieve someone's headache, earache, backache or other pain by rubbing or stroking. Mark, though, that to remove pain in this manner does not necessarily effect a cure. It is a means of alleviation and easing of discomfort; in a word, it is natural healing at its simplest, no more than this. The real spiritual healing when rightly explained and practiced is a very different matter.

"If one wants to demonstrate spiritual healing on himself, wait for one of those agonizing bumps on the head or bangs on the chin or a twisted ankle, a nasty fall or any painful occurrence of this nature to which we are all occasional victims. This is the time to put self-healing to the test. In Christian Science parlance, let the victim *declare the truth.* In other words, let him focus all his will power,

---

[3]Ivan and Grace Cooke, *Healing.* The White Eagle Publishing Trust, New-Lands, Liss, Hampshire, England, 1955.

determination, concentration, soul power, and the light of his spirit on that pain. Let him with *all his might* declare that he is one with spirit, therefore no pain or any injury can touch him that cannot be immediately dispersed by the power of divine love. Let him keep on declaring this with all his might and main and sure enough, that pain will disappear in an incredibly short time. In fact the trouble will disappear far more speedily than if the victim becomes cowed and yields to pain."

Dr. Catherine Ponder mentions that "healing hands" can result from healing thoughts. She tells that when she was writing her book, *The Healing Secret of the Ages,* she felt increased vibrations pouring through her own hands. However, her particular method is not to use the laying on of hands, but as she terms it, the laying on of ideas. In any case the law of vibration can work through the hands or through thoughts or through sounds in the form of words. Dr. Ponder says, "Every word brings forth after its kind; first in mind, then in body, and later in the affairs of the individual."

Another method is to use imagery. Gordon Collier[4] was considered incurably ill and was bankrupt as well. On the verge of committing suicide, he met a friend, another businessman, also previously considered incurable, who had not only been completely healed but was in the process of making a fortune as well. He had learned the secret of health, wealth and happiness and the formula, according to Gordon Collier, was this: "Any picture firmly held in mind, in any form, is bound to come forth. This is the great unchanging Universal Law which, when we cooperate with it intelligently, makes us absolute masters of conditions and environment." Thus by visualizing yourself as perfectly well, and using this daily imagery with love, you can bring forth a changed condition in your own body.

---

[4]Gordon Collier, *Make Your Own World*. Robert Collier Publications, Inc. Tarrytown, New York.

Another method used by the Concept Therapists who have witnessed this kind of healing is that ". . . a person closes his eyes and 'summons' from etheria or the world of ideas the greatest surgeons, chiropractors, masseurs, medical doctors, teachers, philosophers, and clairvoyants to assist him. . . . He asks the etheric clairvoyant to inform him of the trouble and what kind of assistance is needed. Then all of a sudden an idea will come to him bringing the needed answers. . . . How can you enter into this inner world and be able to command this great power to do my bidding? Thoughts fail one every time. Imagination, however, wins out."[5]

One of the doctors who works with Concept Therapy proved this for himself. His four-year-old daughter accidentally swallowed a safety pin. X rays showed that the pin was open and in the most dangerous position. He immediately went into action. He fed this child bread, and then he imagined that the safety pin was being rotated and facing upward so that it would pass harmlessly through the child's bowels.

The doctor x rayed his daughter every four hours, a process which actually showed the safety pin following the exact direction he had imaged. Eventually the safety pin came out and the child had not suffered any injury from the experience. Others have seen these amazing x rays, which prove the effect of imagery.

Harold Sherman[6] tells how imagery was responsible for his healing: A hard cyst had developed on his right eyelid, inflaming the eye. He told his wife that he was going to use suggestion on that eyelid and activate his own healing powers. He said, "Each night during my period of meditation, I visualized my natural healing faculties as concentrating a blood supply in the eyelid area, and carrying

---

[5]William Wolff, *Psychic Self-Improvement with Concept Therapy.* Grosset and Dunlap, New York, 1968.
[6]Harold Sherman, *How to Make ESP Work For You.* Fawcett Crest Book, Fawcett Publications Inc., Greenwich, Conn., 1964.

away whatever did not belong there. These thoughts were repeated positively and clearly each night, and in a few weeks, the cyst was entirely gone."

Affirmations also work. Kingdon L. Brown[7] who holds a Bachelor of Science degree from Northwestern University and is the minister of a Detroit church, says, "Affirmations are a form of deep directions to one's own mind. . . . Saying affirmations does help many people. . . . Affirmations are designed to reverse negative thought patterns. They work."

But remember that the power of the *spoken* word is greater than the silent one, though the silent word, too, commands and carries power. Recall how, in an earlier chapter, Dr. John Heller saw the effect of sound on molecules through his microscope; the sound actually changed their helter-skelter pattern into an orderly procession. So, when you use an affirmation, speak it aloud with force, whenever possible. Kingdon L. Brown recommends finding a place in the house where you cannot be overheard and shouting your affirmations at the top of your lungs.

Agnes Sanford believes that the Father within doeth the works, but His healings are projected by the word of power. So speaking a command aloud helps to focus that power onto the problem to be treated. An example, by Agnes Sanford, "I direct and command the forces of the body to throw off this disease and be well. Let it be so! Amen!"

Dr. Joseph Murphy[8] tells of his cure of a disturbance in his early life. He affirmed as follows: "My body and all its organs were created by the Infinite Intelligence in my subconscious mind. It knows how to heal me. Its wisdom fashioned all my organs, tissues, muscles and bones. This infinite healing presence within me is now transforming

[7]Kingdon L. Brown, *The Power of Psychic Awareness.* Parker Publishing Co., West Nyack, N. Y., 1969.
[8]Dr. Joseph Murphy, *The Power of Your Subconscious.* Prentice-Hall Publishing Co., Englewood Cliffs, New Jersey, 1963.

every atom of my being, making me whole and perfect now. I give thanks for the healing I know is taking place now. Wonderful are the works of the creative intelligence within me."

Dr. Murphy, minister of the Church of Divine Science, Los Angeles, also tells the story of one of his patients, a twisted cripple going about on hands and knees, who, through affirmation, became a strong, straight, well-formed man. "The man created his own affirmation, mentally absorbing the qualities he needed. He affirmed many times a day, 'I am whole, perfect, strong, powerful, loving, harmonious, and happy.' He persevered and said that this prayer was the last utterance on his lips at night and the first in the morning. . . . When thoughts of fear, anger, jealousy, or envy drew his attention, he would immediately start his counteracting force of affirmation going in his mind."

Dr. Edna Lister wrote,[9] "Affirmations or declarations, taking only a few seconds of time, by-pass all old patterns and install a new pattern for the subconscious mind to follow in the future. It works as a miracle when it is backed up with a feeling of conviction. It cannot set bones or perform operations, but it can set up a vibration for perfect healing. As we continue to do this at all times, we finally erase every old picture pattern from the subconscious mind. With the old patterns gone, a new deal takes the place of the old subconscious pattern."

Dr. Frederick Bailes[10] gives his method of healing: "People with poor eyesight or hearing should remember that an intelligence built those organs to function properly. It can restore eyesight and hearing, and will if it receives proper cooperation.

"Mind also provides for the repair of the body. Many people are often stricken with disease without ever know-

[9]Edna Lister, *Eternal Youth at Eighty and Beyond.* NCS Publishing Co., 16324 Hawthorne Blvd., Lawndale, Calif. 90260, 1969.
[10]Frederick W. Bailes, M.D., *Your Mind Can Heal You.* Dodd, Mead & Co., New York, 1941.

ing anything about it, such as in the case of TB. The lung has been invaded by the tubercle bacillus which sometimes the individual did not find out about until many years later. If the person has not enough calcium, phosphorus, or other repair materials in his blood, his case would probably go on into active tuberculosis. If he has sufficient minerals and vitamin D, mind calls upon the repair forces of the body to rush up their reserves to the invaded lung area.

"Some things are helpful in keeping the sense of the ingrowing presence alive. Practice the presence of God. Look for it everywhere. Recognize it, cultivate it. Learn to see God everywhere because He is everywhere. He cannot be divided. Learn to see God at the very spot where others say they see disease. Declare this presence. It heals. It brings happiness. It harmonizes.

"One turns completely away from any contemplation of illness to contemplation of the healing presence within. He declares that this presence has the only rights in this consciousness and he welcomes it. He invites it to make itself felt. He fills his consciousness as quietly as he can with the thought of spiritual perfection, which is the only thing that can manifest through the spiritual substance which is his body. He calmly speaks his word knowing it is the word of the spirit. Then he lets go and lets God do it."

Eleanore Thedick, another friend and spiritual teacher, is a dedicated but practical woman who sees and works with angels. She, too, gives helpful information on healing. She says, "There are far too many asking prayers and not enough thanking prayers to balance the power. When you appear to lack health, give thanks for the abundance of health and strength and it will be given unto you according to your faith. If you wish anything, give thanks for what you now have — do not beg God for what He has already given you; give thanks for that, however much or little it is.

"Also, whatever organ in your body is not doing its job as well as it should, should be given encouragement.

Bless it daily, tell it what a wonderful job it is doing, and like a child it will respond to praise by becoming normal.

"Remember to always bless your body, or a part of it, needing help. Never criticize it."

The angels can also be called upon for healing help.

Geoffrey Hodson[11] writes about the role of healing angels: "The healing angels under their mighty head, the Archangel Raphael, being filled with love for their human brethren, pursue their work continuously. Their presence by the sickbeds of men is a reality, though the minds and hearts of the majority of those responsible for healing of sickness are closed against them. Many who suffer and have suffered know them well. They stand by the thousands in the spiritual and mental thresholds of every sickroom in hospitals or homes, eager to enter in. Hitherto, few have succeeded. The barriers upraised by human minds are often insuperable; should they break through these in spite of opposition, the precious healing which they bear in outstretched arms would be lost, dissipated in the effort to overcome resistance."

Flower Newhouse adds, "The healing angels respond to prayers for healing. A definite appeal for aid brings them to the side of the sick. I have watched these workers, whose auras are a medium blue, while they comb the auras of the sick for whom they were summoned. . . . When the astral or physical bodies are stirred by cleansing, the life force enters harmoniously and the ill become well again. Healing angels also work with those who do not seek spiritual healing. They inspire doctors and direct nurses how to care for those in their charge, telepathically advising the right administrations for each case. However, when the particular cycle under which the human labors reaches its culmination, whether that be in childhood or maturity, the healing angels do not interfere with the laws governing transition.

---

[11]Geoffrey Hodson, *The Brotherhood of Angels and of Men.* The Theosophical Publishing House, London, 1957.

"If someone is working with a relative or a friend, ask that the doctors be divinely guided and directed for healing for this person."

This reminds me of a late beloved elderly friend, Louise Snyfeld. She was a counsellor and one of the most spiritual people I have ever known, although her only professional training was that of a trained nurse. She had become blind in her youth, and her father, a medical doctor, went from physician to physician seeking help and hope for his daughter's vision. All the doctors said hope was impossible; that she would never see again. Finally, she decided that she would ask God to be her witness and heal her. She prayed incessantly and her prayer was eventually answered; her vision returned. It is true that she used glasses for the rest of her long life, but she could see through them perfectly. She later guided and shared her beliefs with, and enormously helped, others.

One man came to her, and when it was clear that a brain tumor would require surgery, she promised him that she would pray for his doctor to be guided by divine light during the operation. The operation was an amazing success, but what occurred afterward is of greater consequence.

During the patient's recovery, the doctor came one day to visit the man. He said, "Something happened during that operation which has never happened to me before and I wonder if you can give me an explanation. While I was handling the scalpel, I saw blinding white light surrounding it and I felt the same light was surrounding me. Instead of unnerving me, it gave me confidence. Can you explain it?"

The patient smiled. "That was the result of prayer, Doctor, which a friend promised she would ask in your behalf for a successful operation."

Agnes Sanford would, of course, call this the healing light. She says,[12] "If God makes plain to us that we need a

[12]Agnes Sanford, *The Healing Gifts of the Spirit*. J. B. Lippincott Co., Philadelphia and New York, 1966.

doctor, let us rejoice in the opportunity of cooperating with him. Let us bless the doctor himself so that he may be guided in helping us and we may be guided in helping him, for of all men on earth the doctor will be most benefited when he comes to understand in full the marvelous power to heal that God has given him."

Viola M. Frymann,[13] D.O., speaks to doctors themselves: "If we believe in a greater intelligence within the body, then we should trust it, we should listen to it in treating our patients. A doctor who was treating a patient of mine told me her own story: she herself had suffered an overwhelming coronary occlusion seven years ago, she was cyanotic, requiring oxygen continuously. The cardiologist informed her that an internal mammary transplant was her only hope, if she were to be anything but a complete invalid. She thought it over and decided she would not subject herself to this sort of surgery. She is a Mormon and she said, 'We called in the elders of the church and they prayed with me and anointed me with oil, and before they had finished I no longer needed the oxygen.' And today she no longer has to consider her heart. Experiences like this are becoming more and more frequent. We must recognize them. We are not practicing total medicine if we don't recognize and accept them."

Agnes Sanford gives an example of a healing resulting from prayer alone. A woman's car had skidded on ice into a tree. The woman was bleeding from her eyes, ears, nose, and mouth. Her lungs were filling. Her pelvic bone was broken in five places and she had internal injuries. Agnes was called to the hospital, prayed for her, and used laying on of hands. The patient's trained nurse who was also her sister, believed in prayer and so did her mother, grandmother, and aunt. One of these was with her constantly, while the others continued praying. In five days, although no medical or surgi-

---

[13]Viola M. Frymann, D.O., "What is Man That Thou Art Mindful of Him," *The Pacific Coast Homoeopathic Bulletin*, September, 1970.

cal treatment had been possible, she was well. X rays showed no broken bones or internal injuries, and all her body processes were normal. She walks today with no limp.

Agnes Sanford[14] says, "His angels and spiritual messengers are also working through us. And it is often given to us to be conscious of their cooperation and support. . . . As we pray for His indwelling and for the cooperation of His saints, we become aware of the inrush of power. Some of us feel an actual current of life entering into the center of the body and rising through the spine. So forceful is this vibration or stream of life that we are forced to keep the spine erect and the breathing light and even. For a little time we cannot speak. We are so filled with the fullness of Christ that there is no room for words. Being so filled with His life, we must needs send it forth. So the next step of intercessory prayer is the connecting of the healing force to the one whom we would heal."

Agnes Sanford states that in cases of successful healing she has definitely been conscious of a heavenly "presence" near her and the patient during the time of the healing. She says, "Most of us need every day to enter into God's presence and focus our attention first upon Him, then upon the area that needs healing. After which, we may say 'Thank you' instead of 'Please.' We may then use our creative imagination to make a picture in our minds of that perfection which we hope will be ours. And finally we may look steadily at that picture until it is accomplished.

Ann Ree Colton[15] writes, "St. Anne sends out help unto those who come in their weakness and simplicity. Those who are helped by St. Anne have tried everything in their physical power to be healed. They come and turn to her and on this last part of faith comes a great fire from above which gives the power in healing and in health. No healing is accomplished alone."

[14]Agnes Sanford, *The Healing Light.*
[15]Ann Ree Colton, with Jonathan Murro, *Islands of Light.* De Vorss & Co., Los Angeles, Calif. 90015, 1953.

Ann Ree Colton, who wrote the book, *The Human Spirit*,[16] believes that healing prayers should be uttered not directly from person-to-person, but should be an angel-to-angel request. This seems to confirm the belief that the angels know better than man how, and how much, healing power the patient needs and can take. The mediative healing technique as practiced by Mrs. Colton's group, Niscience, is as follows:

1. Keep minds cleansed and emotions free of any selfish thought. Be loving and willing to serve and dedicated as an ethical channel for healing light, life and love.
2. Pray according to your desire.
3. Gently close your eyes and hold the feeling of love in your heart for approximately 10 seconds.
4. Visualize light rising to the level of the brow instilling your thoughts for approximately 10 seconds.
5. Now raise or visualize the light rising to the crown of your head. Hold this light and then visualize the person to be healed, as standing or sitting or lying in the light for a period not longer than five minutes.
6. While holding this person in the light, speak an angel-to-angel mantra.
7. Conclude by speaking a mantra such as this:
    "Beloved, my angel speaks unto thy angel
    If it is the will of the Father,
    May you be healed
    In the name of the Christ."

The foregoing technique is, of course, adapted to the healing of another person. Niscience members (the group of which Mrs. Colton is leader) find this technique extremely effective for others. Mrs. Colton believes that if you ask an angel for self-healing, the request should be accompanied by a proviso that when good health is granted to you, it be used for the good of others, not for selfish purposes.

[16] Ann Ree Colton, *The Human Spirit*. ARC Publishing Co., P. O. Box 1138, Glendale, Calif. 91209, 1966.

Please note that in the angel-to-angel healing technique, the qualification of healing should always be tempered with this phrase: "According to the will of the Father." This is a safety device whereby you or the angels will not interfere with the free will of the patient, or with God's will, a very important point in an individual's growth and evolution in his life. Mrs. Colton says: "For every pain, God has given a remedy. For all suffering, God has given stamina and compensation. For all sorrow, God has given comfort and wisdom. If one will obey and listen to the will of God, the mercy of God shall send a wave of release from pain. Reverent prayer and sustained faith will inevitably disclose the lesson within the sickness.

"If you wish to be healed through the help of the angels, call upon the Luminosity Angel. The first step is to ask the Luminosity Angel to reveal to you the cause of the illness, and how you can eliminate it. The second step is to ask the Luminosity Angel for healing according to the will of the Father."

Mrs. Colton used this mantra (similar to an affirmation) to free herself of pain. She repeated it until the pain had disappeared:

"The Divine Spirit
In His mighty power
Is healing me."

If you definitely feel the need for a spiritual healer to help you lift your load or turn the tide in the right direction, I suggest that you ask the angels to direct you to one. Then give thanks and allow time for fulfillment. By this means, when I needed it most, I was led (1) to a healer I had never heard of (through a letter from a friend); (2) to a healing group in England (from a periodical sent me by another friend), and (3) to a book the announcement of which came in the mail. In each case the help received was unusual, effective, though new to me, and proved to be exactly what I needed at the time for healing.

Agnes Sanford advises, after a healing prayer, "Don't look into yourself to see how this is working. When you plant a seed, you don't keep pulling it up to see whether it is growing roots. This is the seed of a new life planted in you and it is bound to grow."

Mrs. Sanford advises:

"If you have a lot of ailments, begin with one only and connect with the light, energy, or God's power.

1. Choose one of your symptoms or ailments for first.
2. Give your body a suggestion that the condition is being healed. Do not mention the ailment. To ask to be freed of headaches causes it to be focused upon.
3. Make a picture in your imagination of what you wish to accomplish, but do it lightly. Don't strain. Play it as if it were a game. If symptoms re-occur at first, say consolingly to the body, 'Never mind; here is the picture of what should be and we are on our way to it.' Healing takes time. Don't panic if it doesn't happen instantly.
4. Give thanks that God's power is entering you, working to make you whole in every way according to His will. Be sure to use the terms: '*according* to his will,' not '*if* it is the will.' 'According to' suggests faith. 'If' suggests doubt, it is a weak word. And you do give thanks before you see healing take place."

Agnes Sanford concludes, "Healing is answered prayer and anyone can learn to pray."[17]

---

[17]Agnes Sanford, *The Healing Gifts of the Spirit.* J. B. Lippincott Co., Philadelphia, N. Y. 1966.

17 Why Some Prayer Is Unanswered

Ann Ree Colton once told me, "I have had every prayer I have ever made, answered." This is quite a record. But there are reasons why she has been so successful. First, she knows how to pray. Second, she knows what to do when a prayer is not answered. Third, she does not always expect instant results. Some prayers need more time for the angels to complete. This is particularly true when other people are involved. Like the parking problem I mentioned in Chapter 14, it takes time for the angels to get one person to move his car out of the way in order to make room for another. I believe that this maneuvering on the "other side," for angels to bring answers to prayers, must resemble a chess game. It is often necessary to get one person to make a move before another one can. And, remember, the angels cannot shove or push or interfere with free will. They work by gentle nudges, to get someone to *want* to do something. This takes time and can hold up the show. There is another reason for unanswered prayer: the prayer answer may be only delayed, not unanswered, *because the person is not ready for it;* or it may not be answered at all because *that prayer is not right for that person!*

Catherine Ponder writes, "When you pray, do not insist upon immediate results or rewards. They will come as and when you are ready to receive them." And they usually come in most unexpected ways.

I know a woman who prayed for a husband. She picked a candidate she considered ideal. She used every feminine wile at her disposal to win the man. Meanwhile she kept on praying. The man of her choice proved completely resistant and she had to give up. Later, she met and married another man who was so far superior to the first one, that when she looked back, she shuddered to think how unhappy her life might have been with the man *she* had chosen as a mate. God, or the angels, knew her needs better than she, and when they were *given a chance* and *sufficient* time, produced him! This is why prayer experts warn always to qualify your prayer with a rider, "according to the will of God," or "not my will, but Thine be done." Otherwise you may get what you think you want and bitterly regret it later. It also explains the wisdom of the statement, "Let go and let God (do it)." So when you pray, give thanks that it is being done "according to the will of the Father," then turn your attention elsewhere. Forget about it. Don't get in the angels' way. Let them do it their way. Many people report that they did not have their prayers answered until *they gave up* completely!

But what about people who are sick, suffering and miserable, and still don't receive the health they are praying for? Has God forgotten them? On the contrary, He may be remembering them. Here is why:

Stephen Sanders,[1] who was first an army officer, and later a successful business man, suddenly experienced, without warning, a spiritual illumination and transformation. No one could have been more surprised than he, but his life was changed within minutes. He received understanding which answered all questions and completed life's puzzles for him. He has since devoted himself to helping others, and his book contains some of these priceless helps.

He explains, "Somewhere and somehow, somebody

[1]Stephen Sanders, *To Him Who Conquers.* Doubleday & Co., Inc. Garden City, New York, 1970.

forgot to pass the word that there is a specific purpose and plan for each of us here on earth . . . there is divine guidance available to lead us each step of the way and show us the road to happiness.

"It is absolutely certain: God does have a plan for each of our lives and He does reveal it at the proper moment. Before He does 'speak' to us, God must test us severely and condition us for the holy task that He has prepared especially for us to do for Him in this world."

There are no happenstances. As you look back in your life, you can see that all unrelated happenings actually formed a pattern, or ladder. "It is almost unbelievable to realize the exact precision of the universe and to know that every occurrence and experience is only a preparation for a definite and divinely created role that each of us must inexorably play in this world. . . . It is also a paradox that he whom God calls, He sacrifices, by taking him to the depths of hell and then exalting him as His anointed or chosen one.

"We remain in a perverted state until some time when we surrender completely unto the spirit of God. . . . But we must pass all tests of faith. There are no 'free' passes or reduced rates. . . . Man is an empty glove until God places in him His Holy Spirit. Only when this happens does man awake from his 'sleep' and begin to see the truth around him.

"It is often difficult for each of us to find the truth. The way is tortuous, twisting, turning. . . . It is only through the act of complete and absolute surrender that one receives life everlasting. . . . Only a truly humble, repentant and contrite heart can open the door of happiness. You see, God selects or chooses *us*. We do not choose Him.

"When we fully surrender to God, in total, He sends His will to help us conquer and solve all our problems. Our will is never strong enough to do the job alone."

Lobsang Rampa adds, "We come to this earth as to

a school. Humans have to undergo stresses which drive
them almost, but not quite, to the breaking point, so that
their spirituality may be tested and their faults may be
eradicated. People learn much more quickly and more permanently by hardship than by kindness."

Mrs. Thedick agrees. She says, "Pain and suffering are
often blessings in disguise, coming over and over again, to
teach us sadly needed soul lessons.

"In this great School of Life we have the blessed opportunity of learning lessons and graduating from one grade
to another. No person or condition can hold us back but
ourselves. As each experience comes to us, sometimes
through the avenue of pain or grief, we must look carefully
for the lesson the experience has come to teach us. As we
learn the lesson we find that something wonderful has taken
place."

Ann Ree Colton adds: "When one opens his mind as
to *what* is being said through sickness, and would consent
to healing, he will receive the power of healing manifestation. If one consents not to the reproving within sickness,
he will experience continued illnesses, and will fail to respond to healing. If he wishes not to live, or has a secret desire to flee from life, disturbances will continue within his
body. Such persons fail to respond to the healing power."

Dr. Edna Lister also believes in this concept. She adds
a different twist, however: "Life is a school with its many
grades, each with new lessons to be learned, new understanding, new laws to be obeyed. To repudiate these lessons
will cause more illness than germs and viruses because they
destroy our immunity to disease: blood corpuscles cannot
reproduce themselves under such conflicts between the
mental, emotional, and spiritual confusion.

"It is only when we are integrated in the conscious,
subconscious, and superconscious, that we become whole.
Everyone is required to go through trials and tests. Sometimes we repudiate such a trial or blame it on someone or

something else instead of accepting it as a needed lesson. Prompt acceptance of whatever comes to us, whether we feel it deserved or not, will pay us the largest dividends, for it saves us the necessity of having to meet the same situation many times until the lesson is learned.

"When something seems repetitious we should ask this question: 'Why does this thing always happen to me?' Then if we have refused to seek the hidden lesson in it we will know that a repudiated lesson will be presented again and again until the ego accepts it as some kind of message, sent only for the good of the soul and for its strengthening."

As I was writing this paragraph and was thinking, "I wish I had a true example to help drive home this point," the phone rang. A friend, Joanna Briggs, said, "I wonder if you have a minute to listen to a healing I just received?" Naturally I was all ears. And though this may seem incredible to you, it is not surprising to me now, since this kind of thing happens often, no doubt due to the angels who are really in there pitching. Joanna said she had been "nudged" to call me, then told me the following story which illustrates *exactly* what I had just written prior to the phone call.

Joanna has had among other illnesses, a chronic back condition since childhood. She has been in and out of hospitals and suffered excruciating pain as a result. She has finally learned that when she overdoes, as she is inclined to, including heavy lifting, her spine seems to become misaligned, she suffers from pinched nerves and she is immobilized by pain. She has had operations; she has been in traction in hospitals; but she finally discovered that a spinal manipulation and adjustment is the easiest, quickest, and most beneficial method of relief. She trusts only two doctors to do this, since they understand her case.

As I write this, it is Sunday morning. Joanna told me that probably because she had been overdoing again, this time in her garden, when she awoke at 8:30 A.M., she found that she was frozen with pain, and could not move.

Her legs wouldn't budge and she couldn't even flex her hands. She realized that since it was Sunday, she knew the doctors could not be reached. She said she lay still and began to pray. She said over and over, "God make me well." She waited, and then tried to move. Nothing happened. She kept this up until finally she heard the clock strike 9:00. One-half hour had passed and her prayers were not answered.

Finally she gathered all the force she could muster, largely from frustration, and said explosively, "God, what *lesson* am I supposed to learn to be free from this pain? I want not only to be freed from the pain, but in some way want to be able to pass the word along to help others so they won't have to suffer as I do!"

Suddenly, she said, she received the illumination that there was really nothing wrong with her body; it was basically perfect (in spite of the many illnesses she had suffered from all of her life). Her trouble, she felt, was that her *thoughts* were interfering with how her body worked. In other words, she, not her body, was at fault. Thus, by *letting go*, instead of trying to run the show herself, her body could and would relax. And at that moment, she said, something clicked. She couldn't recall how this click felt, but it was something she felt in her mind, not her spine. And at that moment, the pain stopped completely. She stirred cautiously and found that she could move her legs, she could flex her hands and she was completely well.

Several things are evident here; and Joanna has discovered this before, though like the rest of us, she sometimes forgets it. She has had other dramatic healings but not when she asked for them in a wishy-washy manner. When she summons *all* her force and then asks, something happens. Another point is that this time she asked not only to be healed, but to learn a lesson as well to be of help to others. (This is another "Open Sesame," as Ann Ree Colton has pointed out.)

Joanna admits to being a born skeptic. In spite of past

healings, when she has need for help, she always begins by thinking, "It can't happen this time." But not until she is pushed to the wall and has no other recourse (i.e., the doctor was unavailable, the pain was unbearable and she lives alone and could not even move her arm to use the telephone by her bed) is she forced to turn to God. And the moment she did *in complete surrender*, the skepticism, as well as the pain, vanished.

Strangely enough, Joanna did not know I was writing at that time, but she was nudged to call me and give me her story at the exact moment I needed it to help others. Coincidence? Not on your life. All of us who are trying to learn how divine power runs this universe when we give it a chance, have seen too many examples to consider them coincidences.

But suppose you are a chronic invalid; perhaps you have been born crippled? What can you do about it? This is where, in my opinion, the concept of reincarnation comes in. I had never thought about reincarnation until I met Edgar Cayce and had several readings from him before he died. He did not like to make predictions because, as he said, there are many conditions which can be changed. When a prediction is made, a person may consider it absolute, resign himself to his fate, and not do anything about it, whereas with prayer and positive thinking he might change the condition for the better. However, my Cayce readings, which I treasure, did point out the general path I was to follow, if I chose (which I did). More than that, the readings gave me instances from previous lives to show *why* I was doing what I am doing; and why I was presented with problems (of which, believe me, I have had my share). It seems that these problems I have brought upon myself, or I had not finished solving in another life and could not run away from them until I had paid the debt. The whole idea of reincarnation now makes sense, to me, at least, and explains life more satisfactorily than anything else I have found. I now truly believe that sooner or later we reap what we sow. This is known as "karma." As a friend, Arthur McMillan, says, when the going gets rough, "My karma runneth over."

The law of sowing and reaping, of course, applies to good as well as bad. There is good karma as well as corrective karma.

Any good you have ever done does not go unnoticed by the angels. This good is deposited to your account where it collects interest. Dr. Edna Lister said, "To open a new account in the Bank Universal and to begin to draw upon it now is the thing to do. . . . We should sing praises for what we have right now." We can also increase our deposits by helping others wherever and whenever we can. And sometimes, when you least expect it, these dividends will pay off. Someone will do something for you; some good will come to you which will make you ask: "Whatever did I do to deserve this?"

This is your payment, with interest for a forgotten service rendered in the past.

Grace and Ivan Cooke of England write about corrective karma,[2] "There is no case of bodily suffering that cannot be healed, although the right conditions must be provided for perfect healing to take place. In spite of the fact that karma created in a past life has to be made good, nevertheless there is a cure for every disease when once the soul is ready to receive God's light and power within its being, for then a transmutation of karma takes place, the soul having absorbed the lesson its karmic outworking came to teach, be that lesson humility, forgiveness or truth.

"Man can put aside his hasty rebellious self and even something else instead of accepting it as a needed lesson. while suffering, turn to look within to ask in humility what

[2]Grace and Ivan Cooke, *Healing*. White Eagle Publishing Trust, New Lands, Liss, Hampshire, England, 1955.

lesson his sorrow comes to teach; what gift it proffers; what treasure it may reveal. And always he can be helped. That is why there are such things as angels and why they draw near; why they plea to help you. They offer themselves, and each man must decide to accept or reject this help. Disabilities may have originated during one's present life or they may be the outcome of something done or left undone in the past. But every disease, every form of sickness of the body is really intended to bring home to your soul a certain knowledge and understanding of the spiritual law now working out or becoming externalized, which it at present lacks.

"Doubtless it will be very difficult for a sick person to believe these things, although it makes no difference whether that person accepts what we say or not. It still remains the truth. Your own part in becoming whole will be *to let go,* meaning that you are not to think too much about your symptoms; indeed need not to think about them at all. Concentrate instead on the Source of all light and life from whence alone can come peace and tranquillity of spirit.

"Often the soul inherits a body that is prone to disease because it has chosen [before birth] to follow that particular path. It recognizes it will only learn what is necessary through suffering and pain in some incarnation.

"We cannot therefore live serenely until we glimpse *why* we are living and *where* we are going. The beginning of understanding is the beginning of healing.

"What proof is there of reincarnation? Teachers such as Krishna, Gautama Buddha, and Jesus gave out this truth to their followers. Belief in reincarnation was widely held in the East so that almost automatically it became incorporated in the early Christian church. Not until about the year A.D. 500 when Christianity became the official religion did the Fathers of the Church suppress the doctrine of reincarnation.

"Many have found the belief in reincarnation deeply

satisfying because it unravels many a tangled skein. Does a soul always incarnate in one sex? Man or woman? The soul chooses the kind of body which will enable it to gain the particular experience which it is seeking. This may be male or female. A choice is offered, for the soul retains its free will within the law of God. It will usually reincarnate with its companions of former lives because it has again to contact those whom it loves and also those to whom it owes debts, for every debt has someday to be repaid. At this very moment and with every day of your life, you are making new obligations. Without a shadow of a doubt you can so order your life so that you no longer contract bad debts, or karma. This is true wisdom because every bad debt must eventually be faced and worked out. This is not a threat but a statement of the law. So unless man studies and in the end grows fully to comprehend the law of incarnation, he cannot begin to understand the purpose that his life must serve.

"Without this comprehension there can be no continuity, so that any search for the truth of man's being must come to a dead end. The answer is through the continuing discipline of many physical lives that surely means eventual growth, since the finest soul discipline of all is the daily rounds, the common tests. If you will accept the fact that the purpose of reincarnation is to teach man to bear sorrow bravely, to meet success with a humble heart, to share his happiness, it will help change your outlook, help your acceptance.

"Should a soul *choose* to come back into a body which may be malformed or diseased, or to bear some other handicap, it must learn first and foremost *not* to resent this condition. It may have been brought about to enable the sufferer to learn a special lesson.

"You do not necessarily have to wait for another incarnation to see results. Indeed, the more advanced the soul, the quicker will be its reaction. Indeed, we have known karma to rebound in a few days.

"So with courage and determination declare every day of your life that God within you can overcome your difficulties and problems. No longer concentrate on pain and the limitations of the physical. Analyze yourself honestly and you will know then that you, yourself, possibly through selfishness or self-pity have been preventing this manifestation of the perfect life."

Mrs. Thedick adds, "Everyone has difficulties to meet each day, but if you permit yourself to be irritated or annoyed, it affects your physical and mental body. It is unwise to give way to depressing thoughts of worry, fear, disappointments, restlessness, or criticism. All these negative thoughts take their toll on your body and mind. Do not struggle or try so hard against them; just relax and let the harmony of God flow in and through you. Ask the unseen helpers to work with you and they will."

Stephen Sanders suggests, "Just live one day at a time and God will show you every step to take. It takes a world of patience and waiting, but the day comes when you are in step with Him all the time and then you know what happiness really is."

Some people, who are crippled, are embittered and repel those around them. Others, and no doubt you have seen them, appear to be the happiest people on earth. You need only to look at their illumined facial expressions, observe their patience, and their ability to console others far less fortunate than they, to be convinced that they have risen above their suffering.

The concept of reincarnation may explain such people as Helen Keller. Even though she was blind and deaf, she made the most of her infirmity and did so much more for humanity than those with perfect vision, that she was considered a near-saint.

Manly Hall says, "The annals of life show that our

greatest sinners have made the greatest saints, not because they made mistakes, but because they learned through experience to correct them. We should all thank God that we have the power to suffer, for through pain great souls are born."

Joanna Briggs states that her many illnesses and sufferings duirng her life have turned out to be her greatest blessings! She has learned more, and grown more, spiritually as a result, she says, than by any other route.

Manly Hall lists many of the negative traits which we must learn to overcome for growth, success and true happiness:

HATE	ANGER	SELFISHNESS	PRIDE
FEAR	SORROW	EGOTISM	ATTACHMENT
GREED	PASSION	DISLIKES	CONTENTION
EXCITEMENT	LUST	SULKINESS	ARGUMENT
EMOTIONALISM	DISHONESTY	LYING	DEMANDS

Quite an order, isn't it? However, Manly Hall concludes, "Adversity disciplines the spirit and tests the resolve. With the mastery of adversity, courage is born."

In your seeming adversity, you can also call upon the angels for help. Ann Ree Colton says that you can ask your luminosity angel to help you bear your suffering; to help reveal the cause of your illness; to rectify your karmic debts; but you *should* ask your luminosity angel for healing so that you may be able to help others. It may come as a surprise to learn, according to Ann Ree Colton, that your angels stay with you from one incarnation through another. That means forever! No wonder they understand your problems and how to help you, if you will only let them.

Dr. Edna Lester says, "There are millions of Angelic Ones whose work is entirely with prayer. Do not become discouraged when you pray and do not seem to get an answer. Have faith and keep on praying. No prayer is ever lost. If a person prayed for does not use a prayer, it is placed in the Bank of the Universal. Someday the person can draw upon that prayer and receive his good.

"Often, when a prayer is not answered, it is because the ingredient of thanksgiving is missing or that it is not the 'will of the Father.' However, your gratitude to Him for all good gifts opens the door for you to receive your own good. Bless your body, your affairs. When you pray with thanksgiving and a heart filled with gratitude, you are making the work of the Prayer Angels much easier."

If you did *not* come into this life as a cripple, thus bringing a karmic condition with you, but have acquired a resistant illness somewhere during your lifetime, there is a surprising method of handling it. We will discuss it in the next chapter.

CHAPTER **18** *How to Handle a Resistant Illness*

During the years of research in connection with this book, one of my biggest surprises was to discover how those who have been so successful in spiritual healing have overcome resistant illness, either in themselves or the people whom they helped. It is a technique which the religions in which I was brought up did not include. Frankly, I did not believe in it. But after learning that those who used this technique really got results, I took a second look. When I realized it was actually a factor in psychology, the explanation finally became clear.

Grace and Ivan Cooke write, "In the olden days sick people always resorted to the temple to obtain their answer. They did not go to doctors. There were no doctors. They sought the priest. They were often told by the priest that their complaint was primarily spiritual, originating from some shortcoming or sin of theirs. The priests were specialists. Some were herbalists, some trained in surgery, some employed in massaging. Others did spiritual healing. The priests were men of great and trained spiritual power themselves. But they began their healing by making the patient understand *why and how his sickness had come about. The results were often amazing, for complaints which threatened months of sickness or early death were sometimes healed in a few hours* [emphasis mine]."

How can such clarification help this type of healing take place so quickly? Through confession.

Carl Jung,[1] the great psychiatrist, said, "Confessions have a great effect with simple people, and their curative results are often astonishing. . . . For we are all in some way or other kept assunder by our secrets.

"It is obviously not always enough for the patient to know how and why he fell ill, for to understand the causes of an evil can do very little towards curing it. . . . This does not disappear until it has been replaced by other habits, and habits are only won by exercise, and appropriate education is the sole means to this end.

"Experience shows that many neuroses are caused by the fact that people blind themselves to their own religious promptings. . . . A religious attitude is an element in psychic life whose importance can hardly be overrated."

Catholics have the advantage over the rest of us by going to regular confessional and "ventilating" their sins or misdeeds. Sometimes we who are not Catholics must use our own methods of confessing our sins and asking for forgiveness in order to remove a block in our subconscious, and thus a block in healing. Catherine Ponder[2] says, "You must clean up your life if you truly want your prayers answered. The 'skeletons in your closet' that you think no one knows about have got to go." And she cites cases of people who did not receive answers to their prayers until this so-called "unforgiven sin" was dissolved.

Dr. Harry Douglas Smith,[3] author and minister of the Church of Life, Hollywood, California, states again and again that if you wish healing of the body you must first cleanse the mind. Obviously he is referring to the subconscious mind. He also believes success can be accomplished by confession. He says the statement "confess thy sins and

---

[1]C. G. Jung, *Modern Man in Search of a Soul*. Harcourt, Brace & World, Inc., New York, N. Y., 1933.
[2]Catherine Ponder, *Pray and Grow Rich*. Parker Publishing Co., West Nyack, N. Y., 1968.
[3]Dr. Harry Douglas Smith, *The Secret of Instantaneous Healing*. Parker Publishing Co., West Nyack, N. Y. 1965.

repent" does not mean that we should fall down in humilia-
tion, but rather that we should *do something constructive*
about changing the condition. In his opinion the "confession" of our sins is really a secret admission that we have
allowed ourselves to by-pass God's law. He says, "The so-
called 'confession' can be a frank, sincere discussion with
a minister or practitioner or it can be a completely private,
personal revelation to oneself of what one's problems and
their causes are. It is done with the recognition and admission that God does not create the causes of our troubles, and
then punishes us for them; but that *we* create them and then
suffer for them." Dr. Smith believes that confessing and
asking forgiveness for our mistakes releases our hold upon
the negative thoughts or conditions, thus sets the stage to
release a block in our healing.

There is agreement in many quarters. The problem is
how to cleanse the mind. Agnes Sanford admits that after
she had hit a dry run in her healing work, she was advised
to use confession, which was something quite foreign to
her way of thinking. Yet, when she tried it, it did work. She
went to a minister, asked for forgiveness and absolution for
any past sins which she may have committed. The minister
read to her an appropriate prayer, and this seemed to solve
the problem; she felt an almost immediate release from her
temporary block, and her healing powers returned. She
says,[4] "I worked out a practical method which, with slight
modification, can be used by anyone. . . . We ask God's
Spirit to come into us and guide our memory. Then we look
back over the week and write down every sin that comes
into our mind.

"This is not so difficult as one would think for God is
very merciful and He guides us in what we remember. He
does not show us at one time all the faults and failings of
our subconscious. He shows us only those wrong deeds or

---

[4]Agnes Sanford, *The Healing Light*. Macalester Park Publishing House,
St. Paul, Minn., 1955.

unworthy thoughts that He wants us at this time to correct.

"Having seen our faults we then ask Him what He wants us to do about them. The Bible tells us that if we have defrauded any man, to restore it fourfold, so the least we can do if we have shortchanged anyone, is to restore it. If we have cheated anyone or underpaid anyone, we should make it up to them in cash. If we have lied, we should apologize for the lie and correct it. If we have spoken rudely or unkindly to anyone, we should say that we are sorry. . . . There will be some things on our list that we cannot correct by our own efforts. Gossip once started cannot be stopped. Lost opportunities for kindness and helpfulness cannot be regained. Hate or wrongly directed love cannot be atoned for by apology. There is nothing we can do to take out of our minds the sting of these things. But there is One who can do it for us, and He is willing to do so on one condition, which is that we accomplish an act of repentance for them.

"Then let us learn to repent. It begins by being sorry for our sins, but it ends with joy, because it ends with a changed life. Let us ask Him, then, to send his love into the very depths of our subconscious minds and there wipe out the thought impressions of our sins. . . .

"To end this act of repentance, and of acceptance of forgiveness at a definite time is a very important thing. If we do not do so, we may fall into a permanent state of a repentant attitude and nothing can be more unhealthy than that. Repentance is a powerful cathartic and we do not wish to take too much of it . . . or if one wants to make doubly sure that he will really receive the forgiveness of Jesus Christ in this way, he can ask a spiritual friend to pray for it to happen."

Mrs. Sanford believes that it is extremely important to swing back from an attitude of repentance to a state of mind of joyful acceptance of forgiveness. "To denounce oneself as a miserable sinner once each Sunday is excellent, if one recognizes oneself as a joyful Saint immediately afterwards, and strives throughout the week to do His work."

She gives an example: "One young man had remained in a perpetual state of self-condemnation because of his guilt feelings and the thoughts of his guilt would not seem to leave him. So I tried to help him and apparently did help him with God's help in this way. I said, 'In the name of Jesus Christ I command those thoughts to stop.' Finally I stated through faith and the redemption of Jesus Christ that I knew that this young man's sins were forgiven. Then he made a confession and I pronounced the absolution, although neither of us had the least idea of what we were doing. It worked. But as the weeks passed the thoughts gradually crept back into his mind again. This time I suggested that he go to church on Sunday morning especially to receive the forgiveness of his sins and I told him that I would be there praying for him at that time. We kept this assignment with the Lord, and in spite of many ups and downs he has been a new man ever since."

Ann Ree Colton explains that in Niscience the technique is as follows: At the end of each day, take inventory of what you have done during that one day alone. Look back upon the day, beginning at the end of the day, and going back hour by hour, counterclockwise, examine each hour quickly to see if you committed a so-called "sin" at any hour of the day. If so, then the obvious solution is to ask for divine forgiveness for this deed.

But many people find that sometimes a healing or other solution to a problem is blocked because of a hidden feeling of guilt over some misdeed which has long been buried in the subconscious. In this case, Mrs. Colton suggests the following technique: Divide your life in periods of seven years. Beginning with the present time, work backwards and take each seven-year period and examine it carefully. If there is a stumbling stone hidden in the depths of the subconscious, ask that it will be made clear to you. And, she says, it will. Certain experiences will stand out, and as these experiences come to your attention, Mrs. Colton advises that you ask God to forgive you for this misdeed so that it may be erased.

However, if a situation has occurred that seems to be impossible to erase, for example, a chronic condition which will not yield, or cannot be expected to yield such as a dismemberment of the body, then ask God to give you strength to live with this disturbance which came as a result, possibly, of your misdeeds or karma. Otherwise, by retrograding seven-year cycle by seven-year cycle you will be able to see your entire life and to clean the slate.

Still another and even quicker method has been used by Dorie D'Angelo. For some time she was a member of a group which was helping the dissolution of guilt problems in the subconscious by the use of cybernetics. The method apparently was successful, but it was a long drawn-out process to reach success. Dorie accidentally discovered a short cut and people were able to dissolve these hidden guilt problems or receive absolution after confession, not in years or months, but within a few minutes. And here is the technique: Ask an angel to bring into your consciousness the cause of a condition which has refused to heal. When the cause comes (it may appear before you like a moving picture) then say, "I will relive this experience or cause three times until it is erased; then I will be free of the problem." According to Mrs. D'Angelo, this can be done in about 10 minutes.

She, herself, who is now beautiful, radiant, and healthy, was ill for many years and was unable to digest any food. Finally, through the long way (cybernetics) she learned what her own stumbling block was. When it was released, she immediately became well and has remained so ever since, an inspiration to everyone who knows her. However, she says, the short method has done as much for her friends as the long method did for her.

Eleanore Thedick suggests another fascinating method.

She advises taking a pencil and paper, sitting in a quiet spot, then going back through your life, year by year. Beginning in the present year, ask yourself, "Is there anyone who hurt me, or whom I hurt during this year?" If so, write down the name. Continue this as far back into your childhood as you can remember. Then comes the surprise! After forgiving those who hurt you, and asking to be forgiven for those whom you hurt, burn the paper! If you haven't a fireplace, or if the list is too big to burn in an ash tray, burn it over the sink and put the ashes down the drain. Voilà, your sins are gone!

Jesus said, "Forgive us our trespasses as we forgive those who trespass against us" and "Thy sins are forgiven thee. Go and sin no more." Forgiveness is one of the hardest lessons that humanity has to learn, but as man forgives, so he himself is forgiven. It is not so difficult to forgive the big things, but it is the little things in life, the hasty judgments, the impatience with human frailties . . . when hasty emotions threaten to overwhelm you, just forgive.

In addition to forgiveness, there seems to be a secret ingredient necessary as a follow-up, to use as a catalyst and dissolve the harm done to another person, to yourself, or to your own body.

Agnes Sanford writes,[5] "The mind and body so interrelate that the unforgiveness acts as a poison within us. . . . A specialist in arthritis found he could not heal the body unless he could help the patient heal the poisoning resentments in the subconscious . . . but there is a quick and miraculous way of being set free . . . to ask for the love of Christ to be poured through you."

Catherine Ponder reports, "It has been estimated that 70 percent of all disease is caused by suppressed emotion. Regret, sorrow, and remorse tear down the cells of the body. Thoughts of hate . . . can be neutralized by love. All disease

---

[5]Agnes Sanford, *The Healing Gift of the Spirit.* J. B. Lippincott Co., Philadelphia, New York, 1966.

comes from the violation of the law of love. Resentment and anger act as boomerangs producing sickness and sorrow.

"Psychologists have found that people who know how to express love are healthier; they tend to get sick less and recover more quickly. They age more slowly and have better color, clearer skins, better posture and circulation than do the depressed, cynical, bitter types of people. . . . Love causes a beneficial, chemical change to take place in the body . . . bringing peace to both mind and body."

Dr. Edna Lister agrees: "Love released, upon its return, fills in all the old places where wrinkles have been. Every criticism and blaming thought makes a line somewhere, first in the soul, then in the face and body."

Dr. Ponder continues,[6] "Many chronic diseases are manifested upon the body because of some secret rankling in the feeling nature of the person which results in unforgiveness. Love and forgiveness are the two great solvents in the heart of man that dissolve gallstones, cancers, tumors, and other diseases that are usually considered incurable. New thoughts make new cells. Loving thoughts make curable cells.

"Love is a healing energy . . . as you begin to meditate on divine love, it comes alive in the heart and lung area. It will flow through your body temple, cleansing, purifying, and harmonizing it. It will flow through your emotional nature, quickening the feeling of love there and bringing peace of mind. It will flow into your relationships with understanding and harmony, and as you begin thinking of yourself as a radiating center of divine love, you will find that love has made you a magnet, attracting good to you from all directions presently changing your world."

Dr. Ponder believes that learning to radiate love to others will relieve tension in the heart, the body center of love, and that shortness of breath, weakness and pain may

---

[6]Catherine Ponder, *The Healing Secret of the Ages*. Parker Publishing Co., Inc., West Nyack, New York, 1967.

very well be resolved. And she cites case histories as proof. She says one of the easiest ways to generate love is merely to repeat the word over and over: "Love, Love, Love."

You may often wonder why someone is so radiant. Whether this person realizes it or not, it is because he or she is a loving person. Loving people are the most popular; they are also the most beautiful and the most handsome.

Grace Cooke writes,[7] "Light in the soul is a result of being constant in practicing divine love towards every experience which life offers. When the person is feeling the emotion of love, the face lights up. The constant emotion of divine love or Christ-love imparts to the face, and indeed to the whole being, a spiritual radiance. The smile becomes a light with spiritual beauty; the very texture of the skin has the appearance of a light shining behind it. . . . The whole Christian teaching is based upon the love of man for man and the love of man for God. Love more and the light shines more brightly."

Mrs. Colton's group, Niscience, contains more radiant and beautiful people than any one group I have ever seen. Their skin is beautiful, their eyes shine, and their manner is loving. There is no mystery about it: Niscience's teaching is based on practicing divine love. Mrs. Colton says, "Failure to respond to healing is caused by the incapacity to love."

If one has the choice in life between intelligence or love, or, stated in other terms, between the head and the heart, cast a vote for love, or the heart, every time. There is a saying,

> "The fabulous look o' of Irish
> Is *more* than that, 'tis said . . .
> Have ye ever noticed how they listen
> With the *heart* more than the head?"

You may be a brain, but don't make a thing of it. Play

---

[7] Grace Cook, *Meditation*. The White Eagle Publishing Trust, Liss, Hampshire, England, 1965.

dumb, if necessary. Those who pride themselves on their intelligence are usually cold, hard, demanding, unrelenting. Those who put love first, are pleasant, approachable, and often more successful in the long run than their "intelligent" brothers or sisters. So if you do have brains, and pride yourself on them, hide the fact. Cultivate your feelings of warmth and love and let them show instead.

I have told two stories in my book, *Stay Young Longer*. One is the story of a schoolteacher whom I seemed to irritate and who showed her resentment toward me in front of the class, causing me much embarrassment. I was advised to silently beam love toward her, saying, "I love you" over and over. Within a short time, her attitude toward me changed so dramatically, I became almost equally embarrassed because I had become her "pet."

The other story is that of a woman with an irascible mother, whom none of her married children could abide. When one of them was told to beam loving thoughts to her silently, her mother's attitude became pleasant within the hour. And the same technique worked on irritable husbands and children.

Make a habit of radiating love. It will be felt by others. Go armed with love to every group meeting you attend. You will be surprised at the response from others. Cultivate the habit of radiating love.

If you can't love, bless. Bless everything, everyone, every situation. Bless your friends. They will increase. Bless your garden; it, too, will increase. Bless your family; they will love you. Bless your body; it will improve. Make a practice of blessing (silently for the most part) wherever you go. Don't do it mechanically. Put *feeling* into it.

Once I was having a conference with Louise Snyfeld at her home. She was besieged with a spate of phone calls that day. Every time we were in midsentence, the phone would ring, and she would have to get up, and go into the other room to answer it. I am sure both of us felt irritated.

Just as I was ready to blow my top, the phone rang again. She got up, turned to me with a dazzling smile, and said, "Let's bless, not damn that phone." I shall always cherish that lesson.

Sometimes a blockade seems to prevent you from doing something you are anxious to complete at a particular time. The more you push, the more you are thwarted. Stop pushing. Turn your attention elsewhere. You will usually find there was a reason for the delay, and a far better solution will turn up later.

So when you are irritated with a situation or person, bless it! If something upsets you, bless it! If you have a pain or an ache in any part of your body, bless it! Look upon it as a learning experience. Damning, hating, and feeling resentful only destroys you, whereas blessing dissolves your animosity and releases you. At night, if you cannot sleep, start counting your blessings instead of sheep or your woes. Before you know it, you will fall asleep.

Dr. Joseph Murphy asked a farmer friend of his the secret of his perennial happiness, and the man's reply was, "It is a habit of mine to be happy. Every morning when I awaken and every night before I go to sleep, I bless my family, the crops, the cattle, and I thank God for the wonderful harvest." Dr. Murphy says that this farmer had made this practice a habit for forty years.

Actually, blessing is a form of love.

How can you find what your assignment should be in this life? How can you receive day-to-day guidance to direct you to do what is best for you and others with whom you associate? How can you make the right decisions so that you will not get into trouble or accumulate more karmic debts? And, finally, how can you enrich your life by working with the tide, rather than against it? The answer to all of these questions can be found in meditation.

We will now see how to use meditation successfully.

19 *Meditation*

Here are the opinions of some experts on meditation:

Ann Ree Colton: "Meditation is the greatest power in the overcoming of human Karma, and the preparation for spiritual discipleship."

Kay Poulton (author): "In deep meditation light is thrown on the path ahead so that with God's help we can make the right decisions whatever problems may face us. For this we need to learn how to detach ourselves from the distractions of the moment in order to listen for guidance."

Richard Hittleman (yoga specialist): "Meditation quiets and relaxes the mind as well as the body. . . . In working toward integration (unity), be aware that all objects, thoughts, everything that is manifested in the entire universe, both seen and unseen, known and unknown, spring from one source, and return to this source. Behind everything is one supreme intelligence, the universal mind.

Meditation renews the energies of the organism; and will help begin to make you aware of the higher consciousness of universal mind. As this occurs, many of the seemingly hopeless problems of everyday life dissolve and they do so naturally, effortlessly, and what is often called 'miraculously.'"

How do you meditate? The usual method is to choose a time and place where you will not be interrupted. Preferably, it should be at the same time each day. The idea behind meditation is to still your conscious mind, ask for help and "listen" for the answers. Most teachers of meditation believe that you should sit up with a straight spine, relax, and let go. Do not try to "get anything," or let your imagination run away with you. Day after day may pass without your receiving anything you consider important. As Kingdon L. Brown advises, put your conscious mind in "neutral."

In the book about Edgar Cayce called *A Search for God*[1] is the statement: "Prayer is man talking to God. Meditation is God talking to man."

Eleanore Thedick says, "To grow and unfold spiritually, it is necessary to have a quiet time daily with the Lord. A daily meditation and communion lasting not more than half an hour, is absolutely essential for soul growth. All health, whether of body, mind or affairs is helped." Her steps in meditation are:

1. Retire to a quiet place where you can be still and uninterrupted.
2. Put out of your mind any material thoughts.
3. Say a prayer, and give praise and thanksgiving that He has heard you.

"To read, pray, and meditate part of the time, using your spiritual knowledge only when you are in trouble will not bring forth an orderly spiritual growth. It is the daily communion with God that is necessary. Not always asking, but listening to what He has to reveal to you, is necessary. Instead of telling the Father what you want or think you need, or how he should supply that need, you must be willing to stop and listen. If you stop long enough and listen hard enough, you will find out what He wants you to do for Him, not what you want Him to do for you."

Richard Hittleman adds, "Do not let yourself become sleepy. During meditation, whenever you find that your mind has wandered, you must bring it back again and again

---

[1] A.R.E. Press. Virginia Beach, Va.

to the quietness or concentration which you are seeking. Always give a mental order to the distracting thought, which says, in effect, 'I am busy, now, and do not want to be disturbed.'" His excellent book, *Guide to Yoga Meditation,*[2] gives the exact information on how to proceed.

William Wolff explains the concept therapist's approach to meditation: "It is necessary to make perfect union with God. . . . Be still. If you are constantly talking on the telephone, no one can get through to you, despite the importance of their message. They will be getting a busy signal every time they try to call and no doubt will eventually forget about ever trying to reach you. Get the analogy? . . . Meditation is a preparation for inner communication. It is vital that we do learn to cease thinking (originating) for periods of time and train ourselves to halt reacting to external stimuli. Doing this opens up the channel for intuition."

In conclusion, here are some of Stephen Sanders' explanations of how meditations can work:

"There is an answer to all the problems of life but we must first learn to hear the voice of God within us that tells us the proper steps to take.

"Miracles will become almost daily affairs and you will be engulfed by this all-powerful presence.

"True prayer is communion of dialogue with the Almighty.

"The secret that I found was to learn how to detect a kind of subtle nudging that showed me the right action to take at the right time. It is all a matter of 'timing.'

"Please remember to never think, but rather listen. It makes a world of difference."

Whenever I need help with a problem, or the answer to a question during meditation, I use the formula which was given me through a Cayce reading for this purpose. It has stood me in good stead for many years. I am sharing it with you in print for the first time. It is: "As I surround

[2]Bantam Books, New York, 1969. Paperback.

myself with Christ Consciousness, may I, in body, purpose and desire, become purified to be the channel through which He may direct me in that which He, the Christ, would have me do."

In the final chapter, I will tell you how to protect yourself from dangers. I will also tell you how John, mentioned in Chapter 1, achieved his full and complete healing.

CHAPTER **20** *How to Protect Yourself*

These are strange times. We are besieged on all sides by crime and violence. A tug of war exists between the forces of good and those of evil and darkness. As a result the entire world is caught in the turmoil.

A friend of mine was lying on her bed one night when she apparently left her body and was taken on a quickie world tour. She "flew" over every country in the world and as she looked down she was impressed by the great amount of darkness. Then she saw a few pinpricks of light. She swooped lower and realized that these pinpricks of light were people, apparently radiating light. Then she became aware of many blobs of darkness. These, too, she found, were people, but they seemed to be wearing bandages which kept their light from showing. She intuitively felt the explanation: we are all a potential source of light but we hide our light under a bushel or a "bandage"; often our negative thoughts prevent the light from shining.

The Cookes, in their book on healing, state that we are all endowed at birth with divine light: "This light is already within you, although it may be deeply covered up, walled in by intellect, smothered by the body and by materialism.

"Nevertheless, every kind of disease afflicting the body is brought about through lack of spiritual light so that the body cannot function as God intended. True healing is always light-giving. Jesus healed only by the pouring forth of the light, the spiritual rays, thereby causing the soul to awaken. This is your goal—you want to be healed.

"There is only one cause behind all the manifold diseases of men, that is *a lack of spiritual light in the life of man.* This being so, there is also only one true cure to be found for all disease and that cure is *the incoming of the light of God into the life of man.*"

Mrs. Sanford believes, too, that most of us have covered over our source of divine light and as a result we reach a point of stagnation or old age, as well as illness. She says, "The remedy for all of this is more of life and light and it is precisely the inflowing of more light and life that we receive through our health prayers and our acts of forgiveness. The spiritual light stimulates the circulation, relaxes the nerves and releases the natural bodily energies. It also strengthens and invigorates the mind and causes the thinking to flow more quietly."

Eleanore Thedick, who is author of the booklet *Light on Your Problems,*[1] is an expert on this subject of light. Those who own this priceless, inexpensive, little book have dog-eared it to the point where they often have to replace it. When I told Mrs. Thedick of the experience my friend had in her out-of-the-body flight, she agreed instantly with the concept. I asked her how one could remove the bandages.

She answered, "We should not give way to negative thoughts. And we also often veil this light by living a selfish or self-seeking life. We can increase the light by unselfish service to God and man." She added, "We should all be individual lighthouses. We should *let our light shine!*"

Mrs. Thedick says, "To let your light shine, you do not need to agonize. Just LET this Christ or divine light shine through you to bless and heal the world. Let it shine at home, at business, in the stores as you enter. Picture His

---

[1]*Light On Your Problems* is available from The Seeker's Quest, P. O. Box 9543, San Jose, California 95117.

light and love flooding you and everything you contact during the day. You activate this light merely by saying the simple prayer, 'Dear Lord, pour your light through me. Let it flow unhindered to all the world. Thank you.' Also ask that it be tempered to each individual you meet according to his unfoldment. It is too intense for some to bear."

When I asked Mrs. Thedick how one could use the light for self-healing, she said, "Remember, this light is already within us. We just need to unplug it (or remove the bandage). Each morning you can start with the top of your head and visualize the light shining through your eyes, your ears, and down through your entire body. Visualize the divine light as the most sparkling white light you can imagine."

Patty Settles (mentioned in Chapter 14) says, "As you direct it to each part of the body needing special help, increase the intensity of the light in that area by visualizing it as if it were being turned up by a rheostat, which can brighten or dim lights; as you turn up your rheostat to its greatest intensity, hold it while you give verbal directions for accomplishing the perfected condition you wish, at the same time imaging it as being done. Give thanks as usual."

Be alert to any ideas which come to you. They may be angelic suggestions showing you how you may play your part to speed your wish-fulfillment.

Patty Settles is an example of this technique. Though she is in her fifties, she looks like a teen-ager. She did not always look this young and radiant. I have seen before-and-after pictures of her, which are almost unbelievable. Her reformation is partially due to regular face exercises (there are many books available which contain them) but mainly due to her use of the light. Patty visualizes the light radiating from the inside of her body daily. She images it as shining through specific areas which need healing. Her skin, she says, is one of her problems. So she visualizes the light shining from within, through her skin and at the same time "sees" her skin smooth, beautiful, and tight.

When you become a beacon of light, you may also become a target for the forces of darkness which would like to snuff out your light. Light provides illumination, but it also attracts moths. There are both black and white moths, and we must be on guard constantly, because light makes us more susceptible, or a magnet for good as well as dark forces. It attracts their attention and is a threat just as light is a threat to darkness! The problem is becoming epidemic at the present time. John, mentioned in Chapter 1, is an example.

John, when we left him last, was ill, and his specialty, nutrition, which helps most people get well, was not helping *him*. But there was something peculiar about this illness. The story I am about to tell you is a strange one. I will not blame you for not believing it. All I can say is that I can vouch for it because, since John is a close friend of mine, I saw it happen. As you will remember, John was responsible for the care of a mentally disturbed individual until the relative had to be removed, finally, to other premises. By that time it was too late for John. First, he had become greatly drained of energy partially due to the stress of the demanding relative. His resistance had dropped to a serious low from which he could not seem to extricate himself.

He began to study other approaches, besides the nutritional, and learned many of the things you have already read in this book. He was aware of feeling resentful because the relative demanded so much of his time and energy. It was a thankless, futile task. But correcting his thinking did not solve the problem entirely. As he studied further, he noticed many unexplainable ESP happenings, until finally, with the help of a professional, who was treating his relative, it became clear that the relative was apparently suffering from possession by some disincarnated entity. Furthermore, it appeared as if that same entity were trying to possess and undermine John! He resisted actual possession, but not the attacks. It was at this time that the professional suggested the removal of the relative, but the damage had already been done to John. Apparently, John, too, was a victim of psychic attack! His symptoms became worse; his energy level refused to rise. Doctors could find no reason for his illness. John began to feel like the effigies used in the Philippines and other countries, where pins are stuck into a doll used to represent a selected person, and serious health problems and bad luck follow.

Even though John was now freed from associating with his relative, his problems continued, even worsened. How does psychic attack work? In several ways.

The invasion of evil entities from "the other side" has long been known, but it is getting more common. Experienced occult researchers tell us that when dissolute characters pass on, instead of going to higher realms as they should, they hover around this sphere, looking for someone to attach to, in order to continue to gratify their selfish wishes. Drug addicts, alcoholics, sex perverts have often turned a normal person into a perverted one. But first, the normal person has to provide an opening. Fatigue, chronic illness from lowered vitality, unbalanced living, and inadequate nutrition create an opportunity for one of these entities (called "threshold spirits" because they hover about the threshold between the living and the dead) which latch onto such a person too weak to protect himself. Even those who experiment with psychedelic drugs are pushovers for possession. Don't fall for the argument that such drugs hasten spiritual growth. Not so. There are no shortcuts to spiritual growth!

Richard Hittleman explains in *Guide to Yoga Meditation,* "Drugs are dangerous. The real danger is not only physical (from the yoga point of view). Even the mildest stimulant used regularly will result in an eventual deterioration of the nervous system and inhibit the natural awakening of the life-force. . . . The change of consciousness, which manifests in varying degrees, according to the drug used, becomes so desirable, indeed so essential to the user, that his dependence upon it becomes gradually permanent.

"When the user is 'on,' he feels that he captures a glimpse of reality, that he is in tune with his true nature. When the effects of the drug have worn off and he is 'down,' the unreality of what he erroneously believes to be the 'mundane' world becomes intolerable. Therefore, he must revert more and more to the use of drugs. . . .

"The crux of the matter is this: what is actually perceived by the user when he is 'on' is not reality; it is a *counterfeit* of reality. It is close to the real thing, but it is not genuine. . . . The spiritual danger is, then, that the more the drugs are used, the more counterfeit reality, which is experience, and the less inclined (and the less able) the user becomes to undertake these physical, emotional, and mental disciplines necessary to experience a *genuine* awakening. A spiritual realization which the drug user believes is drawing closer and closer is, in the long view, actually receding.

"The user of drugs in an attempt to escape the merry-go-round [should realize] that the symptoms, not the causes, must be treated; that drugs numb the pain, do not dissolve it. . . . [Instead] if we would have real peace of mind and body and spirit, we must pierce through directly to the heart of the matter to the *cause* of our dissatisfaction."

Even those people who dabble in some forms of spiritualism, and I've seen it happen to many who have merely played with a ouija board, may have disastrous results follow unless the dabbling occurs under proper supervision, or they know the rules for safety.

Stephen Sanders states, "There is a great difference between psychic phenomenon and first-hand religious experience. Psychic phenomena can provide many mental 'kicks' but it can never nourish the soul to maturity. It will not give the peace . . . that the aspirant seeks so desperately.

Please do not go too far with the ouija board. Many persons have become so involved with sorcery . . . and the ouija board is sorcery . . . that they are unable to respond to the Spirit of God when it finally comes alive within them. . . . Such thrills harden our hearts to the *real* thing, which is Christ within us."

"There is also a vast difference between automatic writing and inspiration," according to the late Eileen Garrett, the internationally known psychic. She says much ESP information can come from the subconscious, the storehouse of memory. "It is true that as passivity of mind is reached, a gradual opening can be channeled through and that an entity can invade the storehouse of memory. From then on remember that you have laid yourself open to visitation and are undergoing the process of suggestion."

If a personage speaking through the ouija board, or during automatic writing, identifies himself as Edgar Cayce, or even Jesus Christ, pay no attention! Threshold spirits or other unsavory or worthless entities will do anything, masquerade as anybody, to entice you into their trap, to use you for their benefit. I will tell you later how to challenge these characters.

There are even those people who are learning about and practicing black magic, which is a means of working with evil forces to encourage them. When these evil forces give their commands or even take over a person's body (called possession) anything can happen.

Witness the increasing numbers of mass murders by one individual, who, when he was questioned, said, "Voices told me to do it."

In addition to possession, instances of witchcraft or black magic are becoming serious; anyone can be a candidate! One group I have learned of is experimenting on people who know nothing about what is going on and are unaware they are targets. They don't know why they are becoming or remaining ill, or are having all manner of bad luck. Sooner or later, practitioners of black magic suffer the same fates they inflict upon others. These group members I mentioned are already experiencing poor health, loss of property, money problems, and business reverses. But usually the victim suffers long before the evils perpetrated on the poor recipient finally boomerang against the practitioners.

Patty Settles tells of an example of how black magic was aborted by her son. She says, "Larry did not believe in God. When he went into the army, I, of course, always surrounded him with light and with prayer. I wanted him to be protected and not open to dark forces. A young man he met had been in the priesthood and had learned about the black mass. He became very adept at black magic, and could do many frightful things through black magic. Larry was greatly concerned about this young man because he liked him very much; but even though they were very close buddies, Larry did not go along with what he did. The thing that really upset Larry was that the young man planned, one day, to use black magic on one of the lieutenants. Larry, being a very fair-minded person, realized that the lieutenant was doing his job very effectively and very well and it would have been unfair to do something evil to him.

"So that night Larry knelt down in the barracks, in which about twenty men were gathered, and he asked God to please not let this young man do something evil to the lieutenant. He said he suddenly felt a great warmth, and as he looked up, there was this great angel. It was St. Michael, the angel said. And the angel motioned Larry to get back into bed and assured him that everything would be all right. So Larry got back into his bunk, and the next morning he could hardly wait to run up to the next floor and see what had happened to his friend. When he got up there, his friend was still sleeping. Larry shook him and said, 'Did you do the black mass last night?'

'No,' the man answered, 'I felt somebody standing

right beside me, near my bunk. I felt so frightened that I covered my head, and the next thing that I knew, you were shaking me.'

"So Larry finally became assured that there is something beyond human experience which can help us when we ask for it.

"Ordinarily an angel, or a being, or a guide, or a master will not help you unless you ask. They do help, though, in this way. They come and shine a light around you. If you wish to assimilate this light into your aura, you may. It might be a very deep purple light which is the color of spiritual faith, or other shades of purple which represent hope. They may place this color around you so that it will raise your vibratory rate to one of hope, should you be in despair. But the helpers would not be allowed to sustain this aid for you unless you asked them to do it."

Harold Sherman,[2] world famous ESP researcher, says an avalanche of letters have come to him from people who apparently have been invaded by disincarnate entities, often through the indiscriminate use of the ouija board or automatic writing. These people tell him when they started they thought they had made contact with a loved one or a highly developed spirit. They also believed that the messages were authentic and inspirational in nature, and therefore were safe to follow. But later, after an apparently trusted spirit had gained control of the consciousness of many of these people, the character of that spirit suddenly changed, began to use vulgar and obscene language, and the person was commanded to do unsavory things, even committing crimes. Later, a person would say, "I don't know what possessed me to do it," or "I wasn't myself, something inside me made me do it." This is just a hint of the kind of thing that seems to be becoming very common. Some people who write Harold Sherman say a voice "which

---

[2]Harold Sherman, "Spirit Possession, Fact or Fallacy." *Fate* Magazine, May 1970.

seems to be a fiend of some sort at times, seems to laugh or taunt or boast of its power over its victim." One individual said, "I am a respected person in my community. If friends and loved ones knew what I am going through, it would be the end of me. How much longer can I hold out? And how can I get free?"

Harold Sherman explains that due to the use of sedatives, pain killers, tranquilizers, and alcohol to quiet or numb the nerves and mind, or due to the psychedelic drugs, many people can become "possessed," and possession is not a respecter of person, age or sex. Once the conditions have been created, wittingly or unwittingly, to attract and permit involvement with an earthbound disincarnate entity, serious results can take place. And cases on record are multiplying like rabbits! Whereas Harold Sherman had formerly received only a few such letters from time to time, he says that now he is receiving an avalanche of letters. People who are desperate, who are frightened, and some who feel that in order to get away from the taunting entity, which seems to inhabit them and is trying to control everything they say and do, say they would prefer suicide to continuing under the domination of this evil spirit. Mr. Sherman discusses the case histories of such people in his book.[3]

Most psychiatrists, apparently, are not able to give permanent help. Many people have not found a prayer which does the job either. So they ask Mr. Sherman, "Please, please help me."

Harold Sherman warns of another threat. So many people are becoming interested in ESP that they are dabbling in it without knowing the hazards. Even telepathy, we are told, is being beamed from one country to another to dominate an individual or a group or even a respected leader in a country. So, in addition to disincarnate or earthbound or threshhold entities, ready to seize upon us when

[3]Harold Sherman, *Your Mysterious Powers of ESP*. Signet Mystic Books, New American Library, New York. Paperback.

we are not looking, or dominating telepathic thoughts coming through the air all around us, is it any wonder that many people are becoming nervous, hysterical, or hopeless, feeling that they are being controlled by something against which they are helpless?

Mr. Sherman usually instructs these desperate people to try to analyze themselves to see whether they are suffering from an "obsession" or "possession." He says an obsession might be defined as a *condition* in which a person is repressing: perhaps strong sex urges, or antisocial acts, thus developing a secondary personality, which he knows is wrong, but which he cannot seem to control.

However, when someone becomes aware of an outside entity trying to control the person's thought or feelings or filling his consciousness with evil suggestions and lewd mental images, it is very possible that "possession" may be the cause. Here is the remedy Mr. Sherman offers for those who are struggling with this hidden giant, which is torturing them day and night. He advises anyone who needs help against any form of obsession or possession to remember this law: "It has been demonstrated that it is impossible for any evil entity to remain attached to any human consciousness in the presence of the higher God-power within, once this power is reacted through meditation and prayer."

Mr. Sherman offers the following affirmation which he says has proved extremely effective in cases of possession. He insists this must be a part of meditation; merely repeating the words is useless; one must *feel* the thoughts and mean them as well. Here is the Sherman formula which will help the person to be freed of his tormenter: "I am never alone. God, the Father, is always with me. My soul, my identity—that something which says 'I am I' to me—is an eternal gift from God, the great Intelligence. I never can lose myself because this self is a part of God. I am part of God and God has a great purpose in life for me, which He is revealing day by day, as I grow in strength of body, mind and spirit.

I am well and strong; I have the power to overcome all things within me. In God's care no harm can befall me. I now give myself over to God's protection, and I will follow His guidance day by day.

"Get out and stay out! I won't have anything more to do with you any time, anywhere. I call upon the Christ presence in me to throw you out; you are no more!"

There is another method contained in an article I clipped many years ago from one of the earliest issues of *Fate* Magazine (I do not find a dateline). It is called, "My Invisible Protector," and was written by Ann Heller. She tells how, when her father died, he told her that he had faced disaster and death many times, but that he had had a secret formula which he used as a shield. She says, "This, on his dying bed, he bequested to me." He told her, "In the face of danger, cast out all fear. A person afraid is a weak person, out of control. In the face of mental, moral, or physical peril breathe deeply. While the breath is held, press the thumb and the third finger together, and know that you are encircled in a band of white light. Secure now in this wall of your mental construction, command silently but forcibly *with all the strength you can muster* the help of those invisible angels who wait to help all mankind."

Ann Heller tells of the many times that she used this formula. Though invisible, often she felt the presence of these helpers (angels?) and knew she was being protected. She gives the example of one instance in which this formula probably saved her life. She had attended a dance and was walking home alone on a dark street long after others were in bed. There was no one around for protection. At the dance she had met a man who, she discovered, suddenly was following her. He caught up with her and attempted to attack her. She silently drew her circle of white light, and commanded the invisible helpers to protect her. Instantly she felt "something" surrounding her. At that moment, the man's hands which were holding her, seemed to be violent-

ly wrenched from her shoulder. She said silently to her helpers, "Thank you," and stepped away.

As she left, she turned and looked back. The man
seemed to be struggling as if he were being restrained. He
shouted to her, "There is a light around you."

She answered, "Yes, I know," and ran. Later she learned
that this man was a violent escaped criminal. Her protective
formula had saved her from him.

Ann Ree Colton has given me the ring-pass-not of protection. It is this: "May the mighty archangel Raphael protect me from any evil coming from the east. May the mighty
archangel Gabriel protect me from any evil coming from
the south. May the mighty archangel Michael protect me
from any evil approaching from the west. And may the
mighty archangel Uriel protect me from any evil approaching from the north. To Thee, O Christ, be the kingdom,
power, and the glory, ages unto ages. Amen."

If you wish, you can make the sign of the cross as you
say, "To Thee, O Christ" (touching the forehead), "Be the
kingdom" (touching the solar plexus), "the power" (touching your left shoulder), "and the glory" (touching your
right shoulder), ages unto ages. Amen."

According to Mrs. Thedick, the effect of the ring-pass-
not lasts only eight hours; it should be repeated the first
thing in the morning and the last thing before going to bed
at night.

For those who are experiencing actual psychic attack,
Mrs. Thedick says, "You cannot destroy evil; you can merely ask that it be transmuted for good. If you wish help, the
archangel Michael is only too happy to respond to your
call."

Angels must wait to be invited. But demons do not wait
to be asked. They "rush in where angels fear to tread." But
they will obey a firm command to leave if given in the name
of Christ, a word they abhor, due to its high vibratory rate
which they cannot tolerate. Even when uncontrolled

thoughts besiege you, they can be routed by command, as Richard Hittleman explains:

"Remember that it requires a great amount of life-force to think, and much of what flows through your mind during the day . . . is simply not worth this expenditure of vital energy. . . . Whenever you catch the machinelike ordinary mind playing the record, distracting you, filling you with useless thoughts, which consume your valuable time and vital energy, order it to stop! Tell it in no uncertain terms that you are not interested in these superfluous, meaningless thoughts, and that you do not want them to arise again. If you will issue this order whenever you observe the ordinary mind involved in its antics, it will soon stop forcing your attention on these things, but you must be on your guard, and persevere with the practice of this observation technique . . . thus you will more and more be able to quiet the restlessness of your ordinary mind and greatly conserve your life-force."

Hunches can be invaluable, as we all know. The question is, however, when are these so-called hunches reliable, and when are they an attempt for control and devastation by an unwanted entity, masquerading as a good angel?

Agnes Sanford warns,[4] "Guidance alone is not sufficient, for one can misunderstand the voice of God within us. We should pray for the increase of the power within us, directed toward healing, but also for wisdom; subjecting each decision to the judgment of understanding, reason and common sense.

"Premonitions are as apt to come from the devil as from the Lord, and the telling of them (prophesying evil for a person) can be the devil's tool, fastening on the person the foretold disaster.

"Surround yourself with protection. Call upon the light of Jesus Christ to be around you and this power from the

---

[4]Agnes Sanford, *The Healing Power of the Bible.* J. B. Lippincott Co., Philadelphia and New York, 1969.

'enemy' will come up against a surrounding force, and will turn back and go away, for it will not be able to get through."

Mrs. Thedick advises you to challenge *everything*, even if it seems to come from God. By waiting, if it is good, it will come back stronger. Challenge the hunch, nudge, or whatever, in the name of Christ.

"Always forcefully challenge any and all manifestations of your extended senses with these words: 'In the name of Jesus Christ, I challenge you. Have you come in His Name? If not, then leave me immediately.'"

Sometimes the only method to permanently repel psychic attack is through exorcism. Here is Agnes Sanford's method of exorcism. She says, "Times without number I have sent forth the word of power and in the name of Jesus Christ, commanded an evil spirit to leave a person, and it has departed. . . . Sometimes when a demon is cast out another person in the family picks it up, since the demon has to go somewhere.

"After casting out a demon, I pray that the love of Jesus will come and fill up all the empty places where it used to be. And finally I pray that this person be surrounded with the protection of God, so that nothing can come near to hurt him again. In all the years I have prayed this prayer, I have never known the troubling demon or thought form to return to the one who has been healed.

"An English psychiatrist once told me: 'A man may be rightly diagnosed as schizophrenic or manic-depressive, but this trouble on the surface of the personality may be caused by an infiltration of an evil entity from outside. If this can be cast out there would be more hope of healing on the surface of the personality.'"

So, don't sell possession short. If someone says he hears voices and that "they" are after him and follow him, it may be true. Such infiltration is *definitely* possible and is becoming more common.

Whatever the source of the demon, Agnes Sanford

uses the following formula for exorcism with permanent results:

1. She first prays for protection for herself and the person who needs help.

2. With or without laying on of hands, she commands the invading spirit in the name of Jesus Christ to leave the person. She imagines the cross of Christ and the sword of the Spirit (which is the word of God) to be visible and continues the command and exhortation plus any words of power which come to her mind.

3. She give thanks that the evil spirit has departed, places it under the control of Christ and forbids it to ever come back to that person or to any one else on the earth plane at all.

4. She prays that the person be surrounded by heavenly protection.

5. She asks that all the empty places, where the entity used to be, are now filled with the love of Christ so that nothing can ever again enter to trouble the person. She prays for the protection of the Lord to surround the person like a circle of light.

Mrs. Thedick's booklet, *Light on Your Problems*, contains much helpful information, even for the cleansing of your home of unwanted influences. She also gives the "Armor of Light" protective affirmation which has proved extremely helpful for many people. It is as follows:

"In the Name and through the Power and by the Word of Jesus Christ, I put on the whole armor of light. On my head is the helmet of salvation. I wear the breastplate of righteousness. My loins are girded with the truth. My feet are shod with peace and enveloped in the flame of the spirit of almighty God. In my left hand I hold the shield of faith and in my right hand is the sword of the spirit, which is the word of God. The word of God is unassailable and no evil can come nigh my habitation. Thus clad I stand, joyfully expectant, ready to do the will of the Living Christ. Amen."

As suggested before, this should be used night and morning, for continuous protection. It should also be followed with the request that you be insulated from any negative influences. Some people find added help in saying the 23rd or the 91st psalms.

For routine protection, such as driving a car or traveling by plane, Mrs. Thedick's following affirmation (from the same booklet) is simply invaluable. She says, "Whenever you feel the need of protection, say to yourself silently or aloud, 'In the name and through the power and by the word of Jesus Christ, a wall of living flame is built around me (or this car, plane, or bus). I give thanks to the Father that it is done. Amen.'"

This affirmation of protection has proved so effective that many of us who have used it would not think of getting into a car or a plane or any other means of conveyance without first making this affirmation of protection.

Not long ago I left home hurriedly in the car, and although I usually have a good and safe driving record, that day I had all sorts of small nuisances crop up as I was driving. I ran over the edge of a curb. I backed into a telephone pole while I was trying to park, and a shopper in her car cut across in front of me, causing me to slam on my brakes to keep from hitting her. This is so unusual that I finally asked myself, "What in the world is causing all of these disturbances today?" Then I remembered that I had left home without uttering my usual protective affirmation. I immediately said it, then and there, and continued the day's driving without further incident.

There is another cause of loss of energy which, while not actually due to a psychic attack, often undermines the vitality and health of an unsuspecting person. This problem is due to sappers, people who consciously or unconsciously drain your strength. Riley H. Crabb, writing about the Kahunas, says,[5] "Water leaks away and so does vital force. You all know this when you are in a crowd—almost impossible to prevent some leakage here; or if you are in the presence of a vampire type."

Richard Hittleman gives his solution to the problem:[6]

"Another important loss of life-force occurs when you are in the company of certain people. Many persons who do not have sufficient life-force in their own organisms draw on the vitality of those around you. . . . If you know which people have this effect on you, try to avoid their company as much as possible. Associate whenever you can with people who have as much or more life force than yourself to leave you with an elevated, positive feeling.

"Idle chatter is another way in which many people continually use up their life-force. Talking . . . requires great energy, especially idle chatter. This is the reason why monks and nuns of all religious orders take vows of silence so they may conserve their life force and help to quiet the restlessness of the body and mind. . . . Any activity which leaves you physically or emotionally drained and exhausted is to be absolutely avoided whenever possible."

The late Dion Fortune said, "In dealing with a person who saps your vitality, interlace your fingers and lay your folded hands upon your solar plexus, keeping your elbows pressed against your sides. Keep your feet touching each other. You have thus contacted all your own terminals and made of your own body a closed circuit. No magnetism will go out from you while you maintain this attitude. Your friend will probably complain about your lack of sympathy, however kindly you may speak.

"If anyone tries to dominate you by gazing intently

---

[5]*Journal of Borderland Research,* October, 1966.
[6]Richard Hittleman, *Guide to Yoga Meditation.* Bantam Books, New York, 1969. Paperback.

into your eyes, do not attempt to return gaze for gaze, for this only leads to an exhausting struggle in which you may get the worst of it. Instead, look steadily at the spot just above the base of the other person's nose, between the inner ends of the eyebrows. . . . Do not attempt to dominate him; merely keep your eyes on the spot and wait for him to weary of his attempt to dominate you. You will not have long to wait."

Another extremely effective method of protection from anyone who is causing trouble for you is to visualize a thick glass wall between you. Sometimes this works when nothing else will.

Another interesting cause of sapping recently came to my attention. Several members of one family began to experience complete exhaustion for no discernible reason. Two members of the family lived in the immediate area, another 3,000 miles away from their elderly mother who was slowly deteriorating of old age and consequent loss of vitality. Each member of the family cited the same symptoms: they would feel so exhausted (even the member who lived 3,000 miles distant) on awakening in the morning that he was scarcely able to get across the room, to say nothing of leaving the house.

A minister finally diagnosed, clairvoyantly, the cause and suggested the remedy. As her energy waned, the elderly mother was sapping energy (quite unconsciously) from the members of her family. The minister told these people who were being "sapped" to cut the cord. This is done by visualizing a cord connecting the umbilical areas of the sapper and the victim. The procedure is to mentally visualize, using a knife, a sword, or if necessary a saw, and cut the cord. Sometimes, the cord appears to be so leathery and tenuous, it takes a long time to sever it. But when it is cut, the person should instantly say, "I am releasing you with love to a higher power for your source of energy. Go to light!"

The family members experienced almost immediate

relief. Symptoms sometimes reappeared and the process had to be repeated, though it was less difficult to sever the cord on subsequent occasions.

In discussing this incident with two friends whose aged mothers had recently passed on, one said, "I was completely drained of energy for six months before my mother died." The other said, "I was so drained of vitality for a full year before my mother passed away, though it was the last thing she would have consciously inflicted upon me, I often wondered which of us would go first."

Ann Ree Colton advises turning the person about to pass on, over to his or her luminosity angel. The luminosity angel is the one who prepares and helps the departing soul across to the other side.

So John learned, by painful experience, which took nearly three years, the signs of a psychic attacker at work. Kingdon L. Brown has since provided in his book[7] a check list of symptoms which are clues to a psychic attack, whether it be internal (possession) or external (black magic or witchcraft). Here are a few of the clues:

1. Do you have one ailment after another, of mysterious origin, for which no doctor can find a cause?

2. Have you experienced a series of bad-luck incidents?

3. Do you feel so exhausted most of the time that you can scarcely get through a day, week, or month, and often feel like giving up entirely?

4. Do you have nightmares? Do evil thoughts harass you?

5. Do you have trouble thinking clearly, concentrating, making decisions? Do you feel hazy much of the time?

6. Do you feel that people are less friendly toward you, lose patience with you, forget to include you, or on the other hand, intrude on your privacy?

---

[7]Kingdon L. Brown, *The Power of Psychic Awareness*. Parker Publishing Co., West Nyack, New York, 1969.

7. Do you lose your temper often and want to get even with people?

8. Do you hear voices that won't let you alone, or do you feel compelled to do things you normally would not approve of?

9. Do you suddenly encounter "roadblocks" or even lack of interest to prevent you from doing things to help others or starting or finishing a worthy project?

Of course many of these symptoms can be ascribed to other causes. But if you have a combination of several of them, you can suspect they may be due to psychic attack. Fear does not help. It makes you more vulnerable by putting yourself on the same wavelength as your attacker.

Kingdon L. Brown assures us that "the forces of darkness can be cancelled out by the forces of light; it is possible to gain more and more protection from the sources of light and you can build a shield against psychic attack: see yourself bathed in pure white light. Cultivate strong positive vibrations, and reject the negative, since like attracts like."

John finally achieved his healing through a combination of methods set forth in this book. He used exorcism to rid himself of psychic attack. (He protects himself daily to prevent its return.) Due to prayer, visualization, and affirmations for good health, he was unexpectedly led to a diagnostician who discovered a deep-seated and resistant infection overlooked by others. It had evidently taken hold while his resistance had dipped so low during the care of his relative, and the subsequent attack.

Once the attacker was permanently routed, the infection cleared, and his negative thoughts and emotions were brought under control, he began his upward climb, healthwise. His healing was not instantaneous, but chronic disorders usually require time. At any rate, his healing was complete. John believes that, painful as it was, the experience was a blessing in disguise because it provided valuable information to serve as guidelines for the rest of his life. He has made friends with the angels, he has opened himself to divine guidance; he also asks daily to be filled with the Holy Spirit and to radiate divine light to others. He is now healthier and happier and more successful in every way. In short, his life has been transformed.

As you look through this book, you will no doubt be amazed, as I was, on finding how many things can prevent good health. Yet, realizing how intricate our body is, physically, mentally, emotionally, and spiritually, it should really not be surprising at all, since the body works as a whole.

In the words of the Human Dimensions Institute, "Think whole—become whole."[8]

As you arrange your own programming for health, jot down the therapies which appeal and apply to you. If, in the last analysis, you don't know what to do, try asking the angels to help you with any problem you have. They can— if invited—lighten your burdens, help dissolve your fears, protect you, guide you to solve your problem, whether it be lack of supply, or suffering, or poor health.

Be sure to ask for their help in His name, since the good angels exist to do His work for you. Remember to love, thank, and bless them for their untiring efforts. Such appreciation encourages them and helps them to grow in their environment as it helps you in yours.

Your life will become enriched.

[8]Human Dimensions Institute, 4380 Main Street, Buffalo, N. Y. 14226

Bibliography

Bailes, Frederick W. *Your Mind Can Heal You*. Dodd, Mead & Co., New York © 1941. 9th printing.

Bayly, N. Beddow, Laurence J. Bendit, Phoebe D. Bendit, H. Tudor Edmunds, and Adelaide Gardner. *The Mystery of Healing*. The Theosophical Publishing House, London, Ltd., © 1958. (A Quest Book, rev. ed., © 1968.)

Bennett, Clarence E. *Physics Without Fear*. Barnes & Noble, New York © 1970. (Paperback, College Outline Series)

Berne, Eric. *A Layman's Guide to Psychiatry and Psychoanalysis*, 3rd ed., Simon & Schuster, New York, © 1968.

Brown, Kingdom L. *The Power of Psychic Awareness*. Parker Publishing Co., West Nyack, N. Y., © 1969.

Burland, Theodore. *Medical Miracles With Ultra Sound*. Family Circle, October 1966.

Casselberry, Dr. William S. *How to Work Miracles in Your Life, The Golden Secret of Successful Living*. Parker Pub. Co., Englewood Cliffs, N. J., 6th printing, © 1966.

Cayce, Edgar. *Auras*, A.R.E. Press, Virginia Beach, Va. © 1945.

Clark, Linda. *Color Healing*. Devin-Adair Co., Old Greenwich, Conn., © 1972.

Clark, Linda, *Get Well Naturally* (Paperback ed.). Arco Pub. Co., 219 Park Avenue South, New York 10003

Clark, Linda. *Secrets of Health and Beauty*. Pyramid Pubs., New York, © 1970.

Clymer, R. Swinburne. *Making Health Certain*. Humanitarian Society, Quaker Town, Penna., © 1914.

Colton, Ann Ree. *The Human Spirit*, ARC Pub. Co., P. O. Box 1138, Glendale, Calif. 91209, © 1966.

Colton, Ann Ree with Jonathan Murro. *Islands of Light*. De Vors & Co., Los Angeles, Calif. 90015, © 1953.

Coniff, James C. G. "Can You Control Your Heart?" *Family Weekly*, October 11, 1970.

Cooke, Ivan and Grace. *Healing*. The White Eagle Pub. Trust, Newlands, Liss, Hampshire, England, © 1955.

Cooke, Grace. *Meditation*. The White Eagle Pub. Trust, Newlands, Liss, Hampshire, England, © 1965.

Eldridge, Skip. "Prayer," *Pep Talk*. P. O. Box 677, Auburn, Wash. 98002, October 1970.

Family Weekly, October 4, 1970.

Felixmann, M. B. *Acupuncture*. Random House, New York, © 1963.

Fillmore, Charles. *Atom Smashing Power of the Mind.* Unity School of Christianity, Lee's Summit, Mo.

Freeman, James Dillet. *The Household of Faith.* Unity School of Christianity, Lee's Summit, Mo., © 1951.

Frymann, Viola M. "What is Man That Thou Art Mindful of Him" *The Pacific Coast Hemoeopathic Bulletin.* Sept., 1970.

Gross, Nancy E. *Living With Stress.* McGraw-Hill Book Co. Inc., New York, © 1958.

Harlow S. Ralph. *A Life After Death.* Doubleday & Co., Inc., Garden City, New York, © 1961.

Harris, Thomas A. *I'm Ok — You're Ok.* Harper & Row Pub., New York, © 1969.

Heller, John H. *Of Mice, Men and Molecules.* Charles Scribner's Sons, New York, © 1960.

Hittleman, Richard. *Guide to Yoga Meditation.* Bantam Books, New York, © 1969. Paperback.

Hittleman, Richard. *Yoga Natural Foods Cookbook.* Bantam Books, New York, © 1970. Paperback.

Hodson, Geoffrey. *The Brotherhood of Angels and of Men.* The Theosophical Pub. House, London, © 1957.

Houston, F. M. *Contact Healing.* Self published, rev. ed., © 1972. 25.00, available only from Dr. Houston, P. O. Box 51, Highway 80, Guatay, Calif. 92031.

Itard, *Traite des Maladies del'Orielle et de L'audition.* Vol. 1. Paris, © 1921.

Journal of Borderland Research, October, 1966.

Jung, Carl G. *Modern Man in Search of a Soul.* Harcourt, Brace & World, Inc., New York, © 1933.

Keyes, Laurel E. *Toning.* 2168 So. Lafayette St., Denver, Colo. 80210.

Kilner, Walter J. *The Human Aura.* University Books, New Hyde Park, New York, © 1965.

Life. March 7, 1960.

Light on Your Problems. The Seeker's Quest, P. O. Box 9543, San Jose, Calif. 95117.

Lister, Edna. *Eternal Youth at Eighty and Beyond.* NCS Pub. Co., 16324 Hawthorne Blvd., Lawndale, Calif. 90260, © 1969.

Long, Max Freedom. *The Secret Science Behind Miracles.* Kosman Press, Los Angeles, Calif. 90006, © 1948.

Long, Max Freedom, *The Secret Science at Work.* Human Research Pubs., P. O. Box 2867, Hollywood Station, Los Angeles, Calif. 90028, © 1953.

Medical World News. June 3 and Sept. 9, 1960.

Newsletter of the Radionic Magnetic Center, England, Autumn, 1970.

Ostrander, Sheila and Lynn Schroeder, *Psychic Discoveries Behind The Iron Curtain*. Prentice-Hall, Inc., Englewood Cliffs, N. J., © 1970.

Ott, John N. *My Ivory Cellar*. Rev. ed., Devin-Adair Co., Old Greenwich, Conn., © 1972.

Pierce, Frederick, *Mobilizing The Mid-brain* (the technique for utilizing it's latent power). E. P. Dutton & Co., New York, © 1933.

Ponder, Catherine. *The Healing Secret of The Ages*. Parker Pub. Co., West Nyack, N. Y. © 1964.

Ponder, Catherine. *Pray and Grow Rich*. Parker Pub. Co., West Nyack, N. Y. © 1968.

Popular Mechanics. May 1963.

Powell, Eric F. W. *Lady Be Beautiful*. Health Science Press, Restington, Sussex, England, © 1961.

Ramacharaka, Yogi. *Science of Psychic Healing*. Yoga Publication Society, Box 148, Des Plaines, Ill. 60016, © 1934.

Rampa, T. Lobsang. *Doctor From Lhasa*. Bantam Books, © 1968.

Rampa, T. Lobsang. *Rampa Story*. Bantam Books, © 1968.

Rampa, T. Lobsang. *The Third Eye*. Ballantine Books, New York, © 1964.

Sanders, Stephen. *To Him Who Conquers*. Doubleday & Co., Inc. Garden City, New York, © 1970.

Sanford, Agnes. *The Healing Gifts of the Spirits*. J. B. Lippincott Co., Phila. and New York, © 1966.

Sanford, Agnes. *The Healing Light*. Macalester Park Pub. Co., St. Paul, Minn., 19th ed. © 1955.

Sanford, Agnes. *The Healing Power of The Bible*. J. B. Lippincott Co., Phila. and New York, © 1969.

Seabury, David. *The Art of Living Without Tension*. Harper & Bros., New York, © 1958.

Selye, Hans. *The Stress of Life*. McGraw-Hill Book Co. Inc., New York, © 1956.

Sherman, Harold. *How to Make ESP Work For You*. Fawcett Crest Book, Fawcett Pubs., Inc., Greenwich, Conn. © 1964.

Sherman, Harold. "Spirit Possession, Fact or Fallacy." *Fate Magazine*, May 1970.

Sherman, Harold. *Your Mysterious Powers of ESP*. Signet Mystic Books, New American Library, New York. Paperback.

Smith, Harry Douglas. *The Secret of Instantaneous Healing*. Parker Pub. Co., West Nyack, New York, © 1965.

The Boy Who Saw True. anon., ed. by Cyril Scott, Neville Spearman, London, © 1953.

Thedick, Eleanore, *Jewels of Truth and Rays of Color.* The Christ Ministry Foundation, 2222 42nd Ave., Oakland, Calif. 94601, © 1970.

Weed, Joseph J. *Wisdom of The Mystic Masters.* Parker Pub. Co., West Nyack, New York, © 1968.

Westlake, Aubrey. *The Pattern of Health.* Devin-Adair Co., Old Greenwich, Conn., © 1961.

White, Ellen G. *Gems of Thought.* Compiled by R. A. Lovell, P. O. Box 274, Loma Linda, Calif. 92354.

Wilson, George A. *Emotionalism in Sickness.* © 1963. (out of print)

Wilson, George A. *A New Slant to Diet.* Jan. 1950. (out of print)

Wisdom of White Eagle. The White Eagle Publishing Trust, Liss, Hampshire, England, © 1965.

Wolff, William. *Psychic Development With Concept Therapy.* Grosset and Dunlap, New York, © 1968. Paperback.

Wolff, William. *Psychic Self-Improvement With Concept Therapy.* Grosset and Dunlap, New York, © 1968.

Index

Aborigines, Australian, 171
Abramsen, Dr. David I., 120
Acoustical research, 125, 129, 131-32
  See also Music therapy; Sound
Acupuncture, 112
Affirmations, 45, 87, 134-35, 198-200, 247
  See also Mantra
Aged, 30, 88, 238
American Association for the Advancement of Science, 153
American Medical Association, 52-53
  Journal, 112
American Psychopathological Association, 188
Anderson, Reverend Laura Kemp, 134
Angels, 201-02, 205-07, 209-10, 213, 216, 220-21, 227, 258
  types of, 164-66, 169, 174, 175, 202
Animals, 18, 30-32, 34-35, 108, 140-41, 156-57, 182
Anxiety, *see* Emotion
Aura, 145, 148-50, 202, 245
  diagnosis, 147
  human, 147
  plant, 147
  research, 146
  See also Health
Autosuggestion, 37, 43, 47, 54, 56-59, 62, 76
  See also Healing

Bailes, Dr. Frederick W., 81-84, 87-88, 184, 188
Baldness, 32
Bank of the Universal, 216, 221
Baudoin, Charles, 56
Benson, Dr. Herbert, 32
Berne, Dr. Eric, 71-73
Bible, 37, 168, 225
Black, Dr. Stephen, 46
Black magic, 243-44, 256-57
Body, 20, 23, 38, 81, 87, 89, 92, 97, 101-103, 105, 107, 114, 179-80, 228, 234
  blessing, 231-32
  circulation, 182-83
  functions, 81
  invisible zones, 111-12
  needs, 182-83

organs, 29-32, 43, 90, 92-97, 99-100, 135, 184, 191, 201
regeneration, 110, 142-43
  See also Color therapy; Emotion; Healing; Light; "Prana"; Sonic Therapy
Body, mind, spirit (interrelation) 79, 186-88, 223, 247
Boehme, Jacob, 168
Bone conduction, 126
Boston City Hospital of Behavioral Medicine Laboratory, 30
Boston City Hospital, Thorndike Memorial Research Laboratory, 32
Brahmins, 29
Brain, 32, 34, 103, 118
Breathing, 101-05, 108, 142
Briggs, Joanna, 213-15, 220
Brown, Kingdon L., 198-99, 234, 256-57
Brünler, Drs. Grace and Oscar, 118
Burland, Theodore, 119-20

Cancer, *see* Illness
Cannon, Dr. W. B., 187-88
Carpenter, G. D., 115-16
Case histories, 17-20, 32-33, 45-47, 51-52, 54-55, 60-61, 64-66, 73, 97-99, 139, 156-60, 170-73, 186-87, 189, 194-95, 198, 200, 203-04, 213, 215, 226, 230-32, 237, 239-41, 253, 255-56
  animals, 154-55
  children, 133, 160
  Colton, Ann Ree, 175-77, 183
  Cooke, Grace, 163
  D'Angelo, Dorie, 159
  Ellen, 28-29
  Fillmore, Charles, 95
  Fillmore, Myrtle, 95-96
  Harlow, S. Ralph, 161-62
  John, 17-20, 45, 75-76, 79, 89-90, 97, 240-41, 256-57
  Lister, Edna, 47, 101-02
  Settles, Patty, 173-76
  Smith, Reverend Dorothy Wynn, 172
  Thedick, Eleanore, 173
Catholics, 4, 163, 223
Cayce, Edgar, 148-49, 215, 234, 243
Cayce, Hugh Lynn, *Venture Inward*, 70-71
"Chakras," 107
Childbirth, 194-95